KILLER CVs
& HIDDEN APPROACHES

"JOB SECURITY IS GONE
FOREVER. THE TIME IS
RIGHT FOR AMBITIOUS
INDIVIDUALS TO TAKE
CONTROL OF THEIR OWN
CAREERS.**"**

KILLER CVs

& HIDDEN APPROACHES

Give yourself an unfair advantage
in the job market

GRAHAM PERKINS

An imprint of **Pearson Education**

London · New York · San Francisco · Toronto · Sydney
Tokyo · Singapore · Hong Kong · Cape Town · Madrid
Paris · Milan · Munich · Amsterdam

PEARSON EDUCATION LIMITED

Edinburgh Gate
Harlow CM20 2JE
Tel: +44 (0)1279 623623
Fax: +44 (0)1279 431059

Website: www.pearsoned.co.uk

First published in Great Britain in 1995
Revised edition published in 2001

© Pearson Education Limited 2001

The right of Graham Perkins to be identified as Author
of this Work has been asserted by him in accordance
with the Copyright, Designs and Patents Act 1988.

ISBN 0 273 65246 X

British Library Cataloguing in Publication Data
A CIP catalogue record for this book can be obtained from the British
Library.

10 9

Typeset by Pantek Arts Ltd, Maidstone, Kent
Printed and bound in Great Britain by Biddles Ltd, King's Lynn, Norfolk

The Publishers' policy is to use paper manufactured from sustainable forests.

THE AUTHOR

Currently practising as a freelance career counsellor and writer, Graham Perkins has a wealth of experience on which to draw when it comes to advising executives on the management of their careers. Graham started life by training as an accountant with a Unilever subsidiary. After qualifying as an ACMA, he joined International Computers where he spent five years, ending up as Financial Forecasting Manager. Then, following a spell as a Financial Controller in the construction industry, he moved into executive recruitment, ultimately heading up the Executive Search and Selection Division of Touche Ross Management Consultants. Graham is the author of a number of articles on career management, and of several books, including *Snakes or Ladders? – an ambitious executive's guide to headhunters and how to handle them*, Pitman Publishing, 1991.

Further information on individual career counselling is available from the author, who can be contacted at:

6 Cherrydeal Court, 165 Forest Road, London E11 1LL

Telephone/Fax 020 8539 6652 Mobile 07773 095 923
e-mail gjp@cwcom.net

CONTENTS

Part Two: Opening the hidden doors

Part Three: Your marketing brochure – the killer CV

FOREWORD TO THE SECOND EDITION

When, six years ago, I was asked to write *Killer CVs* we were still in the depths of the worst recession for many years and very few people had even heard of the internet. Now the economy is in good shape and any executive job hunter who is not 'connected' is beginning to have a serious credibility problem.

It is these two factors which have led to the decision to produce a brand new edition of *Killer CVs*, rather than just another reprint. The original text has been updated in a number of places to take account of the improved economic climate, a whole new section on the internet has been added and material has been inserted into the appropriate chapters on other new developments such as video interviewing.

Interestingly, however, the underlying principles on which *Killer CVs* was based have changed very little, if at all. The delayering and downsizing which took place during the recession have not gone into reverse – far from it: these processes are still going strong. What this means is that there continue to be fewer executive jobs – and that the competition for each and every one of them is consequently still intense. And that, in turn, means that the executive job seeker must be as aware as ever of the second part of the book's title: the *hidden approaches*. Networking, in particular, is becoming more and more important – not just for older executives who face age discrimination when they apply through conventional routes, but also for many younger people, and especially the increasing number who are adopting more flexible approaches to their careers.

And what of the internet? Will it, as many predict, completely revolutionise the process of finding a job? In time, it may well do so, but. . .

There are two main 'buts'. The first relates to timing. At present the technology is way ahead of the back-up systems, the forces which make for an efficient market and, not least, a lot of recruiters. Before the promise of faster and easier job hunting becomes a reality at the executive level of the market, some important developments still need to take place.

The second 'but' concerns the extent to which the internet will affect the fundamental principles of recruitment rather than just the means of communication. Thus far, its effect has been primarily on the latter, the underlying methods – advertising, file search and the use of agencies or consultants – remaining largely unchanged. This raises the question of how far, if at all, the internet will help people who currently find it difficult to get a new job, such as older candidates. Will the use of computers to screen applications, for instance, give them a fairer crack of the whip or simply make it even easier to screen them out?

A further question is the impact on executive search. Will senior executives really be willing to take the time, and to accept the risks to confidentiality, inherent in registering on job sites, or will they still wait to be seduced by the headhunter's call?

A new chapter explores these issues in greater depth and provides tips on how to ensure that the new technology works for – rather than against – you. Each time *Killer CVs* is reprinted, this section will be reviewed and, where necessary, updated because there is at least one thing we can be completely sure of: further technological developments are inevitable and, unless we want to lose out, we all need to keep up with them and see them not as problems but as opportunities.

INTRODUCTION

Are you:

- Tired of applying to job advertisements and not even getting an interview?

- Fed up with waiting for the headhunter to call?

- Annoyed at being told that you are over-qualified for roles that appear to be just made for you?

- Angry at people who do not even have the courtesy to reply to your letters?

- Finding the internet confusing and frustrating?

Then it is high time you changed your whole approach to finding a new job. Time you faced up to the realities of the new employment market. Time you began to manage your career instead of letting it manage you. Time you stopped blaming 'them' and started, instead, to see things from *their* viewpoint, using that insight to get yourself the job you really want.

But how do you obtain that insight? With so many candidates on the market these days, the people who place advertisements – the human resources (HR) professionals and selection consultants – simply do not have the time to respond to requests for independent advice and feedback, while headhunters, thanks to the shroud of mystery within which they work, are even less accessible.

Written by someone who spent 20 years as an executive search and selection consultant before moving into career counselling, this book shows you what it looks like from the other side of the desk, giving you the inside track which will enable you to steal a march on the competition. Furthermore, because the job you do not hear about is the one you have rather less than an ice cube's chance in hell of getting, you will also be shown how to access all the jobs that never find their way into advertisements or pass through the hands of the headhunters.

While it is aimed primarily at the mid to senior level executive, this book will also help those who aspire to such levels but are not quite there yet. It is equally applicable to those who have parted company from their latest employer (whether currently temping or devoting themselves full-time to their job search), those who are still employed but under threat, and those who are simply feeling blocked in their present organisation and looking for the next step up the ladder.

Nor is its relevance confined to one country. The key techniques – a proactive, professional marketing campaign and the use of hidden approaches – are just as crucial to the successful job search in any developed western country with high executive unemployment. Where differences in matters of detailed practice are significant (for example, there is more to adapting your CV for the French market than simply changing the heading to 'Resumé') your attention will be drawn to them.

First the bad news . . .

If it is tough at the top, then it is even tougher getting there. It always has been. Given that most organisations are essentially pyramid shaped, there will always be a lot more people starting at the bottom than ever make it to the top. The further up you get, the more competitive it becomes.

For many years, this difficulty was largely offset by business growth, which meant more jobs and less competition for them. It seemed that the sky was the limit for the ambitious executive. Then along came a deep, protracted recession which added a bunch of threatening new terms to the business lexicon, sinister euphemisms such as:

- delayering;
- downsizing;
- upgrading;
- business process re-engineering.

What they mean, in plain English, is fewer jobs. In particular, fewer management jobs. That is what is different this time round. We are all used to the fact that, every time there has been a dip in the economic cycle, organisations have laid employees off. What was new about the most recent recession is the widespread willingness to eliminate managerial and professional jobs.

Another difference is that the factors that have created executive unemployment on an unprecedented scale are not purely cyclical. They show little sign of going away now that the recession has been succeeded by a new wave of growth. Technological advances, decentralisation and outsourcing, not to mention fierce competition from the world's emerging economies, will all continue to be around, and to exert their pressure on managerial jobs, for as far ahead as it is possible to see.

Even more alarming, to many people, is what follows on from this. Job security is a thing of the past. Gone is the time when a bank manager had a job for life, when a professional qualification such as that of an accountant or lawyer meant guaranteed prosperity for the rest of your days. There are no such guarantees any more, nor are there any signs that there ever will be again.

A recent advertisement for an administration manager attracted 839 replies, of which over 400 were redundant branch managers of retail banks and building societies. At a job-hunting seminar, a chartered accountant in her mid-20s admitted that she had already been made redundant three times, the first occasion being in the middle of her training contract!

Derek Edwards, managing director of leading outplacement consultants Sanders & Sidney, said: 'People are not secure in their jobs any more – and never will be.' Former CBI director general Howard Davies has been quoted as saying: 'Womb to tomb employment, a lifetime spent with one employer, is becoming the exception rather than the rule.'

So, faced with this state of affairs, what do you do? Reach for the whisky bottle? Throw yourself off Tower Bridge? Or is there still hope after all?

Now the good news

Yes, there is a brighter side to the picture. As old jobs are being destroyed, new ones are being created – but they are different jobs, in different kinds of organisations. And, just as jobs and the market for them change, so must you. It is no use relying on old methods in a new and very different world.

You certainly need to keep abreast of developments in recruitment on the internet which, though initially a medium primarily for IT jobs and graduate recruitment, is now making inroads into the professional and managerial jobs market and is a source not just of vacancies but also of information on potential employers. However, the principles underlying internet recruitment are still those either of the agency – matching a pile of candidates to a pile of jobs – or the advertisement, aiming to attract targeted replies to a specific vacancy. The agency approach becomes less effective the more senior you are and advertisements, even now that the recession is over, tend to attract large responses which means that the odds on success remain depressingly low.

Although there are ways in which you can increase your chances of getting an interview rather than receiving a standard rejection letter, you cannot afford to confine your efforts to responding to advertisements. In any case, they account for less than a quarter of all executive vacancies.

Nor can you rely on the headhunter's call. You may, admittedly, be able to increase the chances of receiving that call when the headhunter has a new assignment. There are also ways of getting to meet search consultants for a general chat, rather than just being told, when you write in, that your details have been fed into their database. The fact still remains that only a minority of senior posts are filled by headhunters.

By far the most productive route to a new managerial job is by means of hidden approaches. Given that they account for somewhere between 50 and 75 per cent of all senior appointments, depending on whose figures you choose to believe, it seems incredible that so many executive jobhunters fail to use them at all. To some extent this may be because such methods are relatively new, and people either do not know about them at all, or do not fully understand how to use them. In many cases though, one cannot help suspecting that emotional reactions are to blame. Their confidence and self-respect already under threat as a result of career block, job insecurity or having actually been made redundant, people feel more comfortable with the apparent respectability of established methods of seeking a new position than with the element of touting themselves around which they perceive to be inherent in networking and in speculative applications. This is a pity, because the reality is that networking actually does far more for the ego than getting yet another rejection letter in response to an advertisement.

Almost as surprising as the complete failure of many executives to make any use at all of the most effective job search methods is the fact that so many of those who do make the attempt display so little proficiency in its execution.

These hidden approaches are the main subject of this book – rightly so because, in the current climate, you cannot afford to ignore the most productive sources of job opportunities. However, knowing the various routes is not enough on its own. You also have to learn how to navigate them effectively.

Starting, therefore, by ensuring that you are managing your own marketing campaign efficiently – something a lot of executives seem to find far more difficult than you would expect – the book goes on to examine, one by one, each of the routes by which you may find your next job. Then, having made you focus on what you are selling, to whom and through which channels, it helps you to ensure that you have the right marketing literature (the CV and the various letters you may need to use) for each type of approach. Finally it moves on to your sales presentation – the interview. This closing section also leads you through selection tests and assessment centres, deciding whether to accept the job offer, negotiating the remuneration package, and the checking of references, before concluding with a look at how to be better prepared the next time you find yourself on the market.

The next time? Yes. Do not give this volume away as soon as you have started your new job. You are going to need it again. One recent prediction stated that people entering employment today can expect to change jobs at least ten times in the course of their career as a result of factors such as technological advances, internal restructuring and corporate takeovers. To quote Howard Davies of the CBI again, people 'can no longer rely on jobs for life, and must be prepared to move more frequently, and cope with periods of unemployment'.

How to use this book

Just reading this book is not enough on its own. There is also a vital interactive element: questionnaires to challenge your existing assumptions; checklists to ensure that you do not miss key action points; lists of useful words to help you with your CV; and sample letters to assist you in your correspondence.

Most important of all are the insights provided as to how other players in the recruitment game see you: personnel professionals; selection consultants; headhunters; networking contacts; recipients of speculative calls and letters. Take the time to stop and examine yourself through their eyes. The few moments this involves in each case could be the most valuable investment you will ever make.

And so to work. But do you go right the way through, chapter by chapter, from beginning to end, or do you pick and choose?

Deciding the point at which to begin a book like this is inevitably difficult, since different readers will be at different stages in their job search. The order in which the parts and chapters have been arranged assumes that you are starting from scratch, eager to set off on your search but not yet having planned your campaign or conducted any self, or market, analysis.

Those who urgently need to produce a CV, or who have an interview in a few days' time, may wish to start with the chapter which deals with that part of the process, then – unless that application proves successful – return to the beginning. Readers who are still working through the anger, depression or other emotions caused by a recent redundancy will benefit by turning straight to the chapter dealing with those areas.

'Signposts to Success'

As a short-cut to ploughing through the full contents listing, the following table signposts the most common alternatives to starting at the beginning of Part One.

Ageism, how to beat it	Chapter 5
Depression, Anger etc.	Chapter 7
Responding to Advertisements	Chapter 8
Headhunters	Chapter 2
Temporary Employment	Chapter 7
Internet	Chapter 9
CVs	Chapters 16 to 19
Gaps in Experience/Skills	Chapter 19
Interviews	Chapters 20 to 23
Tests and Assessment Centres	Chapter 24
Job Offers	Chapter 25
Hidden Approaches	No short cuts. To find out why, read straight on.

"FINDING A JOB IS
A JOB IN ITSELF."

PART ONE

The creative job campaign

> **"It's time you got one thing straight: no one is interested in giving you a job."**

1 Cobblers' children

Why even marketing executives fail to market themselves

'I am always very uncomfortable', said Chris Cawcutt, managing director of City outplacement specialists Fairplace Consulting, 'when people come in here for their first counselling session and proudly announce that they have already been busy networking.'

He went on to explain why. 'Most of them, at least nine out of ten, haven't the faintest idea of what efficient networking is all about. The calls they've made will almost certainly have been completely mismanaged and, since they will have rung their best contacts first, they will have wasted their potentially most valuable leads.' He spread his hands in a gesture of resignation. 'You don't get a second bite at the cherry.'

Sad though it is, the situation described by Chris Cawcutt is not altogether surprising. It is extremely common, and quite understandable, for people who are seeking jobs, particularly those who have recently been thrust out of work, to become consumed by the need to get on with the task, to be doing something. Nor is it entirely unexpected that they should be unfamiliar with relatively new and widely misunderstood techniques such as networking, and consequently do more harm than good when they attempt to use them.

What is absolutely staggering, on the other hand, is the manner in which the majority of executives go about organising and managing their whole job search campaign. Men and women who have presumably, to judge by their achievements, been highly competent in managing projects for their employers seem to go completely to pieces when it comes to managing their own careers. Even cobblers' children are well shod by comparison!

Whoever first came up with the saying that finding a job is a job in itself was a lot wiser than he or she probably realised. Most people who glibly repeat the cliché take it to mean no more than the fact that seeking a job involves a lot of effort, perhaps so much that it actually becomes a full-time job in itself. In reality there is far more to it than that.

Like any major project, the job search can be handled with varying degrees of efficiency – or inefficiency. And, again like any project you might undertake in the course of your employment as a manager, the most common causes of failure stem from diving in feet first without having done the groundwork. Clarifying the problem, analysing the situation and setting clear objectives ought to be second nature to any competent executive, but they all too often get ignored when managers are dealing with their own careers, rather than with a problem at work.

The situation was neatly summed up by John Woodger, Vice President, International, of Right Associates, one of the world's largest outplacement firms. 'Most executives', John commented wryly, 'do more research on their annual holiday than they do on their career. Having no strategic goal, they base their job moves on expediency, substituting panic for logic. It's like boarding the first bus that comes along – it may be going to the wrong destination, but they hop on anyway.'

It is precisely because so many people get it wrong that this is where you get your first, and arguably greatest, chance to get ahead of the competition. Reining in your enthusiasm, and going through a detailed research and analysis exercise before you even start chasing specific positions or contacts may seem frustrating. That is probably why so many job seekers skip it. In the long run, though, it will provide a far less tedious, more efficient and much faster route to the achievement of your objective.

Speaking of which, what is your objective? A better job? Your ideal job? Any job at all, so long as it pays the bills?

If you answered in any of these terms, it is time you thought again. Time you took a further step ahead by putting yourself in the other person's shoes. Time you got one thing straight: no one is interested in giving you a job. What employers are interested in is how you can benefit their organisation. That is not just quibbling with words. It is a completely different way of looking at things. Forget about your job search. Start thinking about your marketing campaign.

The marketing concept

Sales and marketing are two words which produce an instinctive negative reaction in the vast majority of executives who are not themselves engaged in these areas – and even in some who are. The words conjure up images of door-to-door double glazing salespeople and of television commercials so nauseating that you instantly reach for the remote control. To suggest that you treat yourself as a product to be hawked around a largely uninterested market place seems like the ultimate indignity.

But there is another kind of selling which has next to nothing in common with pushy doorstep salespeople or with ghastly TV ads. It is the kind of approach used by businesses like law and accountancy practices, and firms of management consultants. Because their services are professional, they have to adopt a professional approach to marketing and selling – and so must you. Next to nothing in common? Well, both approaches are, in fact, based on the same fundamental principle: the basic concept of marketing. This quite simply states that you are far more likely to sell something if you understand whether and why potential purchasers might want it in the first place.

If that seems too obvious to be worth spending your time on, just stop and ask yourself whether you have been basing your whole job search on this fundamental concept. The odds are that you have not and that, as a result, you have probably been wasting an awful lot of time and effort. What you need to do now is to stop *wasting* time and start *investing* it – and the first investment you have to make is in learning a little about the professional approach to marketing.

How to become a marketing pro

Any sales and marketing people who are tempted to skip this section had better think again – which may at least give some comfort to those trained in other disciplines. Just as managers seem unable to manage their own job campaigns, so sales and marketing people seem to be no better than anyone else at identifying likely buyers of their services or at closing the sale. Cobblers' children ride again!

Confirmation comes from someone who certainly ought to know. Neil Cameron, managing director of marketing recruitment specialists The Lloyd Group, states quite categorically, 'I see no more evidence of the use of proven marketing techniques being applied to the job search by marketing people than by anyone else.'

But what are these techniques? And can you really market a person the way commercial businesses market their products and services?

Neil Cameron likened the process not so much to the promotion of a new product or service, as to what marketing people call the 'repositioning' of an existing one. You cannot start your career all over again from scratch, so even if there may, for example, be a crying need for brain surgeons that is not going to help you if you have spent the whole 20 years of your working life in retail management. What you can do, on the other hand, is find new markets for your existing skills and experience; to add new skills through training and additional experience by, for example, undertaking consultancy work; and to 'repackage' yourself by improving your application letters and CV, your image and your interview technique.

Neil then went on to point out, 'You can't reposition until you know what you've got to begin with. You need to carry out an audit of what you currently have to offer to prospective employers, then you can look at how their perception of you can be broadened and improved.'

In the next chapter you will find the tools to do just that – questionnaires to help with the audit plus explanations as to how to use marketing techniques like USPs and the SWOT analysis – and in the chapter after that you will be shown how to do something else which Neil Cameron believes to be essential to an effective marketing campaign: understanding who the customers are and what they are looking for.

'Like any marketing professional', Neil explained, 'you have to go through the structured process of market research, product development and the distribution process. The starting point', he emphasised, 'is market research.'

Know thyself

All of this assumes that you already know what sort of job you are aiming for. However, if you or your employers had forked out several thousand pounds on an outplacement programme, the first task you would be set, before looking either at your skills and experience or at the market for them, would be to undertake a comprehensive self-appraisal, concentrating on what you enjoy doing, what you are suited to doing and how these factors relate to the rest of your life – family, leisure etc.

This is not just a way for the outplacement firms to justify their fees. Given the risible career advice most people got when they completed full-time educa-tion and the haphazard way subsequent moves so often take place (e.g. if someone is a good salesperson, researcher or whatever, promote them to man-ager of the department, regardless of whether they have managerial ability or not), a significant number of people end up in jobs they are neither suited to nor enjoy. They would be much happier, and consequently more successful, if – at an earlier stage – they had sat down and given some serious thought to the kinds of questions raised in the self-appraisal process.

This whole procedure is, moreover, an essential preparation for all the sub-sequent stages of the job search, from accurately targeting yourself at the kind of role for which you are likely to be the number one candidate to answering interview questions like 'How have you developed as an individual in the course of your career?'; 'Where do you see your career going over the next five years?'; and 'In what ways can you add value to our company?'.

GET TO KNOW YOURSELF

Try it for yourself. Take a sheet of paper and write down:

- What you like(d) about your present/most recent job
- What you dislike(d)

Distinguish between:

- The actual work
- The organisation
- The people – especially your boss

And do not forget things like:

- How far you identify with what the business does – its products or services
- Where the job is based (city centre, rural environment, industrial estate etc.)
- The length, and difficulty, of the journey to and from work
- The hours you work and their effect on the rest of your life
- Travel involved in the job – frequency, duration and destinations
- Fringe benefits
- Promotion prospects

Beginning to feel that you know yourself a bit better? Then go down a layer and get personal:

- How do you think you are seen by your
  - boss?
  - peers?
  - staff?
- And how about people outside work, such as your
  - spouse/partner?
  - children?
  - parents?
  - friends?

Has that got you wondering whether they actually see you the way you think they do? Have you got the guts to ask them? And would they give you an honest answer?

Stay in the domestic area for a moment. Putting your job to one side, ask yourself:

- What do you find satisfying about your current way of life?

- What do you dislike about it?

- What do you do well?

- What do you do badly?

- What do you like about yourself?

- What are you proud of having overcome?

- What would you still like to overcome or to change?

- What are your most important values?

- What are your most cherished aspirations?

At first sight this kind of complete self-appraisal may seem a long way from the simple task of defining the objective of your job search. Surely, if you have got a big mortgage plus crippling private school fees to pay, and you have been in the same type of job all your working life, what choice do you have but to look for something else in the same line? In practice it is rarely as black and white as that. While some people have fewer options than others, most have more scope than they realise – a very great deal more in many cases! That is why outplacement consultants insist on what John Woodger of Right Associates calls a 'whole life plan', worked out – where appropriate – with the involvement of your spouse or partner.

But, you may ask, what about the financial considerations? When do we get on to them?

The answer is, 'Not yet'. While it is perfectly natural that money should be the first thought on your mind, especially if you are out of a job, professional career counsellors do not bring that into the equation until after they have got you to look at what you like doing and why, at what you have to offer in terms of skills, experience and qualifications, and at who might want to buy your services. The reason is that taking these factors into consideration first vastly increases the options open to you, whereas starting off with the financial considerations closes options down.

The 'money first' mentality is reinforced by the conditioning that comes from thinking of advertisements as the main source of job vacancies. Most advertisements have a price tag on them which rules you either in or out. Hidden approaches which, do not forget, account for far more career opportunities than adverts, operate in a completely different manner. When you make a networking contact or a speculative application, you do not even have to consider money. You start off by finding – or creating – opportunities. By the time money comes into the frame, you already have someone interested in employing you and that puts things in a very different perspective.

A helping ear

While some job seekers initially take a bit of convincing about the value of undertaking a comprehensive self-appraisal, it is the mechanics that causes problems for others. It can be particularly difficult if you are still trying to come to grips with having recently found yourself out of a job, perhaps for the first time in your life. As Siobhan Hamilton-Phillips, chief executive of the Vocational Guidance Association, explained, 'When people are worried about what to do next, their mind shuts down rather than opening up.'

It is, furthermore, difficult to be truly objective about yourself. Enlisting the aid of your spouse or partner, or of a relative, friend or colleague may help, in that they may see things that you do not and may be able to challenge your in-built assumptions. On the other hand, it may be that they know you too well to be truly objective. Furthermore, you may find it difficult to bare your soul to people with whom you are so closely involved. Often it is easier to talk to a stranger.

Outplacement gives you precisely that. A trained stranger with relevant experience – your counsellor – leads you through the self-appraisal, often with the aid of a battery of questionnaires and tests. But outplacement is expensive. Typically, it costs several thousand pounds. Unless your employer is willing to cough up, you are probably going to think twice about doing so out of your own pocket.

Fortunately, it is possible to buy bits of the outplacement service if you cannot afford the whole and, in addition to career counsellors and CV writers, there are firms which offer help with this initial stage of the job search process. For a fee in the hundreds, rather than thousands, of pounds organisations like the Vocational Guidance Association and Career Analysts Ltd will provide a combination of tests and counselling aimed first at ensuring that you consider all of the options open to you, and then at guiding you in the most appropriate, and realistic, direction.

Like John Woodger of Right Associates, Career Analysts Ltd's MD Peter Forsyth insists on the need to take a holistic approach, looking at the whole person. In order to get this complete picture, he and his counsellors, all of whom are chartered psychologists, would look at the following:

- **Interests:**
  What you enjoy doing is usually what you do best. Do you prefer working with numbers, with words or with people? Are you more creative or more practical?

- **Attitudes:**
  What do you look for in terms of organisational culture, relationships with other people, remuneration and career progression?

- **Attainments:**
  What have you achieved at work and, where relevant, elsewhere?

- **Aptitudes**:
  Various kinds of reasoning ability (verbal, numerical, abstract, spatial, mechanical and perceptual), and your attention to detail are tested to assess your flexibility, resourcefulness and potential to develop new skills.

- **Physical Factors:**
  How well do your appearance, manner and speech suit you to different kinds of job?

- **Personality:**
  A personality profile assesses how you are likely to react to different problems and situations. It looks at such questions as whether you are independent or conformist, guided by your instincts or by hard facts, outgoing or self-contained, and whether you are a worrier or not.

- **Circumstances:**
  To what extent are your choices limited by financial, personal and family commitments?

Whether you use a full outplacement service, a careers service or your own resources, once you have obtained a better understanding of your own preferences, the next stage is to consider what you have to offer to a potential employer.

"YOU HAVE GOT TO SMACK SOMEONE RIGHT BETWEEN THE EYES WITH WHATEVER IT IS THAT MAKES YOU JUST RIGHT FOR THEM."

2 Knowing the product

If you have not yet prepared an up-to-date CV, sit down with a piece of paper and describe your current, or most recent, job. If you do already have a CV containing that description, get it out and take a look at it. What does it highlight?

- ❏ Your duties?
- ❏ Your skills?
- ❏ Your strengths?
- ❏ Your achievements?

Far too many people think only in terms of duties. The more aware list achievements, which is what you will highlight when you prepare your CV. Right now, though, we need to make a comprehensive list of absolutely everything you have to sell, rather than concentrating on just one or two aspects. Take a fresh piece of paper then and, thinking not just about your current or last job, nor even about your entire career to date, but about every aspect of your life, including business, community, social and leisure activities, list out absolutely all of your:

- ❏ qualifications;
- ❏ experience;
- ❏ achievements;
- ❏ skills;
- ❏ personal strengths;

❑ ways in which you have developed over the years;

❑ any other assets, e.g. business and personal contacts, which could be
     of value to a potential employer.

You should not have had any trouble with your qualifications. You either
have the relevant examination passes, membership of professional institutes
and so on which give you the credentials that people look for in your particular discipline and business sector, or you do not. If you do not, you may wish
to consider obtaining them but, unless this is a relatively simple matter, like
completing the last section of a qualification, it is not going to help you this
time around and should be put to one side while you concentrate on those
assets which are going to get you your next job.

Experience has two aspects to it – what you have done and where you have
done it. The 'where' part, which covers both the type of business (e.g. manufacturing or service industry, nature of product or service), and the size and kind
of organisation (partnership, family-owned business, public quoted company,
subsidiary of overseas group etc.), should not take you too long to write down.

Listing out the duties or tasks you have performed in the various posts you
have held may be somewhat more time-consuming, especially for those whose
careers run into decades rather than just years. Even so, be thorough and do
not forget to write down what you have done outside work as well. You never
know when it might be just what is required to plug an otherwise awkward
gap. For example, a job you are competing for may call for experience of committee work. Even if you have had no exposure to committees in your business
capacity, you may well serve on one in connection with a sporting or a voluntary organisation.

Did achievements give you more of a problem? Then ask yourself why. If you
are simply feeling too depressed about the whole job search to be able to think
of what your successes have been over the years, that is a situation which
needs tackling right away. Turn to Chapter 7 for some practical suggestions.

If, on the other hand, modesty is the problem, it is time you got something
straight. While, in the UK at any rate, overblown hype may do more to lose
you a job than win it, you will do yourself even more damage by being too
modest. So try again. Think of every accomplishment that has given you a

glow of pride, however small. Do not confine yourself purely to your career. Consider every aspect of your life. Remember that, in an interview situation, for example, responses to questions about your skills and personal attributes can often be strengthened by bringing in illustrations drawn from outside the working environment, such as community or sporting activities.

Talking of which, when you move down to the next couple of items on the list, skills and strengths, analyse your achievements to see which aptitudes and personal qualities contributed to the successes in question. You should be able to make some useful additions to your lists.

In the case of skills, it is also worth going back to your experience listing, to check what aptitudes were called for by the various tasks you carried out. The majority of job seekers undersell themselves on skills. Have you, for example, included all the following?

❏ People skills

– advising

– counselling

– interviewing

– managing

– mediating

– motivating

– persuading

– training

❏ Communication skills

– drafting reports

– reviewing and editing reports

– servicing meetings: agendas and minutes

– writing promotional material, newsletters, brochures etc.

– oral presentations to meetings

– public speaking

– foreign languages

And so on for:

❏ Analytical skills

❏ Computer skills

❏ Negotiating skills

❏ Numerical skills

❏ Organisational skills

❏ Planning skills

And do not forget those skills which, because only a minority of executives exhibit any great proficiency in them, tend to be at a real premium – things like delegation, running meetings and, most important of all, developing new business.

If people tend to short-change themselves on skills, they are liable to be ten times worse when it comes to personal strengths. Is your list a bit thin? Then go back to your achievements and give some thought to just what it was that made the difference between success and failure. Even if you decide that Lady Luck played a big part in a particular accomplishment, explore the situation further – you may well find that you made a substantial part of your own apparent good luck by qualities like persistence or opportunism.

The next heading – the ways in which you have developed – follows naturally on from your strengths. Some of the qualities you have will have come to you via your parents' genes or will already have been acquired by the time you started out on your career. Others will have been developed as you have climbed the career ladder and it is these which a professional recruiter will home in on.

To take an example from the world of accountancy, a financial accountant needs qualities like accuracy, thoroughness and honesty. Progression up the ladder to the position of financial controller will call for different strengths, such as the ability to analyse and interpret the figures, to make forecasts, and to communicate with non-accountants in a way that enables them to understand the relevance of the information. Further progress to the post of finance director will call for the development of vision in order to contribute to the formulation of strategies and policies, and also for the ability to negotiate with financial institutions in order to raise capital for the business.

While each discipline will have its own requirements in terms of personal development, there are certain strengths which ought to be fundamental to virtually any managerial role. Communication skills, staff selection and motivation, delegation, time management, conceptual thinking, and the effective use of meetings all figure prominently in the successful executive's toolkit.

So too, if you really want to get to the top, does business development. That is why the last question on the list was about your contacts. Not just those you have made in the course of your job. List every useful contact you have. Chambers of commerce, Round Table and Rotary, golf and squash club, church, voluntary work, boards of school governors and many other organisations are all fertile ground for meeting people who could be useful either directly or, because they can put you in touch with other people they know, indirectly.

From famine to feast

If you started off by worrying that you did not have much to offer to potential employers, you may now be thinking that you have the opposite problem. So, what are you going to do with all this enormous amount of information?

The short answer is, 'Be selective'. Compiling a comprehensive register of all your assets is a bit like putting together a complete wardrobe. Instead of trying to adapt one somewhat inadequate outfit to suit every occasion from a formal dinner to a day out in the country, and from going to the office to spending the evening in a disco, you can choose on each occasion those items which exactly fit the bill. You will be referring to your asset register every time you:

- apply to a job advertisement;
- get a call from a headhunter;

- speak to a network contact;
- make a speculative application;
- edit your CV;
- write a covering letter to accompany it;
- prepare for an interview.

Right now, though, you are going to use it to deal with a couple of the best-known acronyms in the marketing dictionary – USPs and the SWOT analysis.

Not quite unique

USPs – unique selling propositions – are much loved by marketing people and with good reason. They are what differentiates one particular product or service from all its competitors. And, when you come to think about it, it is not easy to get wildly enthusiastic about promoting a product if you cannot for the life of you see how it is superior to or different from all of the competitive products with which the market is saturated.

Which, of course, is where the relevance of USPs to your personal marketing campaign comes in. If you are one of three hundred respondents to an advertisement, or one of a hundred people on a headhunter's target candidate list for a job, you need something to make you stand out. The odds may be shorter when you are networking, but the principle is just the same. You have got to smack someone right between the eyes with whatever it is that makes you just right for them. If *you* do not know what that is, you can hardly expect there to be very much chance of *them* ever spotting it.

A lot of job seekers suddenly feel rather flat at this point. They really cannot see what they have that other people do not. Maybe the problem lies in the terminology. In reality unique selling propositions are rarely, if ever, truly unique. That is just marketing hype. Different selling propositions would be more accurate, but that would not sound nearly so impressive, would it?

So, forget about the word 'unique' and, for the moment at any rate, think in terms of what makes you different. Do you speak a foreign language? All right, you may not be the only executive in your field who does but, given the appalling lack of linguistic ability, especially among British managers, it probably differentiates you from nine out of ten of your competitors. What else? Are you a wizard on spreadsheets? Have you taken the trouble to acquire a detailed knowledge of the legal issues relating to the business you work in? Or the tax implications?

Go back to your asset register. Look at the business sector(s) in which you have years of experience. Do the same for the types of organisation. Now add some personal strengths. They do not necessarily have to be the sexy, glamorous ones like being a dynamic, entrepreneurial innovator. Apart from being grossly overworked, and 90 per cent pure hype, these attributes are not by any means always the ones employers actually want. If they are looking for a safe pair of hands, reliability may be far more important.

Finally, take just one more look at your asset register and put the icing on the gingerbread by adding in a few carefully selected achievements which demonstrate how highly effectively you have put your special qualities to work to add value to the organisation which has the good fortune to employ you.

Is it beginning to come into focus? Are you starting to see just how different you are? In fact, you are more than just different. Selling propositions may not be unique, but you are. When it comes to your personal marketing campaign, try thinking of USP not as a unique selling proposition, but as a uniquely saleable person.

The other acronym

Defining the qualities which make you unique – and saleable – has, in effect, dealt with the first part of your SWOT analysis. In order to plan an effective campaign, marketing people look at strengths, weaknesses, opportunities and threats. Being an optimistic breed, they do not dwell too much on weaknesses, but they do appreciate the importance of being aware of their product's shortcomings and so, without getting depressed about it, should you be aware of your weaknesses.

There are two things you can do about them. One is to overcome them. If you are aware that your lack of ability in anything from the latest computer application to making presentations at meetings is putting you at a competitive disadvantage in the job stakes, you can very easily acquire that ability by going on a course, teaching yourself or whatever.

If the weakness is something you cannot readily overcome, perhaps an ingrained character trait, then the positive way to deal with it is simply not to waste time applying for jobs where that is an insuperable obstacle – which brings us on to the question of targeting.

It also leads naturally into the second half of the SWOT analysis. If you are either out of work already, or afraid that you soon might be, you will be all too aware of the threats – things like delayering and decentralisation. If you had had the foresight to have carried out this kind of analysis earlier on, you might have anticipated the problem and taken evasive action.

In the future, of course, you will – won't you? But what about this time? That is where the opportunities part of the SWOT analysis comes in. Having looked, in the previous chapter, at what you like doing, and in this one at what strengths people are going to employ you for, the next chapter shows you how to identify just who those people might be.

"THE JOB YOU ARE GOING TO GET IS THE ONE WHERE YOU ARE THE NUMBER ONE CANDIDATE."

3 Knowing the market

'The whole essence of being successful in the job search', according to Kit Scott-Brown, chief executive of leading outplacement organisation InterExec PLC, 'is dependent upon the targeting.' What the job seeker has to do, he went on to explain, is to target where he or she is going to be the number one candidate.

This approach may seem to run counter to everything you have heard about finding a new job. Given the imbalance in supply and demand between the apparently limited number of opportunities, and the vast number of candidates chasing them, do you have any other option but to play the numbers game, continually pumping out applications until one finally comes up trumps?

Yes, you do. It is quality, not quantity, that is going to get you a new position. Jobhunters who shoot from the hip at anything that moves, regardless of their suitability for the vacancy in question, are wasting not only their own time but also other people's. You will certainly not advance your cause by doing that. By targeting yourself accurately, on the other hand, you will be applying your efforts more productively. You will still need to work just as hard, but the period of time for which you have to do so will be very much shorter.

WHAT KIND OF ORGANISATION DO YOU WANT TO WORK FOR?

So, where do you begin? The first thing to do is to define the kind of organisation you would like to be part of. Using the analysis you carried out in Chapter 1, consider the following factors. Take a sheet of paper and, against each factor, list out on one side of the page the types of organisation you would like to work for and on the other those you would not wish to be employed by. Consider the following list.

continued overleaf

WHAT KIND OF ORGANISATION DO YOU WANT TO WORK FOR – continued

- Size
- Ownership – public, private, family, partnership, charity etc.
- Culture – British, American, European, Far Eastern etc.
- Management style – formal/structured, entrepreneurial, laid back etc.
- Products or services
- Location.

Then put the factors that would make an organisation appeal to you into your order of precedence so that you define, at the top end of the scale, the kind of organisation you would most like to work for, then list out all the others that you would consider in a descending scale of preference.

Now do the same thing for the kind of job you would like, answering the following general questions, then adding whatever further considerations are relevant to you personally.

- What activities, functions or responsibilities would your ideal job description include? List at least half a dozen.
- List any activities, functions or responsibilities which you would not want to play a prominent role in your job.
- Would you prefer to be employed in a headquarters or sharp end role?
- Do you want to manage staff? How many?
- Do you prefer to work on your own or in a team?
- Do you like to be able to plan ahead with certainty or do you find it stimulating to be responding to changing demands, resulting in you having to reassess your priorities frequently and at short notice?

When you have worked through these considerations, and whatever additional factors influence you personally, what you will have defined is your perfect role – your ideal job in the ideal organisation. That is the role in which you will perform best, because you will be 100 per cent motivated. However, out in the cold, hard world, nothing actually is perfect. That is why we have left plenty of options open, giving you the scope to modify what you would ideally like to do in the light of two additional factors.

What you have

The first of these is what you are equipped to do. This is where we find out how realistic you have been. Is that perfect job a pure pipe dream? Or have you, perhaps, not been ambitious enough? Have you undersold yourself? To find out, go back to the analysis you conducted in the previous chapter. Review your qualifications, experience, skills, strengths and so on against the ideal job which you have defined.

How easy this is to do varies considerably from one individual to another. Some people's idea of their perfect role is one that they already know quite intimately – their boss's job, or even the position they last had themselves, before they were made redundant. Others, who have been working in a job or organisation that they have hated, may have defined something totally different, even the complete polar opposite – a role for which it will be rather more difficult to assess their suitability.

If you fall into the second category, and are consequently unsure as to whether you meet the criteria for the job in question, there are a couple of things you can do. One is to look at advertisements for the kind of post you have defined, to see what attributes are called for in the ideal candidate. The other is to talk to someone else who might be in a position to shed some light on the matter. Who? Well, the person who will know best of all is, of course, the person who is actually doing that job right now.

If you have already begun to protest that you could not even name a single person who falls into that category, let alone knowing one well enough to bend their ear with such a request, stop being negative and start being proactive. Ring up an organisation where that job exists, ask the switchboard operator for the name of the person who holds it and then ask to be put through. As you will discover when we get on to networking, people rarely mind being asked for advice. Usually they are actually flattered. And, admittedly only occasionally – but it could just happen to you – the person you call is about to be promoted, retire or whatever. The job is up for grabs – and you are in with a chance before the organisation has even given a thought to placing an advertisement or calling in a firm of headhunters.

Once you have a clear idea of what your ideal job involves, check how closely you fit. Remember that the job you are going to get is the one where you are the number one candidate. Go back to your asset register, paying particular attention to your USPs. Are you really right for the job in question?

If you are not, then you may have to go back to your preferences and take a look at your other options. Alternatively, if your ideal really is the only thing that is going to satisfy you, you may need to consider it as your next job but one, and look right now for the position which will provide a stepping stone to that ideal. This is a very useful exercise, and should be considered even by those who believe they can get a job which does satisfy their requirements straight away. Only by looking ahead to the next job but one can you ensure that you acquire the necessary qualifications, experience and skills by the time that you actually need them in order to progress your career. So, when you are reviewing the advertisements and talking to people in the fields into which you wish to progress, keep that further step clearly in mind and find out what action you need to take over the next few years in order to be ready when the time comes.

What they want

If gaps in skills, experience and so on appear to create obstacles for some people, the other factor we have to consider seems to pose a major problem for a whole lot more. Time and again in the current market, jobhunters are heard bemoaning the fact that, although they have all the necessary qualifications, skills, experience etc. – not to mention boundless energy and enthusiasm – the jobs they seek just do not exist. They point to the things we talked about earlier on: downsizing, delayering, decentralisation and so on. They complain about the effects on jobs of mergers, acquisitions and the consequent rationalisation. They wave copies of newspapers around, demonstrating how few jobs are being advertised for people like them. In short, they waste a lot of time and effort doing things that get them nowhere, rather than directing their resources into the creative, proactive activities which will get them some really tangible results.

To be sure, the highly competitive executive job market may mean that you have to modify your aspirations – that is why we built the flexibility to do so into the questionnaires you completed earlier in this chapter – but it will only stop you from getting a job if you insist on confining your efforts to responding to advertisements.

If, on the other hand, you use the hidden approaches, you will be surprised at how opportunities emerge even in business sectors or organisations which appear not to be hiring people at all. For example, a business that is going through a difficult period may have a need for someone who can inject that something extra into the enterprise to steer it through the troubled waters. Having displayed initiative in targeting the organisation and in making a direct approach, and having identified that you have the qualities they need, you may well be seen as just the person to do the job.

Research

Like assessing whether you meet the criteria for your ideal job, identifying target organisations will involve varying amounts of work for different people, depending on their individual situation. If you are aiming to stay in your present sector, you may already know most of the players, since they will be, or have been, either your competitors, your clients or your customers. This is particularly true of 'small worlds' like the City of London where, in addition to being in the same business sector, firms tend to be clustered together within a tightly defined geographical area.

In other cases varying amounts of market research may be required. Prior to the internet, this meant a journey to the nearest major reference library, armed with a large notepad. These days it should be possible to get most of the information you need without leaving your own home, though not all of the reference sources are free, so those who live near a good library and are on a tight budget may still prefer this route, as may those who have not familiarised themselves with search engines and prefer to rely on a helpful reference librarian to point them in the right direction.

Whether you access reference materials on-line, by CD-ROM or in old-fashioned book form, some of the most useful sources of information on UK companies are:

- *Key British Enterprises* (KBE) – covers the UK's leading 50,000 companies, giving financial information plus details of business activities and names of top people.

- *Kompass* – Classified both by products/services and by around 45,000 leading companies supplying them. Information includes sales, numbers of employees, names of directors, addresses and telephone numbers plus details of over 40,000 parents and 130,000 subsidiaries, showing their corporate structure.

- *Kelly's directories* – A number of directories classified both by geographical areas and by business sectors.

- *MacMillan's Unquoted Companies* – Financial profiles of 20,000 companies with sales in excess of £3 million.

- *Who Owns Whom?* – A useful cross-reference of who is owned by, as well as who owns, whom.

- *Britain's Top Privately Owned Companies* – Valuable information, including sales turnover, on companies in a sector which is more difficult than most to research.

- *Stock Exchange Official Yearbook* – Covers all listed companies, giving financial data, company history, and names of directors and auditors.

- *Directory of British Associations* – Useful if you are targeting a particular sector. Covers around 6,800 associations, with details of membership, interests and publications.

- *Dun & Bradstreet Business Register* – 32 volumes, classified by area, covering 1.6 million businesses and providing brief details of nature of business, directors/partners and numbers of employees plus D & B's rating of each organisation's creditworthiness.

- *Extel* handbooks.

- *Price Waterhouse Corporate Register* – Quarterly register of companies listed on the London Stock Exchange. Particularly useful is the section containing biographical details of 20,000 senior executives. Also covers professional advisers.

- *Index to Financial Times* – A monthly and annual index to published information on companies and business personalities.

- *Directory of Directors* – Covers directors of major public and private companies, listing names and appointments.

- *Trade directories* – Available for most trades and industries.

- *Local directories* – Particularly useful for obtaining information on smaller companies. Published by bodies such as local councils and Chambers of Commerce.

- *Occupations* – Information on specific jobs and trades. Produced by the Career and Occupational Information Centre.

- *Classified telephone directories* – Classified both by location and by type of business, *Yellow Pages, Thomson* and other publications can be a valuable starting point for research.

- *Executive Grapevine* – A listing of executive search and selection firms and agencies, with details of specialisation by industry, function, location and salary level.

If your needs still are not satisfied after going through this list, you can always consult *Current British Directories,* a catalogue providing information on over 4,000 other directories, including a thumbnail sketch of the contents of each of them.

For information on overseas business organisations, the main directories are:

- *Kompass Directories* – Available for many European countries and some others, mainly in the Far East and Australasia.

- *Principal International Businesses* – Covers in excess of 50,000 major organisations in well over 100 countries.

- *Who Owns Whom* – Three separate volumes, one each for Continental Europe, North America and Australasia/the Far East.
- *Yearbooks of Foreign Stock Exchanges* – Valuable sources of financial data on business organisations in the countries in question.
- *Europe's 15,000 Largest Companies* – Statistics and financial data.
- *Major Companies of Europe* – Covers several thousand major continental European companies, with details of activities, directors and senior executives, etc.
- *Major Companies of the Far East and Australasia*
- *Major Companies of Latin America and the Caribbean*
- *Major Companies of the Arab World*
- *World Guide to Trade Associations* – classified by country.

The length of the list of job possibilities you end up with will be governed by several factors: how idealistic you have been in defining your preferences regarding employer and job content; how thorough (and how modest) you have been about what you have to offer; how imaginative you have been in identifying reasons why people should want to buy what you have to sell; and how conscientiously you have conducted your research. What we are going to look at next is how to handle long lists efficiently and, where necessary, how to make short lists longer.

"IF YOU'RE NOT THINKING SEGMENTS, YOU'RE NOT THINKING MARKETING."

4 Optimism or realism?

The simple way to handle a long list is to use the salami technique – slice it up into bite-sized pieces. In marketing speak, this is known as segmentation. Harvard guru Ted Levitt once said, 'If you're not thinking segments, you're not thinking marketing.'

What he meant by this is that, in any market, different customers have different needs. These different needs can be satisfied either by different products or by different positionings of the same product. That is where the relevance to your marketing campaign comes in. You need to divide your market into groups of customers in such a way that you can identify the different needs of the various groups. Having understood their different needs, you will then be able to market to each group more effectively.

Your split may be based on any one or more of a whole range of different factors. If, for example, what you want to market is your ability to sort out problems, you could approach not only organisations that are in financial difficulty and therefore need a company doctor but also those whose problems arise from very rapid growth, where the need is for someone to grab systems and administration by the scruff of the neck, and pull them up to the same level as the ever increasing sales. Both types of organisation need a problem solver, but you would target your sales pitch differently in each case.

The same fundamental approach applies if your segmentation is based on business sectors. When marketing yourself to the kind of business you are, or have been, working in, you will obviously stress your many years of relevant experience. If, on the other hand, you want to target other businesses which have similar attributes, let us say you want to move from one kind of service industry to another, then you will play on the fact that you can introduce new concepts which have been proven to succeed in other businesses with similar problems, and you can point out that you will not be subject to the tunnel vision of people who have been in that one narrow area all their working life.

Whichever way you do it, just remember the vital principle of concentrating on what the customer needs. As one job seeker put it, 'You can land more jobs in two months by becoming interested in people's problems than you can in two years by trying to get people interested in you.'

Shooting for the stars

Having sliced your list up into manageable chunks, how do you prioritise them? Do you aim first of all for your ideal and then gradually lower your sights if you are unsuccessful? Does that depend on your own individual position – people who are in jobs may have the luxury of being able to wait for the right job, but what about someone who is unemployed with an ever growing pile of bills to pay?

In reality, the answer comes out much the same for all job seekers, regardless of their situation. This is because the urgency of finding a new position tends to correlate with the amount of time available for the job search. People who are out of work can devote far more time to their search than those who have to spend long hours in the office, fitting the job search into evenings and weekends.

People at both ends of the spectrum should therefore start off by going for their ideal. The difference is that those who are out of work will, if they do not succeed in achieving their first choice, have both the time and the need to progress more quickly to their alternative options.

Those who are actually out of work, or under notice, may find it useful to divide the process into three stages. In the first period, you look for a job which would represent a definite step forwards in your career. In phase two, you consider a sideways move. In the third and last period, you consider any reasonable option to tide you over, with a view to moving on to something better as soon as the opportunity arises. The timing, naturally, depends largely on your financial resources and the length of time you can afford to be out of work.

People who are in work will obviously go no further than phase two, and that only if there is a good reason. For example, a sideways move may be required in order to fill a gap in experience which will then make it possible, in two or three years' time, to get the job you are really after.

In any case, when you are being proactive rather than reactive there is actually far less of a problem. If you have been truly professional about your marketing campaign up to this point, there should not be too great a conflict between what you seek, the organisations on your target list and the job you ultimately get. If you have been accurate in analysing your experience, skills, strengths and so on; if you have defined the kind of organisation in which you are going to be most highly motivated; and if you have conducted your research thoroughly; then the organisations on your list should all be ones you would like to work for. Some more than others? All right, start with those.

Yes, but . . .

What if your problem is not that your list is too long, but rather that it is too short? These are the kinds of reasons people most commonly give for this:

- I've been in one type of business all my life, and it's at rock bottom – no one is hiring.
- They're delayering – they don't want people like me any more.
- I've always been at group headquarters and now everybody is decentralising.

And, most commonly of all:

- I'm too old at 55, 50, 45, 40 etc.

There are two inter-related, though not entirely identical, issues here. One is the question of how transferable your skills and experience are. The other is how to deal with the prejudice which does undeniably exist against the older job seeker. We shall look at both of these issues in some depth but before we do just ask yourself one question. Be honest – have you really been thorough, positive and imaginative in your analysis up to this point? Go back and look again, in particular, at your:

❏ experience/background;

❏ achievements;

❏ skills/aptitudes;

❏ strengths;

❏ other assets – contacts, etc;

and see if you cannot add to the lists you have made.

Turn again to your list of organisations. Even if they do not appear to be recruiting, might there not be opportunities for someone with your abilities to help them out of their difficulties? Or have you been too tight in the geographical restrictions you have applied? For the right job in the right company, would you not be willing to travel a bit further to work? Or even to move home?

What about related fields? For example, one of the most marketable candidates is a poacher turned gamekeeper. The most highly publicised instances of such moves occur when government ministers in such areas as defence or health move, on leaving politics, into armaments or medical concerns, but such moves from a purchaser of products or services to a supplier are by no means uncommon and, when matters of public ethics are not involved, make a great deal of sense from both parties' viewpoints. Further instances of poacher turned gamekeeper moves include Inland Revenue staff going to join the tax departments of major accountancy practices and people joining the offices of ombudsmen or industry regulators on the back of their depth of experience in the business sectors in question.

Though not exactly in the poacher/gamekeeper category, there are many other opportunities to capitalise on the benefits of your knowledge in a given field. For example, firms providing management consultancy, training, executive recruitment and outplacement counselling all like to employ people with a background relevant to the sectors they are working in. So do organisations developing and marketing computer software.

By this stage, provided that you have really applied yourself conscientiously to the task, your list should already have grown significantly. Now it is time to expand it still further by looking at some of those objections that people so commonly raise. The first three were, essentially, centred on the belief that it is no good looking in the areas in which you have been employed because there are no longer any jobs there.

To some extent we have already demonstrated the fallacy of these arguments by showing that even companies which are in trouble and laying people off may be willing to hire someone who can solve their problems, and by illustrating how many options there may be to use your experience in a particular field by moving to a business that supplies goods or services to that sector. Now let us take an even broader look at the transferability of your assets.

On the transfer list

Many people have been brainwashed by job advertisements into thinking that no one is going to be interested in employing them unless they conform to a rigid specification which normally involves highly specific experience in terms of both the industry and the job content. The reasons for these demands have more to do with the method of recruitment than with your chances of getting hired. Given that almost any advertisement for a mid to senior level post will attract a response well into three figures, recruiters write copy with the intention of ruling applicants out rather than in. And, because it is easier to do that ruling out on purely objective criteria such as qualifications, background in a given sector and – yes – age, rather than on subjective criteria like strengths and personality, these are the ones that are used, in spite of the fact that the final decision on whom to select will, almost every time, be taken more on the basis of personal chemistry than anything else.

Headhunters, by the nature of the way they operate, are a little less rigid, but even they start with, and largely work to, a specification which has a significant objective element to it.

You, on the other hand, are not confining yourself to responding to advertisements or to waiting for the headhunter to call. You are making direct, personal contacts with individuals who may be able either to offer you a position or to put you in touch with someone else who can. You can therefore home in on those USPs which, in combination with each other, are going to make you the best possible solution to a particular organisation's problem. That takes some pretty accurate targeting, which in turn comes from thorough work at the analysis stage, but it is that kind of conscientious approach which is going to get you the job you want. Furthermore, in practice it is not nearly such hard work, or so demoralising, as continually getting rejection letters from applications to advertisements just because you fail to match one of the criteria on which the first vicious cut is based.

So, if your target list of organisations is still looking a bit thin even after the further work you have just done, give a little more thought to organisations which, though not in the same fields as you have been working in, may face similar difficulties.

PROBLEM SOLVING

Since it is the ability to solve other people's problems which is going to make them want to hire you, examine the situations you have been in. What problems were involved? Where else could the ability to deal with that sort of difficulty be useful?

To illustrate the process, here are a few typical examples.

- Airlines, theatres and hotels all have one fundamental problem in common, namely bums on seats or – to put it less crudely – high fixed costs, low variable costs and the need to achieve a minimum percentage of bookings in order to break even.

- Accountants, architects and solicitors likewise have the problem of utilisation, in the sense of needing to charge to clients a minimum percentage of each fee earner's working day. They also share another problem, that of the partnership structure with all its attendant shortcomings in terms of communication and decision making or, cynics might argue, the lack thereof.

- Clothes shops, farms and holiday camps are all seasonal businesses.

  These were all instances relating to the type of business. Use your imagination on some other types of problem. Analyse some of your greatest achievements. Identify just what it

continued overleaf

PROBLEM SOLVING – continued

was that enabled you to succeed in each case. Then see how many types of organisation you could apply these qualities to. Abilities such as meeting tight deadlines, managing complex logistical problems and making better use of resources through the introduction or upgrading of computerised systems, all find virtually universal application. Combine them with other factors such as your understanding of the problems of a particular type of business or organisation, your linguistic ability or whatever, and we are back to the uniquely saleable person – and to a list of target companies that now presents the need not for stretching but for segmentation and prioritisation.

While most of you are getting on with doing just that, it is time to turn to the other problem we identified earlier on. Older job seekers may feel that it is all very well having produced a long list of target companies, but is age not still going to be a barrier to them getting a job? Like so many aspects of the job search, it is in practice far less of a problem when you use the hidden approaches than when you confine yourself to the conventional ones like replying to advertisements. It is, nevertheless, a major issue in many people's minds. That is why it gets a chapter all to itself.

> **"THE OLDER YOU GET, THE MORE IMPORTANT IT BECOMES TO CONCENTRATE ON THE HIDDEN APPROACHES."**

5 Bus pass blues

Ageism and how to beat it

The reasons employers most frequently cite for not hiring older people include the following.

- 'Older employees are set in their ways and full of preconceived notions. It is better to hire a younger person, preferably a graduate, whom we can train from scratch in our own ways of doing things.'
- 'Younger people are hungrier. They have more ambition and energy.'
- 'Older people are not up to date technically.'
- 'Younger employees have fewer commitments outside work, so they are more willing to work late and at weekends.'
- 'Older people are more likely to have health problems.'
- 'Younger people do not have to be paid such high salaries.'
- 'Older people cost more in terms of pension contributions.'

This is, of course, a completely biased picture. Not only do these arguments totally ignore the pluses of older employees but at least some of them are pure prejudices which are by no stretch of the imagination true of all older executives. Nevertheless, since people who have raised objections never listen to any other arguments until their own have been acknowledged, addressed and properly answered, that is precisely what you must do if you really want another job. But, come to think of it, do you? And, if so, why?

Do you need another job?

No, it is not really such a silly question. Do you want a job or just a source of income? And, if it is only a source of income that you want, how much do you actually need? Are the children now off your hands? Have years of inflation reduced the real cost of your mortgage to a fraction of its original burden? Or have you even paid it off completely? What about capital? Have you accumulated a tidy sum in savings? Have you inherited money from your parents? What sort of income stream could your capital be turned into?

Sit down and work out the figures. Calculate your annual expenditure, add a bit for contingencies, then gross it up to arrive at the total income you need, before tax and other deductions, to cover your outgoings. How does that compare with what you are actually earning? Could you live quite comfortably on significantly less?

If so, ask yourself some more questions. Do you really want:

❏ The hassle of fighting your way to and from work every day at the mercy of traffic jams or unreliable, overcrowded trains?

❏ The strain of having to be continually struggling to keep up to date in a world in which the pace of change is ever faster?

❏ Your family and social life taking second place to the 'lunch is for wimps' philosophy of the modern executive rat race?

Why sacrifice so much in order to earn more money than you actually need? Why not take a part-time job, become self-employed or work for a less stressful organisation?

An increasing number of executives are taking one or other of these paths and, as a result, vastly improving their quality of life. Some develop portfolio careers, enjoying a varied and stimulating lifestyle by using two or three or even more of the different skill and experience sets they have acquired over the years. Others reduce the amount of time they work, thus avoiding the classic retirement problem of dropping overnight from a (more than) full-time job to suddenly doing nothing at all. The time they free up can be used for voluntary work, extra holidays or a variety of leisure pursuits.

It is not everyone, of course, who is lucky enough to be able to follow such a path, and readers who cannot afford to take any significant drop at all in their incomes may wish to skip this section and turn to page 49 where we look at how you can overcome age prejudice and still get a job, even a better job. On the other hand, the number of people who can afford to consider alternatives to full-time employment these days is surprisingly large, and the following stories demonstrate why they would be wise to give serious thought to the possibilities open to them.

Alan's story

Alan could have retired earlier. His wife, who was nearly ten years younger than himself, had a part-time secretarial job and their only child, now in her late 20s, was happily married to a man with a successful career and no financial worries. Alan, nevertheless, plodded on until his firm's official retirement age of 60, commuting up to central London every day and working under increasing pressure as his employer's business became more and more competitive.

He had looked forward to the opportunities retirement would provide to play golf and take extra holidays with his wife who, being employed within the education sector, had always been entitled to much more annual leave than he had. Alan enjoyed just over a year of that golden retirement. Shortly after his 61st birthday, he died of a heart attack.

He could have retired at least five years earlier – which might have meant rather more than five extra years of retirement, for his wife is convinced that it was those last few years, during his late 50s, struggling to keep up with the increasing pace of his job and enduring the daily hassle of London commuter trains, which took such a heavy toll.

Colin's story

Another man who had left things too late, but in a rather different way, was Colin. Only just coming up to 50, he was a highly successful company director, with earnings comfortably into six figures. He was also very angry. In fact, his knuckles were white as, in the course of a career counselling session, he explained why.

'Every time there's been some important event in my family's life,' he bellowed, 'that *** company has sent me off on an overseas trip at the last minute. Do you realise,' he continued, his knuckles growing whiter still, 'that both my kids are grown up now and I've never managed to get to a single *** sports day.'

The final crunch had come when yet another business trip meant that he was in some remote Eastern European city on his 25th wedding anniversary. It was as a penance for missing that important date that he had, somewhat reluctantly, acceded to his wife's demand that he should talk to someone about the whole question of his career and its impact on the rest of his life.

Colin did not need nearly as much money as he was earning. He never had the time to spend it and his wife was as far from a keeping up with the Joneses type as you could ever find. On the other hand, he was far too young and energetic to be ready to join the pipe and slippers brigade.

Fortunately Colin's story has a happier ending. Through a networking contact, Colin met and went into partnership with a semi-retired professional man who shared his passion for classic sports cars, and had gone into the business of restoring and selling them. He needed extra capital to expand and also wanted someone whose commercial skills complemented his own to share the managerial workload. As it happened, the company's premises were only 12 miles from Colin's home. His wife has already booked a weekend at a rather exclusive country hotel for their next anniversary.

Devil's advocate

Not everyone, of course, is as well off as Colin and, even if they were, it would be important to sound a few warnings at this point. To begin with, when you do your sums, you obviously need to consider not only the position right now, but also the implications for ultimate retirement. While your expenditure may not alter too much, additional retirement outgoings on leisure activities and holidays usually broadly being balanced by savings on business clothing and travel to and from the office, you will have to think about things that have up until now been paid for by your company, like medical insurance, life cover and, most significantly for many people, your car.

An even more important factor is, naturally, your pension. This is not only a crucial area but also a complex one in which no two people's circumstances are exactly the same. It is therefore vital that you take expert advice.

What is perhaps less obvious, and this is where the devil's advocacy comes in, is that while many executives these days will tell you that their life has been transformed by the decision to move out of full-time employment into self-employment, part-time work or whatever, this is not for everyone. Some people, used to the structure and social contacts inherent in employment, find working on their own lonely and demoralising. Others have difficulty with the need to go out and sell their services which self-employment usually involves. Given that, once a mature person has been out of normal employment for a while, it is extremely difficult to get back in, you need to think twice before you burn your boats.

This is even more important when you are thinking of investing part or all of your capital, which you may need to generate an income stream in retirement, in a business venture. While some options, like becoming a self-employed consultant, involve only a relatively small outlay, others call for a great deal more. That pub in the country you always dreamed of running, or the purchase of a franchise, could involve a significant investment – and one which it may not be easy to recover if things do not go as planned. Time and again, business executives pump their redundancy money or savings into such ventures only to find, after a relatively short period, that they have made a mistake. Running a pub, for example, means working all hours, and can soon become terribly repetitive and boring to someone who has been used to the challenge and stimulation of a senior managerial job in industry or commerce.

Anyone considering opting out of corporate life and going into self-employment really should consider investing a few hundred pounds in the service provided by the career guidance companies mentioned in Chapter 1. If you are thinking of investing any substantial sum in a business of your own, it is absolutely essential.

It should also be mentioned that, if you do decide that self-employment is right for you, there are all sorts of other things you need to think about. Should you form a limited company or operate as a sole trader? How much capital will you need? What kinds of insurance? What about your income tax and national insurance position? Who is going to do your accounts? In fact, you need to get yourself a whole book on the subject.

Not for bread alone

This book, on the other hand, is about getting a job. Other options have been mentioned because they do deserve serious consideration on the part of the mature executive, especially the unemployed mature executive. But now the time has come to return to the subject of being employed and to take a look at some of the other things, apart from a source of income, that people get out of working for a business organisation. Consider how much importance you place on:

❑ the stimulation you get from a job;

❑ the structure it gives your life;

❑ social contact with your colleagues;

❑ the change of scene involved in spending part of your time somewhere other than the place where you live;

❑ the challenge provided by your level of responsibility;

❑ the social respectability inherent in being employed compared with the perceived stigma of being unemployed;

❑ the status of your position;

❑ the executive car and other perks;

❑ meeting new/different people – clients and other business contacts;

❑ opportunities for business travel;

❑ social activities associated with the job;

❑ being appreciated;

❑ belonging.

If it is as much for these reasons as for the money that, if you want a new job rather than taking an alternative option such as early retirement or running your own business, you do need to overcome the prejudice against age. Or is it entirely prejudice?

Being honest

Take another look at the reasons given at the beginning of this chapter for employers being unwilling to hire older people. Ignoring the cost considerations, which probably have more than a grain of truth in them and can only be answered in terms of value for money, take a look at the other arguments. Now, be honest. Are you:

- ❏ Open minded?
- ❏ Flexible?
- ❏ Hungry?
- ❏ Ambitious?
- ❏ Energetic?
- ❏ Willing to work long hours at the expense of your family and social life?

If you are not, then maybe you do, after all, need to consider early retirement because you are certainly not going to get a job in today's competitive market.

To illustrate the point, meet Norman. You can spot him a mile off by the enormous chip on his shoulder. Although he is only in his early 40s, Norman attributes all his problems to his age. Until 18 months ago, he held a demanding and very responsible job, managing over 100 staff. Then his employers were taken over by an American company. Norman's version of what happened next is that the Yanks wanted to change everything just for the sake of it and fired everyone who would not go along with their daft new ideas, especially anyone over the age of 40.

If you could hear the other side of the story, you would discover that the British company had become uncompetitive due to its failure, in a fast-moving distribution business, to keep up with modern developments. The Americans had tried to get existing managers and staff to adapt to their more efficient ways of doing things, and some had responded enthusiastically, glad to see a way of keeping the company, and their jobs, viable. There had, however, been resistance from other managers with a 'We've always done it this way' attitude. In order to avoid jeopardising the prospects for the company as a whole, it had unfortunately been necessary to lay off a handful of stick-in-the-muds.

Norman, with his inflexible attitude, his open criticism of his former employers, his increasingly depressed approach and that enormous chip on his shoulder, has still not found another job. In desperation, he has even applied, being the possessor of an HGV licence, for a job as a lorry driver. He was told that he was over-qualified. The chip has grown even larger.

In this case, the prejudices were justified – but what about the many, many cases when they are not? What can genuinely positive and adaptable senior managers do to combat the attitude of potential employers who consider them to be past their sell by date? Read on for James's story.

What sell by date?

James had worked for some years as the office manager/accountant of a family-owned company operating as subcontractors in the construction industry. The company had two locations, the one at which he was employed, near to his home in Ealing, West London, and another in South East London, which he had to visit once or twice a month. When times became difficult, economies had to be made, and it was decided to shut one location down and concentrate all of the activities at the other. Unfortunately, in a difficult property market, Ealing proved to be the more saleable and James's job moved to South East London.

Unwilling to disrupt his children's education and his wife's social life by moving home, James began to drive to and from his new office each day. It was a terrible journey, taking an hour and a half each way. On top of that, James was working longer hours, in order to help the firm through a tough patch. Not wishing either to spend so much time travelling every day, or to leave the firm, James – now in his mid 40s – hit on an original solution. He bought a motor bike. Weaving in and out of the traffic on his two wheels, he reduced the journey time to an acceptable 50 minutes each way.

In spite of the fact that he was still spending much more time both at work, and getting to and from it, than he had previously done, James began to attend evening classes. The reason for this was that his two teenage lads had become computer buffs and James was determined not to be left behind. Within a year he had become a real wizard at spreadsheets, as well as quite a dab hand at computer chess.

Three years later a main contractor went bust, owing James's firm a sum which represented nearly 30 per cent of its total debtors. After a fraught few weeks, the bank pulled the rug out from under James's employers and, now knocking 50, he was on the streets.

Realising that getting a new job through advertisements was an only marginally better bet than winning the jackpot on the National Lottery, he hit the telephone – after, that is, he had analysed what he had to offer and who was likely to buy it. In his networking, he concentrated on getting leads into smaller companies. The rationale for this was twofold. First, by keeping up to date with what was going on in the world of business, he knew that the smaller companies are creating most of the jobs these days. Second, he realised that smaller concerns frequently cannot offer promotion prospects and might therefore prefer an older candidate who would stay with them for ten years or more to a younger person who might just use them as a stepping stone.

Although the construction industry was pretty dead, he homed in on related sectors which might be more lively and, after two or three months, was put in touch with the senior partner of a firm of architects in North London. The practice was growing and the partners wanted to concentrate on fee earning. In order to do this, they needed to divest themselves of the administration side of the business. They were considering advertising for someone to run the back office but were not sure whether they could attract an individual who could not only handle the wide range of duties involved and win the trust of the partners, but who would also be affordable and who would stay with them for a reasonable length of time.

What was intended to be a brief, exploratory meeting between James and the senior partner turned into a session which lasted the whole afternoon. He was then invited back to meet the other three partners. They were all highly impressed by the way he proved that:

- he had a flexible approach and was not at all set in his ways;
- he was still hungry, with bags of ambition and energy;
- he had kept up to date technically, making the effort to go to evening classes to turn himself into an IT (information technology) wizard;
- he was not a 9 to 5 man, as his previous record demonstrated;
- he would accept a salary on a par with candidates in their 30s or early 40s;
- since he could not be admitted to the partners' pension scheme, and they had no scheme for the few other staff they employed, he was willing to pay for his own personal pension.

Having sunk without trace any reservations they may have had about his vintage, he went on to demonstrate how his advanced years could actually be an advantage in terms of:

- reliability;
- the maturity required to gain acceptance by the partners;
- a solution to the problem of there being nowhere to go within the firm.

Their only concern was the awkward journey from Ealing to North London. Challenged on this, James simply asked where he could park his motor bike. When the laughter subsided, he was offered the job.

This, of course, goes to show that you can still get a job, if that is what you really want, in spite of your age – provided that you can show how to solve an organisation's problems and add value to the business. Getting it through an advertised vacancy may be rather a long shot, since – in spite of the fact that they are rapidly disappearing from job ads – many recruiters still use age limits as one of the easiest ways of reducing several hundred replies down to manageable proportions. The older you get, the more important it becomes to concentrate on the hidden approaches.

"You HAVE TO APPOINT YOURSELF MANAGER OF YOUR OWN JOB HUNTING CAMPAIGN."

6 What is your return on investment?

At first sight, the employed and the unemployed may appear to have diametrically opposed problems with regard to time. The first group, and this includes those who are doing temporary work, experience great difficulty in finding enough time to conduct their job search. The second group often feel that they have more time than they know what to do with.

In reality, though, they both have the same problem – that of using the investment in their time more effectively. This becomes even more important when you take a proactive approach to the job search than when you are being purely reactive.

Replying to advertisements imposes its own discipline. Review the newspapers on the appropriate days, and get your applications in. The only way of improving your time utilisation is to be more selective, putting more effort into responding to fewer, but more appropriate, advertisements.

While the hidden approaches are, in themselves, a more effective use of your time, they do also have their hidden dangers. It is all too easy to get carried away by your enthusiasm and to start thinking more about input as measured by the number of calls you have made and the number of letters you have sent, than about monitoring your output measured in terms of tangible results.

Target practice

The ultimate tangible result is, of course, the new job, but you are not going to get a job offer every day of the week, nor even once a week, nor – generally speaking – once a month, so you need to come one step back in the process.

Set yourself a target in terms of the number of meetings you achieve with people who either have a job opportunity for you now, who may have one in the foreseeable future, or who can at least put you in touch with other people who will have opportunities for you. Employed job seekers may well set a lower target than those who are out of work, but then they generally have longer to find a new job. The unemployed should aim for several meetings a week, while one or two a week would be acceptable for those who are in employment – in practice, as you will see, networking can often be combined with normal business activities.

And do you not then have to go back and set further targets for the number of calls and letters you need to initiate in order to achieve that number of meetings? Yes, but . . . the but being that anyone can, within a given amount of time, make a set number of telephone calls or mail off a certain number of letters. In itself, that achieves precisely nothing. What is more, it can become an end in itself. Having been along to the post-box with the week's batch of letters, you sit back and congratulate yourself on having achieved your target, even if it was just another load of junk mail.

Letters and calls are only the means to an end. If you keep that constantly in mind, you will find it easier to concentrate on quality rather than quantity. You will also do far more for your confidence and your enthusiasm. Think about it, which would you rather get: two bites in a hundred (the average for junk mail) or three meetings from just a dozen calls or letters? That kind of average is perfectly achievable if you pay proper attention to your research and targeting.

Budgets and plans

Time needs to be budgeted and planned just as scrupulously as money, arguably even more so, since any time you waste cannot be regained in the way that financial resources can. For those who have full-time jobs, the main requirement is to set aside a certain number of hours a week, preferably at the same times and on the same days each week because that reduces the risk of distractions eroding your precious resource.

Those who have the whole day, every day, at their disposal need to do a bit more planning. The first task is to impose a structure. Just as a day at the office has a structure, partly imposed on you by others and partly set by your scheduling of your own priorities, so must every day that you spend on your job search. An element of routine helps most people although, as in any job, you must be flexible enough to be constantly reviewing your progress, and reassessing your priorities in the light both of the stage you have reached at any given point and in response to other people. As soon as you get an interview, for example, thorough preparation for that meeting must go to the top of your list.

While everyone's situation will be different in one way or another, the following checklists should provide a useful starting point for most job seekers.

Daily tasks

❏ Check diary for appointments, follow-up calls and other reminders.

❏ Deal with incoming mail.

❏ Review newspapers and periodicals for:

   – advertisements to reply to;

   – news items to follow up.

❏ Reassess priorities for day in the light of the above.

❏ Make daily networking calls.

❏ Complete daily quota of speculative letters.

❏ Do your filing – it is essential to be well organised.

Weekly and ad hoc tasks

❏ Visit library for research.

❏ Prepare for interviews and other meetings.

❑ After interviews and meetings:

    – make notes about anything that may be relevant subsequently;

    – review, and learn from, your performance.

❑ Periodic contacts with headhunters, agencies etc.

❑ Keep yourself up to date professionally.

❑ Learn new skills.

❑ Carry out regular progress reviews and diarise whatever action stems from them.

Ignore the last point at your peril. Just as the setting of budgets is only the first step towards the achievement of effective financial control, so these structures and checklists are only the first stage towards the achievement of effectiveness in your job search. Budgetary control involves the regular comparison of actual performance with what was budgeted, the investigation and analysis of significant variances, and the taking of remedial action. Your progress checks should follow the same pattern.

Failure to meet your targets could be due to failure to target in a different sense, that of the accuracy with which you have identified what you have to sell and who is going to buy it. On the other hand, it could also be due to the question raised at the beginning of this chapter, for there is more to using your time effectively than just setting targets, important though that undoubtedly is.

Time management

Most executives are not nearly as good at managing their own time as they like to think they are. If you need proof, just look at the amounts of money that business organisations spend each year on time management courses.

TIME MANAGEMENT

How efficiently do you manage your time? Take a look at the following list of fundamental time management principles. Where could you improve?

- Effective time management, according to Roy Brighton of Time Management International, is not doing things faster or better but doing the right things. The first step should therefore be to identify your key goals.
- The second step is prioritisation – putting those goals into order of importance.
- Important does not mean the same thing as urgent. If you plan properly, you should be able to avoid things unexpectedly becoming urgent and consequently distracting you from those goals which are truly important. Priorities will, naturally, change but ideally only when something is important as well as urgent, like preparing for that interview you have just been asked to attend.
- Having identified the most important thing to do at any one point in time, concentrate on it 100 per cent, to the total exclusion of all else.
- Once you have started a task, always try to finish it. Stress, tiredness, anxiety and loss of motivation are often brought about by the thought of things you have left outstanding or unfinished.
- Do not put off tasks you find unpleasant or difficult. They too will sap your energy – and putting them off will not make them any easier.
- Be aware of when you are at your best. Do the more creative and demanding jobs at these times, and leave tasks which call for less concentration for other times of the day.
- Make large amounts of work manageable by chopping them up into bite-sized pieces.
- The best way to save a lot of time is to spend a little. Always think before you act. Then, once you are clear both about your objective and the best way to achieve it, get straight on with it.
- Save money as well as time when you use the telephone by preparing for each call before making it. Keep your objectives clearly in mind, and have all the paperwork you will need on the desk in front of you.
- Keep yourself well organised with only one job on your desk at a time and the rest sorted into appropriate piles.

continued overleaf

TIME MANAGEMENT – continued

- Set deadlines for everything you have to do – and keep to them.
- Keep interruptions and distractions to a minimum. If this area gives you problems, analyse why interruptions occur, then you will be able to take appropriate action to prevent them.
- Make time to relax and unwind.
- Make sure you know exactly how you are using your time. Keep a log for a week or two. Most people find the results enlightening, if frequently embarrassing (but you do not have to show them to anyone else).

One might be pardoned for thinking that time management when you are working from home, concentrating on just one project – the job search – ought to be so much easier than working in a busy office with endless interruptions from staff, colleagues, clients and your boss, and trying to juggle any number of priorities all at the same time. Whether it is easier or not depends not only on your application of time management principles but also your abilities in a couple of other areas of management.

Facilities management

If you are lucky enough to have outplacement services provided for you, you will have access to a work station, secretarial services and so on. You may have similar advantages if you are under notice but still able to use your employer's office facilities. Failing either of these two options, it is absolutely essential that you set yourself up at home, or elsewhere, in a way which enables you to operate in an efficient and competitive manner.

Start with the room you are going to use. It is no good thinking you can operate effectively by perching on a corner of the dining room table, where you have to move your papers every time lunch or supper comes round. If your home has a study, fine. If not, you are going to have to take over a spare bedroom, or at least a part of a room that can be yours and yours alone during the hours you need it. Do not under-estimate the importance of privacy. Not only must you be able to concentrate, you must also be able to talk on the telephone in a businesslike manner without such distractions as noisy children or a blaring TV set in the background.

Since it is vital to be well organised, you will need an adequate work surface and sufficient storage space for your files. Furthermore, because you are going to be spending a significant amount of time in your new office, you should have a comfortable chair, good lighting, adequate heating and ventilation, and, preferably, pleasant surroundings.

Speaking of the amount of time you will be spending there, it is essential that you establish a clearly defined working day, just as if you were going off to your place of employment. During that time you must shut out the rest of your life, resisting the temptation, when the sun is shining, to potter in the garden or go off for a round of golf. What is more, you must impose the same discipline on your family, ensuring that they respect your need to put in a full working day. You have to make it absolutely clear that, during those hours, you are not available to ferry the children to and from school, do odd jobs or even sit around chatting over endless cups of tea and coffee.

For some people the domestic situation may be a real problem. For example, Luke had four children, two at junior school and two who were pre-school age, and therefore at home all day. On top of that, he and his wife were going through a bumpy patch in their marriage. Working at home, in those conditions, was a virtual impossibility. Luke's solution was to borrow, during the daytime, the flat of his grown-up daughter by his first marriage, who lived only a few miles away. He was even able to use his daughter's PC.

These days a PC, ideally your own dedicated computer, is essential for word processing, e-mail and access to both jobs and company information on the internet. As little as a few hundred pounds will buy you a perfectly adequate machine for these purposes.

Whether to use a PC as a database for such things as lists of target companies is debatable. PCs can impose a useful discipline but, like so many other things, they are only a means to an end. If simple files and card index systems can do the job just as well, beware of spending valuable hours tinkering around with your computer when you could be making calls and sending out letters. To some extent it depends on how much of a computer buff you are. Unless you are pretty keyboard literate, entering large amounts of information can take an awfully long time. On the other hand, if you are completely computer illiterate, it really is time you learned!

Moving on to other pieces of equipment, a telephone which is not constantly in use by other members of the family is clearly a must. So too is an answering machine, unless you really can rely on someone else both being around whenever you are not and also being capable of taking clear messages which never get lost or forgotten about before they reach you. You may also find it worthwhile to invest in a fax machine. They are now relatively inexpensive and having one makes you look just that bit more professional, putting you one more step ahead of the competition. Photocopying, on the other hand, can easily be carried out by a bureau, by using the machines which are available in libraries and shops, or by getting a friend or member of your family to do it at their office.

At the less high-tech end, an efficient filing system is absolutely essential to hold correspondence, copies of advertisements, records of networking contacts and all the other information you may need to retrieve at short notice when someone calls you. It is also worth investing in some good quality business cards – they are not very expensive – and in high quality stationery, although this need not necessarily be pre-printed, given the quality which can be achieved these days using your home computer.

Project management

Having set up your office and organised your time, what else is there to think about? The last thing, and arguably the most important, is to ask who is actually going to manage your job search.

No, that is not meant to be a joke. Think about it. When you carry out a project as part of the job you do for an employer, the terms of reference are given to you by your boss and, while you take responsibility for the project, you probably either delegate at least some parts of it to other people, or organise a team or working party to help you.

When it comes to your own job search, not only do you have to play all of these roles yourself, but you are also the product that you are trying to market. No wonder so many executives manage their own job hunt so badly!

In practice, you may be able to get a certain amount of help from other people. For example, just as, in a business organisation, the accountant tells the other managers whether they are in line with their budgets, you may be able to get someone to make you 'report to them' on your performance against your targets. This could be an outplacement counsellor, the person who runs your local Jobclub, or a friend or member of your family, so long as they are willing to be sufficiently strict with you.

You may also be able to recruit into your team, at least on an occasional basis, a few people to use as sounding boards for your ideas, others – like the reference librarian – to help with research, and, most importantly, someone to turn to when you are feeling demotivated. There is, however, one thing no one else can do for you, and that is to take responsibility for the whole project. Before you go any further, pause for long enough to let the full implications of that sink in. You have to appoint yourself manager of your own job hunting campaign with sole responsibility for running it efficiently and seeing it through to its successful completion.

"CHANGING YOUR JOB . . . IS RECKONED TO BE ONE OF THE THREE MOST TRAUMATIC EXPERIENCES YOU CAN GO THROUGH."

7 Where there's a will

The psychology of success

Even people who are still lucky enough to be in secure employment may find job hunting a disheartening experience. For those who have been made redundant, it can be an emotional roller-coaster ride of nightmare proportions.

However, you are not going to get a new job if you have a king-sized chip on your shoulder, or if you are demoralised, depressed or desperate. After all, would you hire an uninspiring candidate, let alone one who was downright negative?

If you want to make a success of your job search, you are going to have to learn to recognise and deal with any black emotions that are lurking within you, and to find ways of lifting yourself out of the downs so that you always feel – or at least appear to others – positive, well motivated and determined to achieve your goal. All of which is, admittedly, easier said than done.

Along with bereavement and moving home, changing your job, even voluntarily, is reckoned to be one of the three most traumatic experiences you can go through in life. Following the process through will illustrate the reasons why. Those who are still in a secure job can skip the earlier stages if they wish.

When the axe falls

When people are fired or made redundant their initial reactions vary a great deal depending on the circumstances. If the news was unexpected, shock is understandably the most common first response, leaving the recipient dazed. This is often followed by disbelief and denial. As with news of the sudden death of a friend or relative, it takes time for the message to sink in.

When it does get through, there is usually a very visible emotional reaction: grief in some people, frequently expressed in tears; anger in others. The latter is the more likely when the process is mishandled by the company as, unfortunately, happens in far too many cases. Human resources (HR) professionals are trained in the way to give bad news sensitively, but line managers are often not.

The treatment received from colleagues can also be distressing. Due to embarrassment, they often do not know what to say to someone who has been made redundant. Unable, on the other hand, to carry on as if nothing had happened, they frequently chicken out completely and try to avoid their unfortunate workmate, making him or her feel like some kind of pariah.

By complete contrast, in cases where people know that redundancies are in the offing, and believe that their own job is under threat, finally being told can trigger an enormous feeling of relief. In some cases, particularly those where the person loathed their job, their boss or the company, the feeling of release can, for a while, expand into a sense of pure elation.

Whatever the first reactions may be, it is vital to recognise and understand them, and to let them out rather than bottling them up. Until you have worked through them, you will not be able to progress on to the point at which you are ready to take a balanced and positive approach to rebuilding your career.

What goes up . . .

In practice, what all too often happens is that people adopt a knee-jerk reaction to being cast out of employment, throwing themselves straight into a frantic assault on the job market. Like many a furious attack in the annals of military history, the energy of such onslaughts tends to burn itself out as quickly as the optimism becomes dissipated. An untargeted approach, relying solely on volume, is no way to get a new job.

At this point the roller-coaster begins its descent, gaining pace at a frightening rate as it plunges the jobhunter into feelings of:

- emptiness, arising from the loss of their
  - job,
  - status symbols (car etc.),
  - social interaction with colleagues,

   – secretarial and other support,

   – structure to their daily life,

   – identity,

   – direction,

   – morale,

   – confidence;

- rejection, in respect both of their previous employer and of the recruiters who fail to acknowledge letters or advise as to the outcome of interviews;

- insecurity, both financial and due to uncertainty as to how long it will take to find a new job, if one can be found at all;

- the (perceived) social stigma of not having a job;

- being out of control;

- lowered self-esteem;

- guilt, in respect of the effects on dependants;

- apathy;

- gloom and pessimism.

These feelings may be relieved – momentarily – by the odd piece of good news: an interview, or maybe even a place on a shortlist. Unfortunately the euphoria tends to be short-lived. All too soon, the roller-coaster is plunging into yet another hectic descent. What is more, as we all know only too well, it goes down a heck of a lot faster than it comes up.

A smoother ride

While few, if any, people can control their emotions completely, violent mood swings can largely be avoided and periods of depression can be minimised – even when you are out of work. The first thing to do is to acknowledge, without being judgemental, both your current situation and the way you feel about it. Because of the conditioning to which we have been subjected throughout our lives, we often find this recognition and acceptance of our feelings difficult, but it is essential. If you do not know, accurately, where you are now, it is no use trying to plan a route to your ultimate destination, let alone setting off along it.

The best way of overcoming this difficulty is to talk to someone – a friend, relative, former colleague, career counsellor; anyone who will not only listen sympathetically but who will also be objective enough to challenge your assumptions and help you to get to grips with your feelings.

Once you have got things off your chest, gained a better understanding of yourself and put your situation into perspective, you should be able to sit down and take a more balanced, and therefore more productive, approach to your job search. Before you get too far along the line, though, there may be one or two major areas that need to be tackled if they are not to sabotage your efforts at a later stage.

Financial constraints

It is difficult to run a business efficiently if you are constantly being distracted by the need to fend off creditors and to prepare cash flow forecasts for the bank. In the same way, you will not be able to concentrate properly on your job search if your mental energies are being sapped by money worries.

If you are actually out of a job, the first thing you need to do is to work out your financial position. There is no need to waste time compiling a set of schedules fit for a major PLC's published report. All you need to know is how much capital you have, what you owe, how much you need to live on and what income you have now that you no longer have a monthly salary.

The next thing is to talk to the other people who will be affected by the situation: your partner, and any children who are old enough to understand the implications. Quite apart from the fact that they need to know what the position is and how it will affect you all, they may be able to make suggestions as to how to reduce expenditure or increase income.

The third thing is to talk to people who can give advice or help. Depending on your own knowledge of such matters, you may find it useful to consult a financial adviser on how to get the most out of your investments and someone who understands tax to ensure that you get any rebates due to you. If you foresee difficulties in meeting your commitments, it is also better to discuss the matter earlier, rather than later, with your bank manager, building society and any other creditors.

Whether you have immediate financial problems or not, it is important to ensure that you make arrangements to replace insurances which were previously dealt with by your employer, such as life and private medical cover. You should also register for unemployment benefit. Although some people consider this degrading, there is absolutely no reason for this. The amount of income may not be much, but every little helps and do not forget that you have been paying in for years so you have a right to get something back. Furthermore, by signing on you get your national insurance contributions kept up to date, which means that your state pension will be protected.

Pride and prejudice

The sense of shame which prevents some people from crossing the threshold of the Jobcentre can be downright dangerous if it extends to the way they behave towards their family and friends. If you are to conduct a well-motivated job hunting campaign, you are going to need the full support of those around you. To get that, you need to be honest with them.

These days, so many people either are or have been out of work that it is no longer a stigma in the mind of anyone but the person involved. Do not try to hide it from your friends. The worry about them finding out, and the dishonesty involved in concealing something from those you like and respect, will have a far more negative effect on you than their knowledge of the true situation could ever produce.

Even more important is to be completely honest, from the start, with your partner and family. Some people's pride is so great that they even attempt to hide the very fact of having been made redundant from those closest to them.

Peter, who had worked for the same City firm for over 20 years, was a particularly sad case. When he lost his job, he could not even bring himself to tell his wife. Instead, he caught his normal train every morning, spending his day going round to see people who might be able to help him or, increasingly as the days became weeks, sitting in a public library or a bar. The longer he left it, the more impossible he found it to tell his family what had happened. One morning, instead of boarding his normal commuter train, he went to the platform through which the Intercity train roared non-stop, and threw himself into its path.

Peter's case may be exceptional, but any bad news, even if it is only of the need to cancel that exotic family holiday and settle instead for a self-catering cottage in England, is best got out of the way without delay, otherwise it is always there in the back of your mind, distracting you from the vital task of getting on with your job search.

Keeping your chin up

Speaking of which, how far should you change your normal lifestyle? It clearly depends on just how dire your financial straits are, but in general the answer is as little as possible. Avoid extravagances, but try not to make life miserable. It is worth investing, financially and otherwise, in a few things that will boost your morale and, therefore, your chances of getting a job. Remember the following.

- **Keep up an active social life**.
  If this previously came largely from your colleagues at work, either continue to see them or take active steps to make new friends. Job hunting can be a lonely business. Maintain a healthy balance between commitment to your job search and carrying on with the rest of your life.

- **Keep your mind active.**
  Without the challenges involved in your job, it is all too easy to get stale. Develop new skills and interests, either by studying something that may help you to get a job, like computer skills, or simply some subject of general interest. An additional benefit of this is that it provides the opportunity to meet new people.

- **Keep fit.**
  You need a healthy body as well as a healthy mind if you are going to feel good and project the right impression when you meet people in the course of your marketing campaign. Take regular exercise, get enough sleep and do not cut back on the food budget, unless that means cutting out expensive, unhealthy foods and substituting cheaper but more nutritious ones.

- **Keep up appearances.**
  You may not wear a suit when you are at home or in the library, but maintain your pride in your appearance, adopt an upright posture and always have a cheerful smile for people. The image you project outwards onto others reflects itself back onto you.

- **Have one or more people to talk to.**
  It may be useful to have one person to discuss your job seeking strategy and progress with, and another you can turn to if you are feeling a bit down or want to get something off your chest. Help of this kind may come from a friend, relative or former colleague, or from some more formal kind of support.

Support groups

If you are on an outplacement programme, you can talk to your counsellor either about the job market and your campaign tactics, or about emotional and personal issues. To whom can you turn if you do not have the advantage of outplacement?

The closest alternative is a job club. If you are unemployed you can, after a qualifying period, join a government Jobclub. Members receive coaching in topics such as CV preparation, researching and identifying job leads, making speculative approaches, telephone techniques and interviewing skills. They are expected to attend the Jobclub regularly and can work on their job search either on their own or with other members. Members give each other a great deal of support, both in terms of helping each other to get over emotional lows, and by providing an effective network for news items and job leads.

Jobclubs also enable you to access their reference books and newspapers, to use their word processing and photocopying equipment, and to take advantage of free telephone calls, stamps and stationery, the cost of which can certainly mount up as the months go by. While some Jobclubs describe themselves as Executive Jobclubs, the majority welcome people of all backgrounds, skills and experience.

Perhaps the biggest problem about government Jobclubs is that you normally cannot get into one until you have been unemployed for six months. The reason for this is apparently simply the availability of resources. It is, however, worth checking the situation out. If there are more places than people who have been unemployed for six months to fill them, you may be able to get a place at an earlier date. Talk to someone at your Jobcentre. They will also be able to tell you about any relevant courses for which you may be eligible.

Support from the private and voluntary sectors

Not all job clubs are sponsored by the government. Professional institutes are another source. For example, the Institute of Chartered Accountants in England and Wales operates its own careers service providing a telephone helpline, job search seminars and one-to-one counselling. The Institute also disseminates job opportunities through its district society network and runs its own recruitment consultancy, specialising in vacancies for accountants.

If you do not belong to an institute or association which provides such services, you can set up your own job club, getting together with former colleagues or people you know through a sports club, church, or such organisations as Lions, Round Table or Rotary clubs.

While these sources can be an excellent substitute for outplacement and even, through the team spirit they generate, provide something that outplacement does not, you may nevertheless sometimes feel the need for one-to-one counselling. If this need is related to an emotional problem, such as depression, a few sessions with a trained practising counsellor or, for a lower financial outlay, an organisation such as your local pastoral counselling group, may be the answer. Alternatively, for occasional one-off crises, a listening ear is available, 24 hours a day, 7 days a week, completely free of charge from the Samaritans – they deal not only with the potentially suicidal but with anyone who needs someone to talk to and unload onto.

If it is one-off career advice you need, there are both firms who will provide just that part of the outplacement service and also, at a lower cost, individuals with extensive experience of the business world and the job market who will ensure that you are on the right track, and who will give advice on any specific part of the process, including the kind of job you should be targeting, research, networking, CV preparation and letter writing, and interview techniques. Although the occasional session can be useful at any stage, jobhunters usually find this kind of help most useful either right at the outset or when they have reached a point at which they just do not seem to be getting anywhere and need either objective advice or someone to give them a kick start.

Finally, do not forget your own personal team. In the previous chapter you were advised to appoint yourself manager of your own job search. Take a few moments now to consider who you are going to recruit to support you. Treat your family, friends, former colleagues, network contacts, the reference librarian and others as members of a project team whose aim is to find you a new job. Whether or not you tell them that you have done this is unimportant. Looking at it that way yourself will make you think more positively about them, and that in turn will make you appreciate them more, and, consequently, get them to make an even more valuable contribution to your job hunting campaign.

"NETWORKING IS NOT DISCRETE."

PART TWO

Opening the hidden doors

"BE CHOOSY, BE
PROFESSIONAL,
AND BE CREATIVE."

8 The odds against ads

and how to improve them

A recent advertisement for a managing director at a salary of circa £60,000 attracted just short of 1,500 replies. While that may be exceptional, three-figure responses are the norm. Although no one has ever produced an accurate figure for the average number of applications to an executive job advertisement, it is probably in the region of a couple of hundred. Given these odds, and bearing in mind the significantly better chances of success through the hidden approaches, is it worth bothering with advertised vacancies at all?

The answer is that it is worth it – but that 'yes' has to be a qualified one. The main qualification is on the amount of time that you spend on this aspect of your job search. Since advertisements probably account for only about 20 per cent of managerial job opportunities, you should not be spending more than a fifth of your time on them. Part of that budget will be dedicated to a regular review of every national and regional newspaper, trade and professional journal that carries advertisements for the kind of job you might be interested in. Never miss an issue. You can now access back issues of most publications on the internet. The rest of your budget will be devoted to making applications, and making them count.

How do you fit all that in? In practice it is not as difficult as it may appear. The trick is to concentrate not on the amount of time available, but on how productively you spend it. There are three ways you can improve the return on your investment in replying to ads: by being choosy, being professional, and being creative. One or two applications a week which are spot on in every sense will earn you far more interviews than half a dozen a week which are misdirected, poorly prepared and unimaginative.

Being choosy

Unless you are a close fit, which means meeting around three-quarters of the requirements stated in the advertisement, it is usually better not to reply for these reasons:

- A worthwhile application takes time – several hours of it – which you could be putting to better use.

- Most advertisements are placed not by the person making the ultimate hiring decision but by a selection consultant or personnel manager whose job is to reduce a response of, say, 200 to a short-list of about four to present to the line manager. Recruiters do this in an arbitrary fashion, often spending less than a minute on each application and screening out anyone who fails to match the basic yardsticks.

- It is better for your morale to get a couple of interviews from half a dozen carefully chosen ads than only a single interview from 20 – which is about the average.

- Regular advertisers, such as selection consultants, quickly come to recognise applications from people who are replying to anything and everything. They regard such candidates at best as lacking judgement and professionalism, and at worst as desperate. This, plus advertisers' natural annoyance at having their time wasted, counts against such candidates, even when a job comes along for which they are a reasonable fit.

While the '75 per cent fit' criterion is a useful rule of thumb, and will be valid for the majority of advertisements, there will be exceptions – and these represent an opportunity for the proactive candidate. Identifying the exceptions is essentially about the question of supply and demand. In each case you have to take a view on how many replies are likely to be attracted, and how many applicants are likely to meet most, if not all, of the requirements.

Where very rare skills or experience are being asked for, it may well be worth replying even if you only meet, say, 60 per cent of the specification. In the case quoted at the beginning of this chapter, on the other hand, where an extremely attractive job produced nearly 1,500 replies, you would clearly have needed to have been very close to the ideal to have stood any chance at all.

In deciding whether or not to apply, careful reading of the text is vital. Seasoned recruiters (i.e. both selection consultants and HR professionals) go to considerable pains with the wording of their advertising copy, aiming to attract enough replies to be sure of filling the job, but – because of the time it takes to screen the response – not too many more than they need. They are therefore careful to use words like 'must' when a qualification, skill or other requirement is essential. When something is not absolutely mandatory they use terms like 'should', 'preferably' or 'would be an advantage'.

Apart from the tightness of the person specification, response rates will also be affected by the desirability of the job and by the impression made by the advertisement.

TURN-OFFS

Examples of things that may turn people off a job, and consequently reduce response, include:

- job content, for example, only a minority of accountants want to be internal auditors;
- location;
- type of business;
- factors that impinge on family life, such as extensive travel or the unsocial hours involved in businesses like hotel and catering.

The same factors may, of course, also deter you. If they do not, however, you could have identified an advertised opportunity where the odds are considerably better than the average and where the time taken in making an application is likely to be more profitably spent.

The odds are also likely to be greater when an advertisement is smaller than the average size, is tucked away in a bottom inside corner of a page, lacks polish in its wording or has been typeset to a lower standard than most. Small companies which only advertise very occasionally often fail to match the impact of the insertions placed by the selection consultancies and the large direct advertisers. While this may mean that they are also less professional in other ways, that is not necessarily the case and, even if it is, maybe that is the very reason why they need someone like you.

A further category which puts a lot of job seekers off is the ad placed anonymously under a box number. People who currently have a job may be deterred from responding by the fear of writing to their own employer, but those who are out of work need have no such concerns. If the advertisement appeals, give it a whirl.

Being professional

The whirl that you give any kind of ad must, however, be a totally professional one. Recruiters, facing an intimidating pile of CVs, running well into three figures, are not going to have much time for applications that are half-hearted or half-baked. As one selection consultant put it, 'Anyone who isn't capable of producing a decent job application almost certainly won't be capable of writing a professional report for the board of directors'. True or not, it is a perfectly understandable assumption.

 APPLICATION FAUX-PAS

Some of the most common, and most damning, errors listed by recruiters include:

- use of a duplicated, standard cover letter with the title and reference for the job in question filled in by hand;
- just sending in a CV with the job reference scribbled in the top corner;
- failing to sign a cover letter;
- mixing up two or more applications and sending them to the wrong people.

There is, of course, far more to being truly professional than simply avoiding those errors which are patently crass. At the risk of sounding just that, the very first thing to do is to read the ad. No, not just a quick skim on the basis of which you jump to the conclusion that you could do the job standing on your head. Take the ad apart. Sit down with a piece of paper and list out what it tells you about:

❏ **the company**
its size, ownership, culture, locations, products, markets, plans, management style;

❏ **the job**
reason for vacancy, whom the job reports to, how many staff, what are the responsibilities, the performance criteria, the prospects;

❏ **the person sought**
qualifications, skills, experience, personal qualities.

Do not stop at the factual information. Read between the lines as well.

Now, how closely do you fit? Unless the job is one which is likely to attract only very few suitable candidates, it is not enough to say, 'I could do that job'. You have to be able to say, 'I could do it better than anyone else'. Go back to your asset register. Look at your USPs. How could you add value in a way that is uniquely yours?

If you are still convinced that you are a really strong candidate, and that it is therefore worth investing several hours in making an application, get to work. Put yourself ahead of the competition by doing as much research as you possibly can. If the company is named, you will be able to do quite a lot, using the company's website and the reference works listed in Chapter 3, together with your network (see Chapters 11 and 12). Even where the company's identity has been concealed, the business sector in which it operates is normally indicated, so you can at least do some digging into that.

Then, putting together your thorough analysis of the advertisement, your conscientious research and your carefully selected USPs, make a first draft of your application. First draft? Yes – no one gets it completely right first time.

Leave it for 24 hours, then take another look. If you have someone knowledge-able who is willing to offer an objective view, get them to run an eye over it too. You will always find the odd word or phrase which you can replace with something better. Not infrequently you will spot a major point you have either failed to make clear or have even missed out altogether.

Take your time. There is no advantage to be gained by getting your application in early. Many recruiters do not even look at the response for the first few days, knowing that neither busy candidates, nor those who take the time to produce a well thought out reply, are likely to rush their application off on the day the advertisement appears. Once you have made the decision to apply, give it your very best effort. Anything else is a waste of time.

In most cases the format of your application will be a CV plus covering letter (the whole of Part Three of this book is devoted to these matters), but never neglect to read the instructions given in the advertisement, normally at the bottom of the text. For example, organisations in the public sector may insist on an application form, even at quite senior levels.

Application forms? Do you really have to complete them? And what about other apparently unreasonable demands – like age limits, for example?

Being creative

Most people get a kick out of beating the system, especially when the system in question appears to be unfairly loaded against them. However, before look-ing at ways in which you can get around the worst injustices of the advertised recruitment market, a word of warning: never try to buck the system unless you are convinced that you are a front runner for the job in question. Not only would you be wasting time you ought to be spending more productively, but you could also get up the nose of a recruiter who, subsequently, may be han-dling a job for which you really are a strong contender.

There are basically two ways you can annoy recruiters: by not doing what they ask you to, and by bypassing them completely. When is the risk worthwhile?

One of the commonest problems is the demand, in the advertisement, for either your current salary or your salary history. What if you have been earning more than the advertised figure but are willing to take a drop? There is no way of predicting how any one prospective employer will react to this. Some are delighted to get what they see as a bargain. Others may fear that you will move on as soon as the market eases and you can get something better, or may simply be suspicious of your inability to get another job without taking a reduction in earnings. The bigger the drop, the more questions they are likely to ask.

The other side of the coin is the situation where you are earning significantly less than the advertised figure, either because your salary has been held back in the hard times your employer has been going through or because you are right at the bottom end of the age scale. Here the risk is that you will be regarded as at too low a level, ability being equated in the recruiter's mind with earnings.

When the advertisement asks for your earnings without indicating what the remuneration is for the job, you have – if anything – an even greater problem.

In all of these cases, providing the information which has been requested could rule you out, but failing to do so may lead the recruiter to assume either that you did not read the advertisement properly or that you are deliberately concealing something. Stating that the advertised salary, where there is one, would be attractive to you is not only a fudge but also compromises your negotiating position if you are ultimately offered the job – they might have been willing to pay more!

The only way to avoid all of these risks is to say, in your covering letter, something like, 'I shall be very happy to discuss my current/most recent remuneration package with you when we meet' or 'Rather than attempting to explain in this letter what is a somewhat complex situation regarding my current/last salary and benefits package, I would prefer to discuss this with you when we meet'. While recruiters may have their suspicions, you could simply be alluding to the fact that there were complicated bonus, profit sharing or equity participation elements in your package. If you are a close fit to their specification, there is a fair chance that they will respond to the suggestion you have (deliberately) planted and invite you in.

If they do not do that, there is a strong probability that they will at least telephone to clarify the matter – which gives you the opportunity not only to explain the salary situation but also to strengthen your claim to an interview by emphasising your plus points, by asking relevant questions about the job or the company, and by the general impression you make through your positive telephone manner. Needless to say, in order for this to succeed, your files need to be so well organised that, when the call comes in, you can immediately access the advertisement, the copy of your application and the list you made of points you would raise should you find yourself in this situation!

Bypass surgery

But what if, although you genuinely believe you are a serious contender, having all the experience the ad calls for, you lack the qualification it demands? Or perhaps, although advertisements no longer carry age limits, you suspect that age is, in fact, the reason why you keep getting turned down? Assuming that you do genuinely have something special to offer, there are two things you can do.

The first is to telephone the person who placed the advertisement. Rehearse carefully what you are going to say. It is vital that, within a maximum of a couple of minutes, you get across your USPs – the experience, the achievements, the value you can add – which will make the recruiter want to interview you. Then raise the question of the one criterion which you do not match.

The timing of this call is important. It is no use ringing the day the advertisement appears, or even a day or two after. At this stage you will get, at best, a non-committal response because the recruiter will have no idea how strong, or otherwise, the field is. You need to wait until the bulk of the response is in – about ten days for daily newspapers, a fortnight for weekly or monthly magazines and professional journals. By this time, the picture will be much clearer. If the response is so strong that there is no need to bend the specification at all, at least you will be told that. Should the field be a bit thin, on the other hand, and the recruiter be getting worried, you will have called at just the right moment.

The alternative is to bypass the recruiter completely and make a direct approach to the person whom you would actually be working for. This option is, obviously, open only in those cases where the employer is named in the advertisement, but a significant proportion are, so it is well worth considering.

Your first task is to identify the target individual. If the advertisement names the title of the person to whom the job reports, a call to the switchboard will readily produce the name. Failing that, try using your network contacts or, as a last resort, calling the recruiter and asking about the reporting structure. To avoid undue suspicion, and to help you in your approach, you may want to check out any other information you need at the same time. It is not uncommon for candidates to ring up to ask for further details about an advertisement to which they are thinking of responding.

Once you have identified your target, the best approach is the warm, rather than the cold, one. If you can network your way into a personal introduction, so much the better. Be persistent. It may take a few calls to achieve, but it is worth it. The ideal is someone who knows the target personally and will make a call on your behalf, but even a name you can quote as a door opener is better than nothing.

All is still not lost, however, if you have to go in cold. Take the time to compose a letter which, preferably on a single page, summarises your USPs in respect of the job in question. Do not include a CV (which will not only include additional information less relevant to the job in question, but will also make it plain that, for example, you lack the required qualification) and do not refer to the advertisement, or it will be obvious that you are trying to buck the system.

Assuming that you really do have some value to add (and if you do not, it is no use wasting either their time or yours), there is a very good chance that the line manager will go straight to the recruiter with a comment like, 'Guess what landed on my desk this morning? Could be just what we're after. Certainly looks worth an interview.'

More often than not, the recruiter will feel obliged to comply. At worst, for example where there is a strong response from the advertisement or the recruiter insists on getting some more details about you before calling you in, you will at least have created an opportunity for a telephone conversation which, providing you have prepared properly, you should have a good chance of converting into a meeting.

The whole process is, theoretically at least, rather simpler in the minority of cases where the advertisement is placed by the person who will actually make the hiring decision. Assuming that you can get hold of what is probably a very busy senior executive, which may mean fighting your way past a dragon-like gatekeeper (see the techniques outlined under networking, in Chapter 11), you stand a good chance of making a strong impression with your carefully pre-pared, concise presentation.

The dreaded form

When you are called for interview, or sometimes even at an earlier stage, you may be asked to complete an application form. If you feel that this is an insult at your level, or an unnecessary duplication of information already provided in your CV, what should you do?

A few candidates refuse point blank. A somewhat larger minority arrive at the interview with excuses like 'The form only arrived in this morning's mail' or 'I've been away on business and only got back late last night'. Still more only partially complete the form, putting lines through whole sections with the terse comment, 'See CV'.

This is another area where you can get one step ahead, so long as you are willing to try to look at things from the other person's point of view. These days, generally speaking, companies do not ask people to fill in forms unless or until they believe they have a genuinely valid reason for doing so. This may be simply the wish to have every applicant's key information in a standard format, the need to gather information to form part of a personnel file should you be hired or the desire to prove that they are operating an equal opportunities policy.

Given that the form is nearly always seen before you are, there is no point in getting off on the wrong foot. Create a good initial impression. Use the follow-ing checklist.

❏ Read the whole form thoroughly. Pay particular attention to such requirements as listing your career in chronological or reverse chronological order. Note whether you are given permission to refer to your CV in certain places rather than unnecessarily repeating information.

❏ Do not write straight on to the form. Draft your answers on blank paper or, better still, a photocopy of the form. Leave your draft for 24 hours before checking it, making amendments and, only then, copying it over.

❏ Pay attention to neatness and layout but do not try to type your answers in – they rarely line up properly and consequently look messy.

❏ Take every opportunity to tailor your answers to the advertisement, the further information you have obtained by research and the value you can add to the company.

❏ Make optimum use of any open questions which invite you to state how you believe you match the requirements of the job or to provide any further information which you consider relevant. All too often candidates, suffering from application form fatigue, fail to make the most of this golden opportunity. Take advantage of other applicants' short-sightedness and use these sections to get another step ahead.

And, finally, a word of warning. Application forms can be used to expose matters which candidates have accidentally, or deliberately, omitted from their CVs – things like gaps in their employment history, health problems or the lack of a driving licence due to a court ban. Failure to answer a question is an invitation to the interviewer to probe it. Lies are liable to be uncovered, at least at reference checking stage, and the dishonesty in itself will almost certainly be damning. An open approach, volunteering the facts but providing an explanation of the circumstances, will usually give you the best chance of limiting any potential damage.

The value of feedback

Both outplacement counsellors and people who write books and articles on job hunting are prone to advising people whose applications earn no more than a standardised reject letter to phone up the recruiter and ask why they have been turned down, so that they can use this information to improve their chances in the future. Unfortunately it simply does not work like that in practice.

Put yourself in the recruiter's shoes. With literally hundreds of applications to every job, it is bad enough just having to look at each of them once. Having people call up after you have closed off their file is a pain. You have to retrieve their papers and check out the reason why you rejected them, which may well have been a somewhat arbitrary one. If this was the case, or if you have the feeling that the caller may be persistent, you give a reply calculated to get them off the line as quickly as possible, for example, 'We had an enormous response to this advertisement and, although you have a lot of relevant experience, there were a few candidates who were just that bit closer to our ideal specification.'

With luck, that gets rid of them. If they persist, asking in what way exactly the others were closer, you reply, 'I'm afraid that professional confidentiality prevents me from discussing the details of other candidates with you.'

The only time you stand a reasonable chance of not getting fobbed off with half truths or outright lies is when you know a recruiter reasonably well and consequently have a more personal relationship. Failing that, you would make better use of your time by discussing apparently unjust rejections with friends or network contacts. They are likely to give you both more time and greater honesty.

If you still feel that, in spite of only applying to jobs where you fit very closely and of having been totally professional in your application, you have nevertheless lost out in the lottery of the screening process, what can you do? In the case of blind ads, very little. But, where the company is named, you could use the techniques described under 'Bypass surgery', even when there is not a problem such as age or lack of qualifications to be overcome. Where you have an existing contact in a company placing an advertisement, you would presumably have used it anyway. When you get onto networking, in Chapter 11, you will see how easy it often is to generate contacts, even in organisations in which you currently have none at all.

"NOT HAVING AN E-MAIL ADDRESS THESE DAYS GIVES YOU THE SAME KIND OF CREDIBILITY PROBLEMS AS NOT HAVING A TELEPHONE.**"**

9 The internet revolution

The terms 'internet' and revolution are so frequently linked these days that one might be forgiven for thinking that they were synonyms. In many ways this is justified. The internet will change many aspects of our lives and is – in a number of areas – already doing so. This includes the job market.

However, the reality of revolutions is that they change some things completely, others to a certain extent and leave yet other things largely – or even completely – unchanged. Job hunters who are keen to make the most of every tool that can give them a competitive advantage but who need to prioritise the way they spend their time consequently need to dig down beneath the claim that the internet will revolutionise job search and ask some specific questions, such as:

- What are the benefits of internet recruitment?
- Are there any disadvantages or dangers I need to be aware of?
- When is all of this actually going to happen?
- Is the internet changing the underlying fundamentals of the job market or just more superficial aspects, like the way I send my application?
- In a competitive recruitment market, will the internet make it easier or more difficult for me to find a job?
- What specific tips do I need to follow in order to get one step ahead of other job hunters?
- Given that I have only a finite amount of time to spend on my job hunt, how do I balance my use of the internet with other methods?

Win, win

The internet promises major benefits to both job seekers and employers. From the candidate's viewpoint the advantages it claims include:

- **Speed**
  - instead of having to plough through pages and pages of job advertisements, you can click on your requirements and have suitable jobs listed out on your screen in a matter of seconds
  - the time you save can then be used to research companies more thoroughly before making your application
  - vacancies can be accessed 24/7 (24 hours a day, 7 days a week) – you do not have to wait for the day the job ads appear in the press
  - applications made by e-mail speed up the whole process

- **Convenience**
  - you no longer have to trail around agencies – you can access them via the internet
  - because applying for jobs on the internet is faster, you can make more applications
  - some job boards even offer, once you have registered your requirements and CV, to notify you by e-mail every time a suitable vacancy arises

- **Range of jobs**
  - it is claimed that it will be possible to access a greater number of job vacancies including, thanks to the global nature of the internet, positions in other countries

- **Information**
  - the vast amount of information available on the internet, together with the speed and power of search engines, should enable you to conduct far more efficient research and thus to improve the quality both of your applications and of your performance at interview

- some job boards also provide tips on job search and CV preparation, chat groups and other useful facilities.

Since employers are the people who are generating vacancies and deciding how to go about filling them, the internet will of course need to appeal to them too and there are a similarly impressive range of advantages claimed:

- **Cost**
  - compared with the sums spent on advertising or the fees of agencies or headhunters, the internet will result in savings of anything from 50 per cent to as much as a staggering 90 per cent

- **Speed**
  - vacancies can be posted on the internet at the click of a mouse button

  - no need to wait days, or even weeks, for a press advertisement to appear

  - applications start to come in within minutes of the job appearing on the internet

- **Convenience**
  - e-mailed applications can be circulated to everyone involved in hiring without the need for photocopying and they can be stored digitally for future retrieval

  - the tedious and time-consuming process of screening large piles of applications down to the much smaller number to be interviewed can be carried out, at least in part, by computers instead of people

- **Range of candidates**
  - a vacancy posted on the internet is accessible to candidates right across the UK and worldwide

  - employers will be able to access 'passive' job seekers – people who are not actively looking for a new job and who therefore may not be reading press advertisements – through databases built up via the internet.

Too good to be true?

Unfortunately, every silver lining does have a cloud: there is also another side to the coin. What is more, although some of the disadvantages of the internet – like simply getting logged on at all, especially at times of day when the USA is highly active – are no more than minor irritations which will, hopefully, be fairly short-lived, others are more serious and may take quite some time to sort out. For example:

- **Confidentiality**
  - What happens when you send your CV to a job site? Who does it go to? Could it end up with your own current employer?

- **Speed**
  - It may be quicker to access one job board than to scan through all the advertisements in a newspaper or professional journal, but how many of each do you need to access? Most job seekers need only to look in two or three publications to be sure of finding virtually all the vacancies that they might be interested in. On the internet there are, at the time of writing, around 200 job boards, a figure which has increased by nearly 50 per cent in just one month, and employers' own websites number many, many more.

  - Interrogating job boards can actually be less efficient than scanning the recruitment pages. The search parameters are often far too imprecise. Some boards do not even let you define the salary range you seek, geographical criteria are frequently much too broad, and if you enter the job title you want you inevitably get any vacancies containing the word or words you enter, many of which are complete mismatches.

  - Some boards involve extremely long-winded and tedious registration processes, one – which requires you to fill in a lengthy and repetitive questionnaire - taking an hour or so.

  - Because vacancies can be posted at any time of day, on any day of the week, you have to keep going back to each job board (by no means do all boards e-mail you when a suitable new job is posted) which can be more time consuming than just going through a newspaper or magazine once a week.

– Advertisers seem to be slower at updating vacancies than they are at posting them - a common complaint is that many of the vacancies on job boards have been filled by the time candidates apply.

– The ability to shoot off your CV at the touch of a button can encourage you to make a lot of poor quality applications rather than a smaller number of well-targeted ones.

- **Range of jobs**
  – With the exception of one or two areas like IT and graduate recruitment, it is extremely doubtful whether the range of jobs on the internet is as comprehensive as that in the press or with agencies. Cost is not the only factor influencing where employers place vacancies – they also want to be sure that a job will come to the attention of the vast majority of the potential candidates. In the press, one or two publications in most sectors, disciplines or geographical areas have established market dominance. With 200 job boards, none can claim that on the internet.

  – Access to jobs in other parts of the UK, or overseas, is fine if you want to relocate. If you do not, all it means is more candidates competing with you for jobs in your area.

- **The personal touch** Computers are more efficient than people when it comes to dealing with hard facts, but
  – If an advertisement in the press does not provide all the information you need in order to decide whether or not to apply, you can pick up the telephone and have a dialogue, which you cannot always easily do with the internet.

  – Computer screening of applications may save time for the employer, but how do you know you are not being rejected for purely arbitrary reasons, or because you did not include the right key words on your CV?

– If you do not get an interview, it is much more difficult to obtain feedback on the reasons why when you are applying to an internet job board.

– Visiting agencies may be time consuming, but at least you can have a dialogue with another human being and make sure that your individual job criteria have been clearly understood – you are not confined to the search parameters on a job board. In the long run, this could actually make the process faster, as well as more accurate.

How soon?

Whilst the technology exists to make all of the benefits of the internet available right now, the difficulties outlined above may take some time to be resolved.

A particular problem is the sheer number of job boards. From the job hunter's point of view what is needed is a major process of rationalisation so that a single board – or at the most two or three – has all the vacancies in a particular sector, discipline or area. At the moment, far from being rationalised, the number is increasing at a rate of knots. In the long run, the solution will probably be the emergence of niche job boards which attract directly, or bring together from generalist boards, all of the vacancies of a particular type.

There is also a need for the search parameters on job boards to be made more precise so that they respond accurately to the needs of job seekers. This should be a much easier problem to solve, but job boards do need to become responsive to the needs of their users. At present the absence of personal contact seems to be resulting in a total lack of feedback – or of any noticeable interest in seeking it. The situation is not helped by the fact that, just as rates charged for press advertising increase with the circulation of the publication, so can internet boards charge more if they are getting a greater number of 'hits', i.e. visits. This naturally encourages them to go for quantity rather than quality, putting sheer volume before service.

Until these problems are recognised and resolved, the spread of internet recruitment from its initial success areas of graduate and IT recruitment to the professional and managerial areas may be slower than many prophets have predicted. This view is supported by recent surveys.

The *Top Jobs Recruitment Advertising Survey* by PricewaterhouseCoopers, published in early 2000 and covering 5,000 executives (two-thirds of whom earned over £50,000), showed that whilst 48 per cent had used the internet when applying for a new position, 85 per cent of these had used it to find out company information before applying and 73 per cent had used it to e-mail their CV. The percentage of respondents accessing job sites was much lower, only 25 per cent visiting potential employers' web pages, 31 per cent visiting those of recruitment consultancies and 33 per cent visiting job boards.

Furthermore, a survey of the author's own career counselling clients, spanning the period of October 1999 to April 2000, showed that even when professional and managerial job hunters did use job boards they found:

- few jobs at their level
- virtually no jobs which were solely on the internet – most of the jobs were also advertised in the press or available through agencies.

Consequently, although executive job hunters ignore the internet at their peril, they also need to keep it in perspective and continue to use the older-fashioned but – for the moment, at least – in many ways more effective approaches.

Same difference?

In any case, even if the internet does at some point in the future come to dominate all levels of the job market, it is important – if you are to get the best out of it - to understand the extent to which it is affecting the underlying fundamentals of job search, as opposed merely to the more superficial aspects of it. From the job hunter's point of view, conventional job search involves three basic stages:

- Identifying – or generating – job opportunities
- Making an application
- Going through the selection process - being interviewed and, in some cases, participating in tests, assessment centres, etc.

Job sources can be considered under the following headings:

- **Advertisements**
  - An advertisement on the internet is fundamentally no different from one in a newspaper, magazine or technical journal: it still tells you about the employer, the job, the type of person they are looking for and how to apply.

  - In both the press and on the internet there are some advertisements which are well written, containing information carefully selected to help you decide whether or not to apply. There are others which tell you next to nothing and whose specifications are riddled with clichés. Interestingly, the internet can accentuate both trends.

  - On the one hand, the facility to provide information for downloading and to insert hyperlinks to further sources such as the employer's website can increase the amount of information available.

  - On the other hand, the assumption that people accessing the internet have a sound bite mentality all too often leads to a minimalist approach to content.

- **Agencies**
  - Just as agencies use press advertising to attract candidates, so they are now using the internet. In both cases they tend to provide only very brief details of vacancies and, by the time you apply, those particular jobs may well have been filled.

  - Matching of candidates against jobs has for some time been done at least partly by computer in many agencies. The main change with the internet has been in the inputting of CVs. When computers first began to be used, this was done by manual keying in, then scanners were employed, and now – with e-mail – they can go straight into the system.

– The claim that the internet will cut out the need to go to the agency for an interview raises the question of how common this is anyway. A frequent complaint from employers has always been that a significant percentage of the candidates put forward by agencies have often never been interviewed.

– Whether agencies will eventually be squeezed out by the internet is another interesting question. Up till now they have survived – and, indeed, grown – by being able to provide scarce resources, such as secretaries, IT staff and professional people, more efficiently than employers can do for themselves. Only time will tell whether the internet will enable employers to cut out an expensive middle man.

- **Executive (advertised) selection consultants**

  – Some commentators question the impact of the internet on their future too.

  – Employers basically pay for the executive selection consultants' expertise in filling managerial and professional positions and for the time they save in sifting large volumes of applications down to a short-list for final selection.

  – From the job hunter's angle, however, there is little difference between applying to an ad inserted by a consultant and one placed directly by an employer, except that in the latter case you usually know the identity of the employer – which is often not the case when consultants are used – so you can do more research at an earlier stage. Again, therefore, the internet is not changing the fundamentals.

- **Executive search consultants (headhunters)**

  – Most experts consider it unlikely that, at least at the more senior levels, busy executives who are in employment and who are used to being telephoned and seduced by headhunters are going to take the time, and lay themselves open to the confidentiality risks, of registering on job boards.

– If passive job seeking really takes off, an e-mail may replace a headhunter's call at lower levels, but only if it proves to be as effective in persuading them to proceed with an application for the position in question, which is open to doubt.

– In any case, it will have to reach the stage where a trawl of CVs on a database provides as accurate and comprehensive a coverage of the available field of potential candidates as the proactive research into target companies and individuals which is currently undertaken by search consultants. The internet should make this research process faster and more efficient, which will benefit the headhunters' clients, i.e. the employers, but candidates will not notice any difference.

- **Direct applications**

  – Company websites are a genuinely new phenomenon of the internet and have already made a big impact on the way the recruitment of graduates and IT staff is undertaken. They are, however, more suited to

  – volume recruitment

  – large companies.

  – Smaller companies, and even larger ones seeking to fill one-off, senior posts, are still tending to use more traditional methods.

  – The main problem with company websites is attracting candidates to them – or, from the job seeker's angle, locating them. This is not a problem with a major multinational like Shell, but it is an obstacle in the case of smaller companies. Candidates wanting to make direct applications may still find it more efficient to identify target companies in a given sector via sources such as *Key British Enterprises* rather than search engines which throw up either too many or too few responses.

  – Once target companies have been identified, however, their websites should make it easier to research them and make a well-focused application.

  – To the extent that employers will find it easier to create their own databases of CVs, direct applications may be retained for longer and accessed more easily and accurately when a vacancy does arise.

- **Networking**
  - Those for whom the conventional job sources are ineffective, e.g. due to age discrimination, are still going to need to rely heavily on networking.

  - Since networking calls for two-way, rather than one-way, communication it is, by definition, a face-to-face or telephone activity rather than one which can be conducted by mail – of either the snail or e- variety.

  - The internet is therefore unlikely to affect it greatly, although it will be a useful source of information for research on companies, and thank you letters to those who have helped you can be sent more quickly and cheaply by e-mail.

At the application stage of the recruitment process there is much talk about online applications to speed up and simplify initial screening. Although some employers have been using telephone interviewing for quite a while, most have, in the past, relied on written applications, so this genuinely is a major change. Applying online is quicker for the candidate, but gives less time to think and there is no opportunity to draft an application, review it and polish it before submitting it. That apart, online application procedures are essentially little different from filling in an application form or doing a psychometric test. At present, online application procedures are, in any case, rarely being used for professional and executive levels of recruitment, although they are being encountered increasingly by graduates seeking their first job.

As for the interview, some commentators are suggesting that it may be completely eliminated, with employers speeding up the recruitment process to the ultimate degree by posting a vacancy on the internet, computer screening responses and dealing with offer and acceptance procedures by e-mail. Whilst this just may happen with jobs like computer programming where selection is entirely down to hard skills, and where the aim is to hire contractors who, if they are found on day one to be unacceptable, can be told to go away again, it seems highly unlikely that the interview – for all its well-publicised shortcomings – will be ditched in the vast majority of cases where personal qualities and the ability to fit into a team are important considerations. If, one day, we all end up working from home and never communicating with colleagues, clients and suppliers other than via the internet or video conferencing, things could change – but that is a long way off yet.

What is more, much though some candidates may dislike or even fear interviews, few would wish to accept a job without having the chance to see the place where they will be working and to meet their future boss.

Friend or foe?

The question of whether the internet will make it easier or more difficult for you to find a new job needs to be viewed from two aspects:

- market forces
- your attitude to the internet and your proficiency in using it.

In some areas – primarily the hiring of IT staff and graduates – the internet is already becoming the favoured channel of recruitment and some employers are refusing to accept applications by any means other than e-mail. Since applicants in these areas also seem to favour the internet, it clearly has advantages to both parties, although the fact that making an application may be easier does not actually increase your chances of success – that is a matter on the one hand of supply and demand and on the other of how you, and your application, stack up against the opposition.

In other areas, the same dynamics of supply and demand also have a significant influence on which sources of vacancies are most appropriate to any given job seeker. Secretaries and recently qualified accountants, though very different commodities in many ways, share the fact that the demand for their services often tends to exceed the supply, so they can leave an agency to do all the leg work of getting them a new job and often find this less of an effort than applying to advertisements. Unless finding a job on the internet can be shown to involve less effort than using agencies, such candidates are unlikely to switch their allegiance.

People who are in a less advantageous supply to demand situation, which includes many job seekers at various levels of management, tend to use advertisements as their main source of vacancies. Assuming that the stage is reached where the number of job boards is rationalised, specialist boards achieve dominance in various areas and search parameters become more precise, the internet will be beneficial in making the process of applying for jobs easier and less time consuming – but we are not at that stage yet.

Those who are severely disadvantaged by conventional job sourcing, e.g. older candidates who tend to be rejected by both agencies and advertisers, are unlikely to find things any easier on the internet – after all, it is at present basically another form of agency or advertised recruitment and, even if the ability of employers to trawl internet databases of CVs increases, those employers are still going to have the same prejudices. Such candidates, therefore, will still have to rely heavily on the hidden approaches: networking and direct applications.

Within each category, on the other hand, there will be the opportunity to gain competitive advantage by looking at the internet as an opportunity rather than a threat and by making the effort to become familiar with the powerful tools and facilities which it puts at the job hunter's disposal.

Taking advantage

At the time of writing this new chapter, there are still job seekers who are not even on the internet. The message for them is to get connected right away. Even if you are the type of job hunter whose best bet is going to be networking, not having an e-mail address these days gives you the same kind of credibility problems as not having a telephone.

CHOOSING AN ISP

On the subject of e-mail addresses, it is also worth giving some thought to your choice of Internet Service Provider (ISP). There are three main considerations:

- Efficiency – both the ease of connection and the time it takes for e-mails to be sent and received seem to vary considerably. Check the experiences of other internet users whom you know for tips on performance.

- Cost – the UK is moving towards the situation which already exists in the USA whereby calls to an ISP are free. However, it will probably take a while before everyone can get completely free access to the internet and at present (June 2000) users need to check carefully the various offers being made by ISPs to ensure they get the best deal.

- Image – at the more senior levels of the job market in particular, recruitment consultants and potential employers may judge you by your e-mail address, just as they form first impressions based on your clothes and your speech, so you may wish to avoid an ISP which gives you an e-mail address bearing the name of a grocery chain or one which has a down-market image.

If you are sharing a PC with other members of your family, do set up your own separate e-mail address. Given the need to have access at any time, your own PC is, however, advisable, especially if you have children who enjoy surfing or who play computer games. For reasons of access, and the image created by your e-mail address, it is not really on to use either facilities provided by internet cafés or public libraries or, if you are in employment, your PC at work.

Once you are connected, you should be prepared to invest some time in familiarising yourself with the powerful new tools at your disposal. How much time depends on your existing knowledge of:

- e-mail
- word processing
- search engines
- using job sites.

How you go about this will be governed partly by your existing level of knowledge and confidence and partly by your preferred learning style – some people like to pitch straight in and learn by trial and error whilst others prefer first to gain a conceptual understanding of the principles involved before attempting to apply them. There are various options available, including:

- Manuals which come with your PC and books which can be purchased from generalist or specialist stores, or (often more cheaply) over the internet. The choice can be somewhat bewildering, so be prepared to spend a little time browsing to ensure that you get books which are pitched at your level and which really do provide the answers to your questions.

- The help facilities on your PC. Those new to computers may find these take a bit of getting used to but it is worth investing the time and effort.

- More knowledgeable and experienced friends. Do, however, make sure that they go at your pace and give you the chance to do things for yourself rather than just demonstrating their own expertise while you become progressively more lost and less confident.

- Courses run by either local adult education institutes or commercial providers. Those who have previously made little or no use of PCs may well feel somewhat fearful and need to gain some confidence by attending an 'introduction to computers' course, whilst job hunters with no experience of word processing may find a WP course more effective than trying to pick it up for themselves. Courses are, however, the most expensive learning option so a judgement has to be made as to whether the benefits justify the costs.

Some points to be borne in mind in terms of what you need to know include:

E-MAIL

- Unless you get people's addresses 100 per cent correct, your e-mails will not be delivered. Far too many fail to get through due to a small detail like a dot in the wrong place.
- Some e-mails arrive but cannot be read. Send them in straightforward formats and, if in doubt, check both that they have been received and can be read. In fact, there is no harm in including a standard request for the recipient to acknowledge receipt.
- E-mail tends to be informal, but when making a job application it is better to err on the side of formality. Do not start off with 'Hi' rather than 'Dear' and confine e-mail abbreviations and particularly emoticons (or 'smileys') – face-like characters used to express emotions – to social communications.
- Avoid 'shouting' – typing messages in capitals – it is annoying and difficult to read.
- Do not forget to run the spell check over your e-mails.
- Whenever possible, send your CV or other enclosures as attachments rather than pasting them onto your e-mail.

WORD PROCESSING

- You will need word processing primarily for letters/e-mails and CVs. The former are relatively straightforward, the latter a bit more complicated.
- CVs look better if you use indents but these can be thrown out of line when you e-mail your CV. In order to minimise the risk of this happening it is best to use either the tab key or bullet points, rather than the space bar, columns or tables.
- Page breaks can also be thrown by e-mail. Try e-mailing your CV to a few friends with different systems to check that its layout is not being fouled up.

continued overleaf

WORD PROCESSING – continued

- Word processing packages provide powerful facilities which can make a world of difference to the appearance of your CV. Do familiarise yourself with them. You never get a second chance to make a first impression.
- Word processing also allows you to customise your CV with very little effort each time you use it. It is easy to have a slightly over-long CV on a master file. Save it as a new file each time you use it. Edit text by clicking on it and either deleting items which are not relevant to a particular application or changing the order in which, for example, bullet points appear in order to place the most relevant points at the top of a list.

SEARCH ENGINES

- Different search engines may be more effective for different kinds of search.
- Think carefully about the words you type in, otherwise you are likely to end up with either too few or – more likely – too many responses. One job hunter who simply typed in 'jobs' got 600,000 entries!
- Recommendations and hints from friends and fellow job hunters can save you quite a lot of time, so do ask around – and keep up to date, nothing stays still on the internet.

JOB SITES

- The two main categories are employers' own websites, and job boards – which are essentially advertising media for vacancies posted either directly by employers or by agencies and selection consultants.

- If you do not already know the names of potential employers whom you wish to target, you can identify them by using search engines, reference books, trade associations or the recruitment advertisements in newspapers and trade and professional journals.

- Job boards are advertised in the conventional press and elsewhere but, given the proliferation of them, ask around for recommendations as to which are most useful.

- Take the time to familiarise yourself with the extent to which job boards allow you to edit any CV you register or to place more than one version of your CV on the board.

- Pay as much attention to an e-mailed cover letter as to one you would send in the post, aiming for a highly focused response to a careful analysis of the requirements specified in the advertisement.

Time management

Every job hunter should have an action plan – just a page of A4 is fine, you do not need a 20-page bound document – which lists out all the relevant job search options and places them in order of priority, bearing in mind the amount of time available, which obviously differs greatly depending on whether or not you are currently in a job. (Action plans are discussed in greater detail in Chapter 6.)

The amount of time allocated to the internet will vary from one individual to another depending on factors such as the sector and discipline you are in, your marketability and your age. For most people it will involve an initial, relatively high time input in order to achieve the requisite level of familiarity. This will then be scaled down to an ongoing input based on the relative usefulness of the internet compared with other job sources. The proportions of time allocated may need to be reviewed in the light of experience.

The ways in which internet time itself is allocated will also need to be considered. Some people may use it mainly for e-mail, others for applications via job boards and yet others, especially those who are doing direct applications, predominantly for research. The important point is to make a conscious decision based on an open-minded approach, neither being a Luddite who misses the help it can give you nor getting so carried away with it that you neglect other powerful routes to a new job, such as networking.

"HEADHUNTERS ARE IN THE BUSINESS OF FINDING PEOPLE FOR JOBS, NOT JOBS FOR PEOPLE."

10 Don't call us, we'll call you

Headhunters and agencies

If only job seekers understood how headhunters really worked, they could save themselves a great deal of time and effort which is currently completely wasted. The lack of understanding which causes this waste is due in part to the veil of mystery in which the executive search business loves to shroud itself, and in part to the outdated conception which the average lay person has of headhunting and its practitioners.

Back in the 1960s, when headhunting crossed the Atlantic and began to make inroads into the UK market, a fair number of the people who went into the business were executives who may not have been particularly successful in their chosen fields but who had extensive contacts – made and maintained largely through their patronage of bars and clubs. Their method of headhunting was, in effect, just an extension of the old boy network which had been in use for years.

There was, however, also a more professional approach to executive search. On being briefed by a client, the search consultant would undertake research into the sector in question and compile a target list of companies in which candidates were likely to be found. Then, often after discussing the target companies with the client, further research would produce a list of named target individuals, people holding appropriate positions in the target companies which made them likely candidates for the job in question. These candidates would be discreetly approached, initially by a telephone call, and – if there was mutual interest – a meeting with the consultant would be arranged.

Given the competitive nature of modern business, it is hardly surprising that it is this more professional approach which has prevailed. David Shellard, managing director of Russell Reynolds, one of the largest and most prestigious search firms, stated quite categorically, 'The old boy network is dead'. Although he made it clear that he was referring to the top end of the market, many smaller firms operating lower down the market are also very largely research driven.

This situation raises a question of vital importance to the jobhunter. If search firms only approach people identified by this targeting process, how do you get a look in if you are either working in a different industry to the one being targeted or, worse still, if you are not employed at all?

Let us begin by exploding yet another popular misconception. What you do not do is to blast off copies of your CV to every search firm listed in *Executive Grapevine*. In the early days of outplacement, some of its practitioners did encourage this approach. The fact that they no longer do so is only partly due to the cost to the outplacement firms in terms of stamps and stationery. The plain fact is that bulk mailouts to headhunters simply do not work.

Researchers and databases

In order to understand why bulk mailshots to search firms are a waste of time – and to discover what does work – you need to know a little more about the way the modern headhunting industry operates.

As the search business became more heavily research based, some simple economics came into play. Since consultants' earnings (including performance-based incentives) can run well into six figures, search firms started to employ full-time researchers – who could be hired for a fraction of that kind of sum – to produce the lists of target companies and individuals, and, in many cases, to make the initial telephone calls to prospective candidates. The search consultants could then devote their time to generating business, fronting up to the client on the conduct of the assignment and doing the interviewing.

Hand in hand with the rise of the researcher came the development of the computerised database. This in turn spawned the twin myth that, if you write in on spec to a search firm, your details will automatically be entered on their database and will then be retrieved whenever they are briefed on a suitable opening for you.

To begin with, many search firms only enter on to their databases details of about 20 per cent of the candidates who write in. Those 20 per cent are the ones they reckon may be useful to them, either as candidates or in other ways. The rest get a polite letter which probably ducks the issue of whether they have been entered on the database with some ambiguous phrase like 'We will be in touch with you if we have anything of potential interest.'

The second part of the myth is that the database is used to find candidates for jobs. In practice, no more than about 5 per cent of search assignments are filled from candidates who are already on the database. The rest come from original research, which includes both desk research and the use of sources.

Sourcing and sources

Researchers are remarkably resourceful, some would say devious, people. In order to identify target individuals, they will subject switchboard operators, secretaries and other staff in target organisations to tactics that range from sheer cheek through con tricks to, if need be, manoeuvres that verge on industrial espionage. There are, however, more straightforward means too – namely the people known as sources.

If you have ever had a call from a headhunter that went something like, 'I wonder if you might happen to know anyone who would be interested in a position . . .' and wondered whether this was just a roundabout way of asking whether you would be interested in the job in question, the ambiguity was probably intentional. They may have been interested in you, but equally it could just have been your contacts they were after.

Often, however, sourcing is done far more overtly. Most headhunters have a network of contacts whom they can tap when the need arises. Far from objecting to being used in this way, sources actually tend to like it. To begin with, there is an element of flattery involved. By asking for your help, the headhunter is acknowledging that you are a well-connected individual who knows a lot of the key players in your particular business. Then, of course, there is always the thought that the headhunter just might, one day, return the favour by coming up with a plum position for you.

It is primarily for sources, rather than candidates, that search firms go to all the time and expense of maintaining databases.

Shapes and sizes

Before turning to the way in which you, the job seeker, should approach executive search firms, we just need to look at one further aspect of the business: its structure and the players within that structure.

Although the leading firms – Russell Reynolds, Spencer Stuart, Korn/Ferry, Heidrick & Struggles and so on – are the largest and best known, there are literally hundreds of smaller organisations too, any one of which might be handling the appointment for which you could be a strong contender. Some of them, particularly the medium-sized firms, are – like the leading players – generalists, covering the whole range of disciplines and business sectors. Others, including many outfits with just two or three consultants, and even a sprinkling of sole practitioners, make a living by specialising – more often by business sector than by job function. How they manage to do this without breaching the off limits code which prevents headhunters from targeting employees of companies which are, or have recently been, clients need not bother you too much as a candidate.

The top firms tend to attract the blue chip clients and, as a result, only to be interested in candidates of the same calibre. The criteria for being on a target list or for a speculative applicant being entered on to the database tend to include a good degree, the appropriate professional qualification, and a career which both demonstrates clear progression and includes company names which are the most highly respected in their particular industry.

Fortunately for those who do not quite match up to this image, simple mathematics dictate that only a minority of job vacancies can be filled by upper decile candidates. The smaller firms may well be more fertile sources of opportunities, not just because they are handling clients with less demanding specifications but also because you stand a better chance of targeting yourself at an organisation which specialises in the area where your particular experience and strengths lie. Furthermore, because the niche firms make greater use of sources, you are also more likely to be picked up by this route, provided that you work hard on your own networking (see Chapter 11).

The bottom line

The one point you must never forget, though, is that, whatever their size and regardless of whether they are generalists or specialists, all headhunters have one thing in common: it is the clients who pay their fees, not the candidates. They are in the business of finding people for jobs, not jobs for people.

What is more, as in any other viciously competitive sector, time is money. In fact, since most headhunters are incentivised on performance, they are even more aware of the value of time than many other businesses are. The corollary of this is that the last thing you should ever do is to waste their time.

So, to move from their bottom line to yours, how do you establish and maintain the most productive relationship with headhunters?

- The best time to start is before you actually need a job. If you are involved in hiring senior staff, be sure to meet the search consultants your company uses. Do not just leave it to the HR people. If you are approached as a source, be as helpful as possible. It is easier, subsequently, to obtain help from someone who 'owes you one' than from someone who owes you nothing.

- When you do need a job, avoid bulk mailshots. Target carefully those search firms which are likely to regard you as a relevant candidate. If necessary, ask a few people for advice on the right firms to go for. This can be part of your networking.

- There is no harm in asking for a meeting, but remember that the search consultant's time is money. When you do get a meeting, keep it brief and focused. If possible offer something in return, like snippets of news about your sector. Needless to say, information on companies which might be hiring (but not, of course, for a job you would want) is the most prized. In the absence of a positive benefit to offer, at least flatter the consultant by asking for some specific advice.

- In practice there are so many jobhunters trying to get to see headhunters that, unless you are an existing or potential client, you will probably succeed only if you can get an introduction via someone with influence. If you do not already have contacts who can make this kind of introduction, try creating some through networking.

- After a meeting, observe the courtesy of a thank you letter but do not pester the consultant with frequent calls. Apart from wasting the headhunter's time, you will also be causing embarrassment if there are no jobs available.

- Be realistic in your expectations. Each search consultant handles only perhaps 12 to 15 assignments a year. Even with careful targeting, it is unreasonable to expect opportunities to grow on trees.

- When search firms put your details on their databases, they enter only selected information under standard classifications, e.g. up to three industries in which you have worked, and a similar number of functional headings for experience. Make their job easier, and reduce the risk of errors which might adversely affect the chances of your details being retrieved against suitable vacancies, by highlighting key information on your CV.

- Remember that you cannot be seen if you are not visible. Make your own luck in terms of coming to the attention of headhunters and their sources by networking actively, and by taking all other opportunities to raise your visibility (see Chapter 14).

Upmarket, downmarket

While most executives are flattered to be approached by a headhunter, many tend to look down their noses at agencies. Is this justified? Or do you risk missing out on a potentially valuable source of job opportunities? The answer depends not only on how senior you are but also on the discipline, and business sector, you work in.

Agencies have traditionally tended to operate at the high volume, fast moving end of the job market. Whether they have been placing secretaries, computer staff or recently qualified professionals such as accountants and solicitors, they have been dealing with people who tend to find a new job quickly. The agencies' own staff, often earning a significant proportion of their income through commission, and having to compete with other agencies for contingent fees, have been unwilling to waste precious time on candidates who might take months, rather than weeks, to get placed.

This situation has, however, been changing. In the process of filling more junior positions, agencies have forged relationships with top level decision makers and, when a more senior position has come up, they have sometimes been given a crack at it. In some cases such positions are filled by client-paid advertising, bringing the agencies into direct competition with the executive selection firms. In other cases they have been filled from the agencies' registers. This method has several advantages to the client: it is faster; the agency's fee is contingent on success rather than being based on guaranteed stage payments; and there are no expensive bills for advertising.

Operating register search at these levels does, however, have the problem that agencies tend to end up with large files of candidates to be matched against relatively few jobs. This is in contrast to the lower level work where, because there are more jobs to fill and people get placed more quickly, it is easier to keep files to a manageable size.

An exception to this arises where the field of candidates is so small that there is no danger of databank indigestion. In these specialised areas register search may be regularly used at much higher levels than it would be where candidate volumes are greater, and niche agencies have established themselves to service this opportunity. Treasury appointments are just one example. Agencies specialising in this sector regularly handle positions at substantial salaries, few of which are advertised.

Agency use, and abuse

Some of the rules that apply to dealing with agencies, for example those that relate to obtaining and handling meetings, are the same as those for dealing with headhunters. There are, however, a few additional points to look out for.

- Unlike most headhunters, agencies work on contingent fees and there is consequently a direct incentive for them to help you find a job. Make full use of their expertise. As Alan Dickinson, managing director of Michael Page Finance, explained, 'Organisations like Michael Page can help candidates to market themselves. Our consultants know what companies are looking for and can therefore advise candidates on which elements of their experience to highlight.'

- Remember, though, that – if anything – agency staff have even more demands on their time than headhunters. After your initial contact, do not call them more than once a month.

- When you do call, do not ask if they have a job for you. If they had, they would have called you.

- Even if you are getting frustrated by the time it is taking to find a job, do not get aggressive with agencies. They are far more likely to try to bend a client spec for a co-operative candidate than for a stroppy one.

- Since they only make money when they place you, give them the benefit of your market research. Suggestions you make may just spark an idea which enables them to market you to one of their clients.

"THE FIRST BATCH OF CALLS YOU MAKE WILL BE TO PEOPLE YOU KNOW QUITE WELL ALREADY."

11 Networking 1: getting started

What were your feelings as you just turned the page? Delight at finally getting to the chapter which tells you how to use this powerful approach you have heard so much about – or apprehension at the thought of having to ring people up and ask for favours? Maybe your feelings were a mixture of the two. If they were, then you are a pretty normal jobhunter.

The apprehension is usually a combination of embarrassment and fear, the latter being both the fear of the unknown and the fear of rejection.

If you feel embarrassed about asking for help, reach for the other person's shoes once again. How would you feel if someone phoned you up to ask for your advice? Would you not want to give them all the help you could? And, what is more, would you not feel flattered at having been the person they chose to ask?

It is just as natural to experience fear of the unknown as it is to be embarrassed about requesting help. If you have not tried networking before, you probably do not know what to expect. That is why this chapter both explains the techniques involved and ensures that you prepare thoroughly before you make your first call.

Fear of rejection – while understandable – is, in this case, quite unjustified. If you were actually asking people for a job, you might well find that the door was being slammed in your face with depressing regularity. However, when you network properly you never ask for a job, only for advice, assistance or contacts. Such requests are very rarely met with outright refusal.

In any case, we are not going to start you off with calls to total strangers. The first batch of calls you make will be to people you know quite well already.

Not just for the unemployed

Talking of people you know, an additional fear for those who are currently in employment will inevitably be the question of confidentiality. Because of this, a lot of executives who are in jobs at the moment assume that they cannot use networking. Nothing could be further from the truth. They may have to do one or two things a bit differently, but they can certainly network every bit as effectively.

The main difference is that while the unemployed people will ask for advice and contacts to help them in their job search, those in employment will ask for more general career advice, never openly admitting that they are actually looking for another job. They use lines like:

- 'I like this company a lot, but I'm a bit concerned about the career prospects'; or

- 'I'm not sure I'm really getting the experience I need to develop myself fully'; or

- 'Given the pace of change these days, I'm beginning to wonder if I've stayed too long in the same environment'.

Comments like these, linked to a request for advice, can lead to a conversation in which you admit that, if somebody made you an offer you could not refuse, your loyalty to your present company might just be tested.

But how, given the hours you work, do you ever find time for networking? In practice, nothing could be easier. You simply tack it on to all the activities you undertake as a normal part of your job. Chatting to the company's PR firm? Having lunch with a customer? Attending a conference? Visiting an exhibition? Just manoeuvre the conversation round to the subject of careers. The other person may be just as happy to do so as you. Networking works particularly well when it is based on 'You scratch my back and I'll scratch yours.'

What is more, if enough opportunities are not falling into your lap, you can easily create them. Simply make calls and initiate conversations which are either genuinely or ostensibly about valid work matters, but which can, after a decent interval, be edged round to what you really want to talk about.

What? No network?

By this point, those who are unemployed may well be getting jealous. Some may be feeling that they have all the time, but that they no longer have the contacts. The following is a typical case in point.

The outplacement candidate's face fell. 'But', he complained, 'I don't know anybody.'

'Here we go again', his counsellor thought. What he said, however, was, 'You mentioned a few moments ago that you still go for a quick one before you catch the train home, even though you're working out your notice. Do you go to the pub alone?'

'Oh, no. I go with some people from the office, and we usually get chatting to some of the other regulars.'

'And do you play any sports?'

'Well, only golf. I'm a member of the local club.'

'What about voluntary work?'

'Not really – not unless you count being a school governor.'

'I certainly do. I bet some of the other governors will be useful contacts. Any other activities – clubs, societies, what have you?'

'Well, er . . . I am a Freemason actually.'

A smile spread from one of the counsellor's ears to the other. 'And you reckon you haven't got any contacts!'

The candidate looked back in surprise. Then he began smiling too.

Get the point? All right then, now get a piece of paper and start making your own list.

Listing your contacts

Use the following headings, listing the names of as many individuals under each as you possibly can. Do not limit yourself to the categories shown, they are just examples to get you going.

- **Family and friends**
  Immediate family
  Other relatives
  Neighbours
  Friends
  People you were at school or university with
  People you have met on holiday
  Family and friends of all of the above

- **Clubs and leisure activities**
  Sports clubs
  Hobbies groups
  Evening classes
  Community groups
  Church/other religious organisations
  Political associations

- **Professional services**
  Bank manager
  Financial adviser
  Insurance broker
  Stockbroker
  Solicitor
  Doctor
  Dentist

- **Business**
  Colleagues – past and present
  Bosses – ditto
  Staff – ditto
  Customers/clients
  Suppliers
  Professional advisers
  Trade associations
  Chambers of commerce

Professional societies
Regulatory bodies
Management consultants

Now take a couple of different coloured textmarkers. In one colour mark the people you know particularly well, the ones you are going to feel most comfortable speaking to initially, while you are getting used to the idea of networking and are still building up your confidence. Use the other colour to mark the 'connectors'; those people (such as lawyers, bankers, accountants in firms of auditors, management consultants) who deal regularly with a lot of other people in a wide range of organisations. They will be particularly productive network contacts.

Resist the temptation to pitch straight in with the people you have textmarked in both colours. While they will naturally be the most useful of all, begin by practising on some whom you marked only with the first pen, waiting until you have gained expertise and assurance before tackling your 'star contacts'.

In fact, you should never dive straight in, even with old friends with whom you feel completely comfortable. Before you make a single contact, there are several things you must think about. The first and most important of these is to be absolutely clear about what you want to achieve.

Spoilt for choice

Although your ultimate objective is to get a new job, that is the one thing you do not ask your network contact for. While somewhere between 5 per cent and 10 per cent of the people you speak to may be in a position to put an opportunity your way, this means that 90 per cent to 95 per cent are not. Asking directly for a job will not only embarrass them, because they cannot help, but it will also damage your chances of receiving the valuable assistance they actually can provide you with. This could include:

- advice as to the career options open to you;

- ideas about new directions you could take which you may not even have considered;

- information about options you are thinking of pursuing, such as
  - working in a different business sector
  - switching into a new role
  - retraining
  - moving to another part of the country
  - having a spell overseas;
- advice on your CV;
- information about job openings;
- introductions to other people who can do any of the above;
- referrals to people who may have a job to offer you – or be in a position to create one for you.

You do not have to confine yourself to a single aim each time you make a contact. You may, for example, ask both for advice about options open to you and for information about what is involved in one or more of them. In practice communication sparks ideas, and it is essential that you are always ready to be opportunistic, latching on to anything useful which a network contact suggests and developing it further.

However, if you are to develop not just suggestions, but also your network, there is one objective which should be mandatory for absolutely every contact you make.

The numbers game

The list you made of people with whom you might get in touch is not your network. It is just a starting point, a roll call of your initial contacts. An oft quoted maxim is that every time you speak to someone you ask them for the name of someone else you might contact. In this way the network perpetuates itself.

Although the principle of this is excellent, it needs a little refinement. If your network is to achieve its aim, which is to keep generating job opportunities until you find one that you want to accept, then you have got to keep it going. It must not be allowed to run down. On the contrary, you must work actively at expanding it.

Do some simple maths. If you started with just one contact who gave you the names of two more, each of whom gave you another two, how long would it take you to get to a thousand contacts? The answer is just ten steps. Now count up the number of people on your initial list and apply the same multiple – that is the power of networking!

Compare this with what would have happened if you had asked each person for just one name. Some would have been unable to think of anyone at all. Others might have suggested a person who had moved on and could not be contacted, or who proved to be a dud for some other reason. Then, of course, there would have been some which were duplicates. Imperceptibly at first, but with increasing momentum, your network would have begun to shrink rather than to grow.

It is for these reasons that you do not ask for just one name, nor even for only two – not, at any rate, if you want to achieve the multiplier effect outlined above. In order to end up with an average of two valid new contacts (i.e. after allowing for duplicates, duds and people who cannot or will not provide names) you need to ask for three or four. If you feel awkward or pushy about being as demanding as that, try – using your own words – one or other of the following approaches.

- Where the discussion has more than one objective, ask to be put in touch with one or two further people you can speak to about each of them, e.g. help with your CV, advice on a change of career direction, information about a business sector.

- Use flattery – but do not go over the top. For example, 'As a partner in a firm of auditors, you must know a lot of top people. I'd be really grateful if you could open a few doors for me. Even just three or four people I could get in touch with, using your name to open the door, would be an enormous help.'

- Be a giver as well as a taker. Explain to your contacts the networking multiplier principle you are operating. Quite apart from giving you full marks for ingenuity, they will have learned about a tool which they may either use themselves, immediately or at some future point in time, or which they can pass on to other people who come to them for advice.

Networking is not discrete

No, that is not a spelling mistake. The use of the word, which refers to being separate and distinct, rather than 'discreet' with its connotations of circumspection and discretion, was quite deliberate. An important point to be made, in connection with the development of your network, is that networking is not something totally unconnected with the other approaches you are employing in your job search. Quite the opposite. You can both increase the effectiveness of other methods by allying them with networking, and also add new names to your network contact lists by using advertisements and other job sources as a door opener.

Headhunting is an obvious case in point. Headhunters make great use of their own contact network, the people they refer to as 'sources', i.e. not actual candidates for a job but people who might know others who could be right for the position in question. The more of these sources you know – and many of them will be the connectors you have on your own network list – the more likely it is that the headhunters will be dialling your number.

It works the other way round, too. Headhunters whom you network may not be able to put a job your way – we have already seen that each consultant handles only a dozen or so assignments a year – but they do know an awful lot of useful people and may well be happy to give you a few introductions.

The same principle works with advertised vacancies. The more people you network, and who therefore know what you are looking for, the more likely it is that one will spot an ad that you somehow missed. Then, once you do have an advertised position to apply for, you can try networking an introduction to either the ultimate decision maker or, failing that, to the recruiter. Even when you cannot find a door opener, a call to the individual who placed an advertisement may be used not only to check out your relevance to the post in question and, by creating a strong impression on the phone, to increase your chances of an interview, but also to initiate a new networking chain. Whether or not your application for the original position goes further, you can ask if there is anyone you can talk to about similar posts, or request the names of any other recruiters who might be able to help you. A busy recruiter will often give you a few names, if for no other reason than to get you off the phone.

Networking can also help with speculative applications. However industrious and diligent you are, you will never pick up on every single news item which might represent a valuable lead. However, with a small army of people keeping an eye open for you, you can greatly increase your chances. You can also use your network to help in researching 'cold call' targets and their business sectors, so that your letters and calls are more effective. Sometimes this results in finding someone who can open a door for you, so that what you expected to be a cold call actually becomes a networking approach, but this just proves how inextricably linked networking is to the other techniques in your job hunting tool kit.

It also goes to show how powerful networking is and how many benefits it has. Before moving on to the nuts and bolts of calls and meetings, ensure that you both appreciate the extent of these benefits, and take full advantage of them. Check out the following list.

THE BENEFITS OF NETWORKING

- You are no longer competing with hundreds of other people for every job. Sometimes, if you hit that window of opportunity when a job is being discussed but no action has been taken to initiate recruitment, you could be the only candidate.
- Better still, you may even have a job created specifically for you.

continued overleaf

THE BENEFITS OF NETWORKING – continued

- Instead of being arbitrarily ruled out because a recruiter has highlighted one item on a list of criteria which you do not match, what you are focusing attention on are the qualities and strengths which you actually do possess.

- Whereas applying to advertisements is a lonely business, networking provides social contact and stimulation, both of which are of immense value – far more than many people realise.

- Instead of having to go in cold, as a stranger, you always have, at the very least, a name to use to prise a door open for you. At best, the person providing the referral may have personally called or written to introduce or recommend you.

- Openings are often created for you to be flexible and opportunistic. For example, in a discussion which you set up to achieve one objective, such as obtaining information about a given company or industry, your contact may suddenly come up with the name of someone who actually has a vacancy in that field.

- Networking can be rewarding not just in terms of identifying job leads, but also in providing opportunities to put something back by helping others. What is more, network contacts often turn into long-term friends.

- Applying to advertisements is reactive. Networking is proactive.

- Above all, you are in control. You set your own pace and course of action. Being in control is not only less stressful than being at the mercy of others but also infinitely more productive.

"THE QUALITY OF WHAT YOU GET FROM YOUR CONTACT WILL DEPEND, MORE THAN ANYTHING ELSE, ON THE QUALITY OF THE QUESTIONS YOU ASK."

12 Networking 2: getting results

There are three possible ways of communicating with your network contacts: in writing, on the telephone or face to face. Wherever possible, go for a meeting.

Meetings produce much more information and provide many more opportunities. In the course of a face to face discussion, names of people and organisations come out in a way that just does not happen when you are talking on the telephone. So do all sorts of ideas and suggestions.

More often than not, network contacts prefer a meeting too. There is very little difference in the time taken up by a short meeting and a long phone call. What is more, you may telephone just when the contact is trying to complete a task to a tight deadline, is in a hurry to leave the office for an important appointment or is being interrupted every couple of minutes. A meeting can be scheduled for a more convenient, and quieter, time. An additional consideration when your network contacts are people to whom you have been referred, and who have never met you, is that they may be unwilling to provide you with further referrals until they have met you in the flesh.

The only real disadvantage of meetings is that they take up more of your time, because you have to travel to and from the place where the meeting takes place. Wherever possible, therefore, arrange more than one meeting in the same town or city on the same day – but not so many that you arrive late, get flustered or fail to find time both to run over your agenda before each meeting and to make notes after each one.

Sometimes, of course, you will have no option but to settle for telephone conversations, either because the contacts insist on handling it that way or because they are so far away that it would be too time consuming, and expensive, to go to see them. You can still get quite a lot out of a phone call, so long as you prepare yourself thoroughly.

Before you call

The planning you do before a telephone call needs to take into account the fact that you can never know in advance whether you will succeed in arranging a face-to-face meeting or whether that call is going to be the only chance you will get to achieve your objectives with that particular network contact. Therefore, while you always ask for a meeting, you must have to hand a clear list of what you want from the person you are calling. This could include:

- advice about the direction and development of your career;

- information regarding specific industries or companies;

- referrals to further network contacts, in which case you need to know
  - names
  - addresses
  - telephone numbers
  - best times and methods of contacting them
  - as much as possible about them, their organisation and their business sector
  - whether you may use the referee's name as a door opener.

Having clarified your objectives, you can then decide how you are going to lead into them. If you are currently in work you can adopt an oblique approach, using an (ostensibly) genuine business motive for the call. If you are unemployed you need to be more direct.

The opening will depend on whether you are calling someone you already know or whether it is a referral who will probably not even know your name. In the first case you can lead in with something of a social nature, and may well exchange a few pleasantries and catch up on each other's general news before moving on to the purpose of your call. In the second, you make immediate mention of the name of the door opener, assuming that you have permission to do so, then carry straight on to explain why you are calling. If you cannot use the name of your original contact, you will have to say something like, 'I am calling you because I understand that you are an expert on . . .'

Since the people you are calling will almost certainly have many demands on their time, it is vital that you do not waste it. An opening which respects that situation might go something like this:

> My name is Jill Brown. Carol Clark suggested I call you because I am considering developing my career within the country hotels sector. Carol said that you know more about that business than anyone she has ever met, and that you might be able to give me some advice and perhaps a few further contacts. Could you please spare a quarter of an hour or so at some point for me to come and see you?

Only 15 minutes? Yes, that is all you ask for – though in practice you will probably get more like 30 since most people organise their diaries in half-hour slots. The important point is to avoid the classic howler committed by one out-placement candidate. Here is the lament which she poured out to her counsellor at a review meeting.

> I'm not getting very far with this networking business. I've been doing everything you said – prioritising my contacts, defining my objectives, planning a snappy opening to each call – but when I ask if I can pop in to see them for an hour or so, they all seem to have their diaries fully booked for the next month or more!

As I was saying, do respect the fact that, for busy people, time is at a premium.

Making the most of the meeting

Given that your meeting will probably last no more than half an hour, you need to prepare carefully in order to make the most of it. Beware, however, of people who advise you to plan for your meetings by writing out a rigid script, geared to a single objective. Networking meetings are fluid, two-way affairs. While you do need to control them, you must do so with a light hand, not a heavy one. Unless you are flexible, you will find yourself constantly failing to capitalise on the true value of the contact and at times missing out on absolutely golden opportunities.

But how can you plan to be flexible? Is that not a contradiction in terms? Not at all – though what it does mean is that you have to work that bit harder.

The starting point is research. If you are going to see someone you have met before, you should know a reasonable amount about them and the organisation they work for or represent. If you have not met, but have been given an introduction by someone else, then you should have obtained similar information from the person who provided the referral. Do not stop there, though. Bearing in mind the business sectors of which your contact has knowledge, and the various pies he or she has a finger in, jot down all the ways in which that individual may be able to help you, either with advice, or information, or contacts.

The next stage is to give careful thought to the questions you are going to use in order to obtain that help. The quality of what you get from your contact will depend, more than anything else, on the quality of the questions you ask. They are the most effective tools you can possibly use in your job search.

What is more, many of the people you meet will base their evaluation of you on how thoroughly you have prepared for the meeting and how well thought out your questions are. The better the opinion they form of you, the more willing they will be to provide you with further referrals and to allow their own name to be used by way of introduction.

When it comes to introductions, do not fall into the error of setting your sights too low. If you ask up front, your contact may be willing to set up meetings for you with his or her referrals, or occasionally even to take you along to introduce you personally. Not all contacts will be prepared to go that far, of course, but others may be willing to forward your CV, accompanied by a personal letter or preceded by a telephone call. Any of these options will open the door more readily than you will be able to do by calling up yourself and using the contact's name or, worse still, just being given the referral without permission to use the referee's name. Remember the old maxim: 'If you don't ask, you don't get.'

Having done your research and devised your questions, you are now in a position to add the third leg to the preparation tripod. This is a careful selection of the USPs you have to offer, the selection being made on the basis of those qualifications, skills, fields of experience, personal strengths and, above all, achievements, which relate most directly to the areas highlighted by your research and covered by your questions. These should be listed out in full, then you should incorporate those that are particularly highly relevant into a freshly edited version of your CV which you will give to your contact at an appropriate point in the meeting.

Managing the meeting

Although your aim should be to allow sufficient flexibility to take advantage of ideas and suggestions emanating from your contact, you nevertheless need to control the tenor and direction of the meeting, albeit unobtrusively.

To get it off on the right foot, establish rapport. This should present few problems with people you already know. With referrals, break the ice and relax them by using one or two open questions, based on your research, to get them talking about their organisation and the issues facing the sector in which they operate.

Most people will be only too eager to help you, but they may not know how to do so. They will often ask what they can do for you. This is where you need to be ready to pick up the baton, giving a succinct (because you have rehearsed well) summary of your career, your current situation and, in particular, what you have to offer, and then explaining what you are looking for – advice, information etc.

It is at this stage that things start to get interesting. Your mind needs to be working overtime as you absorb everything your contact says. Juggling priorities with the speed and dexterity of a multi-programming computer, you pursue the most useful avenues with pertinent questions, ensuring that you make notes of everything that is going to be of value to you.

Finally, before thanking your contact for being so helpful, do make sure that you have not only got your three or four further referrals, but also as much information about them as possible. If you are to continue to develop your network, rather than letting it run down, you must never leave without those new names. Never? Well, there are just a couple of exceptions.

Windows of opportunity

As you read these words, a line manager somewhere is mulling over some initial thoughts about the creation of a new post. Somewhere else, a proposed vacancy has reached the next stage: a job description and person specification is being prepared. In yet another organisation, a divisional director is reviewing a job/person spec to decide whether to approve the addition to headcount. In a further company, they are running through possible internal candidates to see whether a vacancy which has been approved can be filled without the time and expense involved in advertising, or paying a fee to an agency or to a headhunter.

Actually, all of these events are occurring not just once but hundreds of times over every single day. And it is not just a question of new jobs. There are also those which have to be filled because someone has retired, or been promoted, transferred or fired. The problem is that each of these vacancies is known only to a very small number of people.

Or is it a problem? If you were one of those people, would it not be a distinct advantage? And, of course, through networking you can be. The more networking contacts you make, the more of these small circles of people who are in the know you stand a chance of penetrating. Usually you get in when someone you have already networked gets back to you with the lead, but just occasionally you may have the luck to be told about such an opportunity during the course of a networking meeting. How occasionally depends on how hard you work at making your own luck by working hard at preparing for, and managing, your meetings.

When such an opportunity does come up, you can be excused for not requesting further referrals. Indeed, if the position really interests you, it might be diplomatic not to cast doubts on your commitment by making it too obvious that you are continuing to seek out other opportunities – although, if you are wise, you will go on doing so right up to the time that the one you really want is securely in the bag.

The only other occasion on which you neglect to seek additional referrals is when, in the course of a meeting, your contact raises the possibility of creating a job for you. This golden opportunity – a job for which there is no competition and which is tailored exactly to your talents and interests – is even less a matter of pot luck than the previous example. You will have planted the seed in your contact's mind by identifying problems or needs within the organisation and by showing how you could be the ideal solution to them.

After the meeting

Where a specific vacancy has been identified, the next step will almost certainly be a further meeting. In all other cases, a different course of action needs to be followed.

The most urgent requirement is to follow up any leads you have been given. If, for example, a contact has gone to the trouble of getting in touch with a referral to herald your call, you will not be very popular if he or she finds out, a week or two later, that you have done nothing about it. You need expect no more help from that source.

Equally urgent is the need to observe common courtesy. Whenever someone has given you their time, always write within a day or two to thank them. Furthermore, do not neglect to give them subsequent feedback on the progress of any leads they have fed to you.

Thirdly, do your paperwork. Before you make your first networking call, it is essential to set up a simple but effective system to keep track of all the names on your ever expanding list and of every contact you have with each of them. A chore it may seem, but duck it and you will land yourself in the most unholy mess imaginable.

KEEPING RECORDS OF YOUR CONTACTS

All you need is a record for each contact showing:

- name
- title
- organisation
- contact address
- contact telephone number(s)
- source
- date called/met
- referrals
- other action
- follow-ups
- notes.

Supplementary records should be added for each subsequent contact.

These records can be kept either on a computer or on record cards filed in a box. Computers have the advantage of enabling you to sort the records in a variety of different ways, e.g. alphabetically, geographically or by business sector. Whichever method you use, be sure not only to include a facility to cross-reference records, but also to keep that cross-referencing up to date.

Performance targets

In order to motivate yourself, you need to set yourself targets. If these are to be effective, they need to stretch you a bit but they must not be so impossible that you do not consider it even worth trying to meet them. One job search book – admittedly it was an American one – suggested that you aim for 10–20 meetings a week. Assuming a five-day week, that is as many as four meetings a day! How you would even get to that many, given the time spent not only in the meeting but also in travelling to and from each location – let alone make the calls that generate them, prepare for them and take all the post-meeting action – is something of a mystery. And that is without spending any time at all on other job hunting activities such as advertised vacancies, headhunters and agencies, speculative applications and so on.

Assuming that networking accounts for at least 60 per cent of executive vacancies, people who are unemployed and therefore working full-time at finding a new job should be spending three days a week on this aspect of their search. Since that includes all aspects of networking, three or four face-to-face meetings a week would be reasonable and six pretty good, allowing for the fact that there will, in addition, be some 'meetings' that take place on the telephone.

For those in employment the numbers may vary in proportion to the amount of scope for external contact afforded by their job, but many may be able to achieve similar volumes, given that their networking is being piggy-backed onto normal business contacts.

As with so many other aspects of the job search, however, it is not so much quantity as quality that really matters. The true measures of that are the volumes of worthwhile job opportunities that you generate and the time it takes you to get an acceptable offer for a position you definitely want.

"SOME PEOPLE GET JOBS AS A RESULT OF BULK MAILING. SO, TOO, DO SOME PEOPLE WIN THE NATIONAL LOTTERY."

13   On spec

There was a time when banging out speculative applications was flavour of the month. Nowadays outplacement firms are considerably less keen on getting candidates to spray letters and calls around like slurry from a muck spreader. To be charitable, this is not solely because of the impact on their postage, stationery and telephone bills. Most unsolicited sales approaches get the same treatment that we all give to the unending stream of paper that comes through our letter boxes at home – it gets junked.

But, you may ask, does this matter so long as the odd one gets a response? After all, you do only need one job, don't you?

The answer is that it all depends, and what it depends on is:

- what you mean by speculative applications;
- how you go about applying on spec;
- the kind of job you are looking for;
- what else you have got to do with your time.

Shotgun or rifle?

There are two forms of communication you can use for speculative applications – letters and telephone calls. There are also two ways you can approach this method of generating job leads.

Looking first at mailshots, you can either bulk mail a standard letter to a large number of people or you can send individualised letters to a much smaller number of carefully targeted individuals. Few people would argue about the effectiveness of the second method, the rifle shot: a sniper hits the target a high proportion of the time. The value of the shotgun is more questionable.

To be fair, some people do get jobs as a result of bulk mailings. So, too, do some people win the jackpot on the National Lottery. The odds against a mail-shot producing a job may not be as long as those against winning the Lottery, but nor are they as short as the oft quoted figures for junk mail of around a 2 per cent return. To be sure, you will get a fair number of replies. Considerably more than 2 per cent, in fact. Unlike private individuals, who simply bin junk mail, many business organisations have a policy of responding to unsolicited letters, at least when they come from people seeking a job. What lands on your mat 99 times out of 100, however, is likely to be no more than a standard letter with a 'thank you but no thank you' punch line.

If it takes 100 letters to produce a single meeting (which it easily can), and between 10 and 20 meetings to generate a single job offer – which may not be one you actually want – you can begin to get some idea of the effectiveness of untargeted bulk mailings. Now give a little thought to the time and cost involved. The time it takes to get hold of that many company names and addresses, to key them into your word processor, to print the letters and to fold them, and put them into envelopes. The cost of paper, envelopes and stamps, plus – if you are using bubble jet or laser – the actual printing.

That, however, is not all. If mailshots are to be anything but a complete hit and miss method of generating leads, every letter you send out needs to be followed up with a telephone call. There is no point in just sitting there waiting for the recipients to get back to you. But how can you possibly follow up efficiently if you are sending out 100 letters at a time?

Cold calling

Of course, another question which may be raised by that last paragraph is, 'Why bother with the letter at all? Why not just get straight on to the phone?'

At first sight, this may sound attractive. You will be talking to people, which is more stimulating than the low grade clerical work of keyboard bashing, printer operation and envelope stuffing. Instead of having to just sit around waiting and hoping after a batch of letters has gone out, you will be getting an immediate 'yes' or 'no' – you will be in control. Most important of all, on the phone you can make a personal impact in a way which it is difficult to achieve with a letter.

Unfortunately it is not quite like that in practice. Cold calling in volume presents as many problems as sending out bulk mailshots. For example:

- it is expensive;

- it is fatiguing;

- you need a hide like a rhinoceros to cope with the high percentage of rejections;

- more often than not, you do not even get past the gatekeeper. Busy managers get so many unsolicited calls, from people selling everything from advertising space to life insurance, that the only way to protect their valuable time is to block out all of them, including people trying to find a job.

How many hours in a day?

Perhaps the best way of putting the whole thing into perspective is to look at the way you break down the time available to you. If you are unemployed and spending five days a week job hunting, you should be spending three days a week networking and a day on advertised vacancies. That leaves just one day a week to deal with headhunters and agencies, speculative applications and any other hidden approaches. Those few hours must surely be spent more productively by using your rifle than by blasting away with your shotgun.

For those who are either in a permanent, full-time job, or doing temporary or part-time work, the conclusion is even clearer.

The only qualification to what has just been said is that some jobhunters can justify spending a greater amount of time on speculative applications, well targeted ones that is, than others. What determines this is the kind of job you are looking for and, in particular, the number of such jobs which exist in any one organisation.

If you contact a company and ask if they have a requirement for a managing director, or even for a head of function, such as director of finance, production or sales, your hit rate is likely to be miserably low. On the other hand, if you want a job as a salesperson, and approach companies with large salesforces, you stand quite a reasonable chance. It is all a matter of assessing the likelihood of there being a vacancy of the kind you are seeking.

HUMAN PERSPECTIVE

Take the case of Joanne. A human resources professional, she wanted to go into management consultancy. Her research produced a list of 13 consultancies which either specialised solely in HR, or employed a number of HR consultants, and which also met her other criteria. She was able to network into four of them and this produced one interview with a firm which definitely had a current requirement. She made speculative applications to the other nine, being careful to identify, and apply directly to, the decision makers in each case, and this again produced one interview for a specific job. As it happens, it was the firm she approached on spec which she preferred. They offered her a job and she accepted. The whole process took only a few weeks from start to finish.

Rifle practice

Joanne hit the bullseye. How did she do it?

As her story demonstrates, the preliminary – but vital – stages of the process of making speculative applications are the same as those for networking. If you do not target yourself accurately, and if you do not conduct your research conscientiously, then you might just as well be banging away with that old shotgun.

What is more, when you have done your targeting and your research, you always try to network into a target organisation if you possibly can. It is only when you cannot network your way in that you try a speculative application – and that is when you have to start adapting the techniques you employ.

The normal networking process is to make a telephone call, where necessary using the name of the person who gave you the referral in order to get past the gatekeeper, and to ask for a meeting. The most effective way to make a speculative application is to start by sending a letter, then follow this up with a telephone call, using different techniques to get past the gatekeeper. Again, the objective is, of course, a meeting.

The rationale behind this different approach is based on the fact that, when you network, you stand a good chance of getting a meeting simply by mentioning the name of the person who referred you. When you apply on spec, on the other hand, you have to sell yourself from cold. Generally speaking, you stand a better chance of doing this with a carefully prepared letter which the recipient may find a quiet moment to read with at least a moderate degree of attention, than by trying to get the same selling points across when you ring out of the blue, at what may well be a less than totally convenient time, and have to deliver a make or break sales pitch.

Nowadays, of course, there is the alternative option of e-mail – but is it the right way to go about direct applications? There are both pros and cons. The advantages are that e-mail:

- is cheaper
- is faster
- gets straight to the person you want to target
- can easily be circulated to other people within an organisation.

But there are also disadvantages:

- people tend to delete e-mails once they have been read whereas you want them to keep your direct application in case, although there may not be a suitable job right now, one may arise in the foreseeable future
- the rules of e-mail etiquette say that you should not e-mail someone who does not know you, so – although junk mailers may ignore this – you could be put into the same category and you risk offending the recipient.

If, therefore, you elect to use conventional mail, how do you go about it?

The letter you send should ideally fit on to a single page of typed A4 and must be addressed to a named individual, never to a job title. The first paragraph should say who you are, the reason for your letter and why it might be of interest to the reader.

It is important to grab the recipient's attention and interest within the first two or three sentences, but do not try to do this by means of gimmicks. Most of them have been tried before and the vast majority only cheapen an application. The only way to ensure that someone will want to read on is to show them that there is something in it for them, which in the case of a spec letter means targeting yourself accurately at an organisation with a problem or need to which you are the ideal answer. In this way you will also avoid the pitfall of giving your letter the appearance of being part of a bulk mailout.

Beware, too, of copying samples of letters taken from American job hunting literature. All too often sounding like the kind of over familiar 'personalised' junk mail which tells you that you have got into the final round of a prize draw you have never even heard of, most of these gauche examples of ham-fisted sales literature are totally unsuitable for the British audience. Your objective is not to make the recipient cringe!

In case you are wondering whether you ask for advice or for a job, the answer is that you do neither – at least, not in so many words. Indicate that you would like to know whether the company could benefit from your talents, but do not beg for a job. Use phrases like 'seeking a new challenge', 'desire to develop my career in a sector offering greater prospects' or 'seek an opportunity in an organisation where my experience will enable me to make an impact on the bottom line'.

The main body of the letter should demonstrate clearly and forcibly exactly what it is that you have to offer. It is, in effect, a potted CV – or, more accurately, a few carefully selected extracts from your CV. Enclose your full CV as well if it definitely strengthens your application, but do not be afraid to omit it if it does not.

You end the letter (a sample of which appears in Chapter 18) by saying that you will telephone in a few days' time to see if a meeting can be arranged.

When you actually make that call, you will become all too aware of another difference between networking and applying on spec. In networking mode, whether you are calling someone you already know, or using the name of a person who gave you a referral as a door opener to someone whom you have never met, you normally get through to your target without too much trouble. Not so when you call on spec. Then you have to get past the gatekeeper.

Slaying the dragon

Put yourself on the other side of the fence for a moment. Consider all those times when you have picked up the phone only to have your ear pinned back by someone who subjected you to a solid ten minutes of hard selling before you could even get a word in. Or those calls from smoothies who introduced themselves as financial advisers but were in fact commission-only life insurance salespeople.

What did you do? If you valued your time, you got your gatekeeper to block all calls from people who were not either already known to you or who refused to state openly the nature of their business.

In small companies the switchboard operator may be the gatekeeper. More frequently, however, you get past the telephonist with no problem but hit a brick wall when you get to your target's secretary. Either way, you can bet your boots they are dab hands at getting rid of unwanted callers – fast.

So, what do you do? While there is no magic wand that will work absolutely every time, there are a number of techniques which will vastly improve your chances of success.

- Even dragons have feelings. Avoid treating gatekeepers as 'non-people' in your eagerness to get through to your target. Aim for a balance between being businesslike and friendly. When a telephonist puts you through to a secretary, ask for the secretary's name, so that you can personalise your call.

- Fight shy of open challenges to the gatekeeper's authority. Remember where the power lies.

- Refrain from deceit, e.g. pretending to be someone you are not. More often than not, such deception rebounds on you.

- Show courtesy and respect, but do not grovel. Sound as though you expect to be put through, otherwise the doubt in your voice will be picked up by the gatekeeper.

- Use your target's first name, rather than a courtesy title, e.g. Geoff Smith rather than Mr Smith. You can get this information either from literature such as a company report or from the call you made to the switchboard before sending your letter. (You did call to check that Geoff Smith is still with the company and that his correct title is chief executive, didn't you?) Beware, by the way, of abbreviations. Not every Anthony is known as Tony. This is something else you can check when you ring the telephonist before dispatching your letter.

- Say you are calling from another country. International calls often get put through on the assumption that they must be important. If, however, your target is genuinely not there or is in a meeting, you will have to fend off the 'Can he call you back' line with an excuse (such as that you are just about to leave and will be uncontactable for a while) and ask when would it be convenient for you to call back.

- If, in spite of all your efforts, you get blocked by the sadistic kind of gatekeeper who obviously enjoys eating unwelcome callers for breakfast, try calling when the dragon is unlikely to be there but your target might be: before or after normal office hours, or at lunchtime.

In addition to these techniques, you will need to know how to handle one or two questions that you will frequently be asked, such as:

- *What do you wish to speak to Mr Smith about?*
  Do not say you are looking for a job. Refer to your recent correspondence with Geoff Smith and say that you are calling, as promised, to follow up on that.

- *And the name of your company is?*
  If you are still employed, or have only recently left your last company, give that name. If you have been doing some work on a self-employed basis, you could say you run your own company. Do not say that it is 'personal'. That smacks of insurance salespeople and job hunters. If you

have no other alternative, say that the recent correspondence you had with Geoff was in your private, rather than corporate, capacity.

- *He's in a meeting, can I ask him to call you back?*
  If you say 'Yes', you lose control – there is a fair chance that he won't ring you. Explain that you are going to be difficult to reach (in meetings, travelling etc.) and ask when he is likely to be available to take your call.

Finally, although both telephonists and secretaries can be equally efficient gatekeepers, do remember that secretaries have a far more intimate knowledge of their boss's business and social contacts than the person on the switchboard. Even when you are networking, and using the name of a valid door opener, they can give you a grilling. When making a speculative approach you therefore need to be very careful not to get trapped into revealing that you actually know your target somewhat less well than you are trying to imply. The moral here is 'the less said, the better'.

Through at last

To a large extent, the same applies when you finally do get past the gatekeeper and manage to speak to your target. Senior executives are busy people. Never waste their time.

You should, of course, have prepared yourself thoroughly for the call. The letter you sent a few days ago will have identified a reason why the company might be interested in you. You may have referred to a recent news item about the organisation or you may simply have emphasised the depth of your experience in their sector. Have a two or three-sentence summary of this ready to deliver as soon as you have given your name and mentioned that you recently wrote in.

But are you not repeating yourself? Will your target not already be familiar with what the letter said? Sadly, not. If you really had hit gold, the company would already have been in touch with you. The chances are that your missive is either sitting in the non-urgent tray awaiting a standard response or that it has been passed on to some other department, like personnel.

So, make a strong impression with your concise summary of what the letter said, then ask if you might arrange to pop in for a brief meeting. You will only succeed in getting a meeting in a minority of cases, but the better your targeting and your preparation, the larger that minority will be.

And when you do not succeed in achieving your first objective? Then switch to your second one. Ask for the names of any other individuals, either within the same organisation or in other companies, who may be able to help you. A busy manager may well give you one or two in order to get rid of you.

Finally, always thank people for their time and assistance. It never does any harm and it could do some positive good. You may need to speak to the same person again at some point in the future.

"IT IS NOT JUST WHAT
YOU READ, BUT THE WAY
THAT YOU READ IT."

14　See and be seen

More hidden approaches

While networking must take up the largest single share of your time budget, and you should also allocate regular slots to responding to advertised vacancies, keeping in touch with headhunters and agencies, and making speculative applications, do set aside at least a small part of each week to pursue some of the other routes to a new job.

Your first port of call should be any professional institute or association you belong to. In addition to publishing job advertisements in their own journals, many of them operate some form of register of available appointments. Competition for such vacancies may well be relatively low, since employers may try this service either before or instead of either placing an advertisement in the press or notifying agencies, encouraged by the fact that the professional society's register usually costs them either nothing at all or at least significantly less than the commercial alternatives.

Since such services are operated in different ways by different professional organisations, you are advised to ring up and check the situation out. While you are on the phone, do not forget to ask about any additional help which may be available, such as job clubs, seminars or counselling. If you are unemployed, you may also be able to get your subscription waived until you find a new job.

It's not what you read

Another fertile, but under-utilised, source of job leads is the business press. You should, of course, be keeping a general eye on what is going on in the business world anyway. If you do not, you can easily come unstuck at an interview when the conversation turns to prospects in a given sector, a current or recent takeover battle, movements in stock market indices or the trends in foreign exchange rates.

However, it is not just what you read, but the way that you read it. A company in your industry has just announced results which show that it has moved into a growth phase. That means that they may, sooner or later, need to make some additional hirings. Get in now, before they actually go out on to the job market.

Do not confine yourself to the news items. Look, too, at the announcements of new appointments. An incoming managing director, or head of function, often wants to be a new broom. This could be another opportunity to throw your hat into the ring in advance of jobs being put out on to the open market. Remember also to check the company the new appointee has just left. While the recruitment of a replacement will probably be under way, an appointment may not yet have been made. If the company is beginning to have doubts about the quality of the candidates for the position, your intervention could be perfectly timed.

Try to read, or at least perform a focused skim on, as wide a range of publications as possible. In addition to the *Financial Times* and the business pages of other broadsheets, the *Investors Chronicle* carries a wealth of useful company news. You should also monitor the trade press in your sector and keep an eye on professional journals for announcements of members appointed to new jobs.

If you are worried about the cost of doing this, you can usually find the *FT*, *The Economist* and some of the other relevant publications in your local library; also, a great deal of relevant information is now available on the internet. To save time, you can combine this general reading with your review of the job advertisements.

In fact, you can gain a double benefit from your perusal of the appointments pages if you take a tip from John Woodger of Right Associates. He tells outplacement candidates to read the job advertisements in the same way that they would read a novel. The fact that a company is seeking a new MD, or appointing a director to head up finance, production or sales, points to the fact that it may be going through a process of change, and that could mean opportunities for you. Sometimes the nature of the change is actually spelt out in the text by way of references to, for example, expansion, restructuring or an export drive.

Do not confine yourself to advertisements for jobs in your own functional discipline. Scan those in other areas, too, looking for indications of growth or change that could spell job opportunities elsewhere in the organisations in question.

Once you have identified a lead, the best way to exploit it is naturally to try to network your way in. Failing that, a well-targeted speculative application is definitely worth a try, as the following case clearly shows.

Jenny had worked her way up to a senior position in a fairly large housing association. When management restructuring resulted in the loss of her job, she was initially despondent at the lack of advertised opportunities in her discipline. However, she did notice a newly established housing association advertising vacancies in various other functions. She wrote to them, highlighting her experience and achievements, and asking if there might be any foreseeable openings for her as the organisation developed. Realising that an as yet small association might not be able to afford someone like herself on a full-time basis, she also suggested that they might like to consider employing her for a couple of days a week initially, which of course would have enabled her to continue looking for alternative opportunities.

Her letter resulted in an interview at which she obviously created a good impression. So much so, in fact, that although the organisation could not yet justify a position solely in her former function, they actually created a full-time job for her by combining this function with another one which, likewise, would only occupy two or three days a week, given the size of the association. As a result, the new job which Jenny found herself is actually much broader and far more interesting than her old one.

Naturally, this approach cannot be expected to result in an immediate job lead every time, even when you do – like Jenny – largely make your own luck. There will, however, be some cases in which you may have planted a seed that will germinate in a few months' time – especially if you diarise a follow-up – while in others you should at least be able to add some new names to your network.

Getting into print

In addition to reading what other people have written, how about getting your own name into print? A lot of senior people get approached by journalists wanting to obtain an expert view on some business topic. Their desire to give an article authority by quoting your name naturally raises your profile, which does your career prospects no harm at all. As one executive search consultant put it, 'The people most likely to be called by headhunters are those who are already highly visible within their industry.'

While such requests may tail off if you are out of work, there is nothing to stop you – assuming that you have been sufficiently wise and well organised to keep the journalists' names and phone numbers – from contacting them with a view to getting further press coverage by giving your views on either the business or discipline in which you are an expert, or some interesting aspects of the process of finding a new job.

In the absence of such contacts, another way of getting into print, and therefore raising your profile, is by writing articles yourself. So long as you know your subject, you do not need the literary talents of a Booker Prize-winner. While you may find it difficult to break into the national newspapers, trade magazines and professional journals are often receptive to relevant material. You are in any case likely to derive greater benefit from putting your name in front of people in your particular sector.

If you go back to your asset register, and take a look at your experience and achievements, you should be able to come up with plenty of potential topics. Alternatively, you could write about the experience of hunting for a new job, but if you do this be sure to handle the subject in a positive or humorous way, rather than whingeing. Keep in mind the fact that while the immediate objective of writing articles is to raise your visibility, the ultimate purpose is to get a job. It is not a matter of attracting attention at all costs, but rather of being seen in the desired light.

It is also important not to overlook the benefits which can arise out of the actual process of putting an article together, before you even see your name in print. Researching material for your literary gems provides yet another opportunity to do further valuable networking, quite possibly opening the door to some contacts you would not otherwise have made.

Furthermore, the money you ultimately receive for your work will, of course, be welcome. The rates of payment for business writing will never make you a millionaire, but every little helps.

Since you will naturally not want to waste time which could be used more profitably on other job hunting activities, you will be well advised to contact the editor of your target publication before you even start assembling ideas or conducting research, let alone putting pen to paper – or, rather, fingers to keyboard (word processed output is essential). Submit a brief synopsis and ask whether your proposed article will be of interest. It will need both to be relevant to the target audience and to have a fresh slant. Some kind of topical tie-in will be an added bonus. If you get the thumbs up, be sure you check the required word count. There is no point producing a piece twice as long as the journal in question ever publishes.

More detailed advice can be found in the *Writers' & Artists' Yearbook* (A & C Black), a copy of which will probably be in your reference library. It also includes listings of newspapers and magazines with details of the kind of material they seek, together with the name of the editor, and the publication's address and telephone number.

If you do not feel up to producing full-length articles, or if you lack the time to do so, you could still consider the letters pages of trade or professional journals. They are widely read and, although people do not always pay great attention to the names of the writers, they are more likely to do so if you are controversial. You may even set a train of letters in process on a subject and, in consequence, put yourself in touch with supporters – or even opponents – of your views who could be useful to you, either as network contacts or, if your luck is really in, direct job sources.

Yet another way of being seen is to place your own advertisement. Some newspapers and journals actually run a 'Situations Wanted' section. Generally speaking, this approach is not to be recommended, the only beneficiary being the publication in question which cheerfully pockets the charge for the insertion. The only circumstances in which it might be worth considering are to advertise your availability for contract or part-time work, or to publicise the fact that you have specialised skills or abilities which very few people possess. In these cases use trade, professional or local publications which are targeted directly at the audience you wish to reach and which also cost far less to advertise in than national newspapers.

Appearing in public

Another way of raising your visibility, and demonstrating your expertise in your chosen field or business sector, is to speak at conferences and seminars. In addition to bringing yourself to the attention of the audience in question, and perhaps having the opportunity to meet key people afterwards, you may well obtain further publicity from the reporting of such events which often appears in some detail in relevant trade publications.

If you do not feel confident enough to address gatherings of Nuremburg rally proportions, you can start by giving talks at events like local meetings of your professional society. Your audience may be smaller, but it is likely to contain a high percentage of potentially useful people and you will often have the opportunity 'after the show' to speak to a good proportion of them.

Professional societies, trade associations and the like provide further opportunities to raise your visibility if you can get yourself on to their committees or if you accept some honorary office. You normally have to take this step while you are still in employment, and it may involve a certain amount of voluntary work, but you do not get anything for nothing.

Another way of meeting people is by attending conferences, exhibitions, and the various meetings of trade and professional groups. Participating in workshops on a whole range of subjects can keep you stimulated as well as enabling you to make new contacts, while alumni associations, especially of MBA classes and the like, can be a particularly useful way of meeting influential people.

However, since merely being present does not put you in the limelight in the way that being a speaker does, it is essential that you take the initiative to introduce yourself to as many potentially useful individuals as possible. If you already know one or more people at the gathering in question, you can improve your hit rate by getting them to make a few introductions for you.

Exhibitions provide unlimited opportunities to talk as you wander from stand to stand, but at events where much of the time is spent in a lecture theatre listening to speakers you have to make optimum use of openings provided by tea and coffee breaks to do your chatting up. Some extremely useful introductions have even been made in the loo, which just goes to show that you should never miss a single opportunity.

When it pays to volunteer

Professional and trade organisations are not the only ones in which it may be worth taking on an unpaid office. A school's board of governors, sports clubs, and charitable or leisure groups all provide opportunities for you to become known and to meet other people. In many cases the individuals with whom you come into contact may either be prominent in business themselves, or be capable of providing you with referrals which enable you to do some useful networking. Some executive search firms actually encourage their consultants to get involved in such organisations as a means of extending their networks, so you could even end up rubbing shoulders with a headhunter.

In fact, you do not always have to wait for a suitable committee place or honorary office to become available. Just volunteering your services to a charity can produce surprisingly good results. Peter, a training manager whose job had been made redundant, became a volunteer with the local branch of an organisation providing a counselling service to members of the public in his locality. Within his first few weeks he met three fellow volunteers who all had extensive networks of contacts within the local business community and who were in a position to make useful introductions for him.

In addition to these specific benefits, voluntary work also provides opportunities for enjoyable social contact and gives the unemployed jobhunter a feeling of doing something worthwhile. The importance of these factors in terms of their effect on confidence and morale should not be underestimated. It all goes to show how helping the community can, in return, help you in your efforts to find a new job.

A final tip

It has been said that any publicity is good publicity. That may be true in show business, but it most certainly does not apply in job hunting. You are wasting your time raising your visibility if you fail to get the right message across. Just as in all the other approaches to finding a new position, you must prepare yourself thoroughly before you meet people, so that you never waste any opportunity that arises to promote yourself.

It is all too easy in quasi social situations to have a pleasant chat that gets you precisely nowhere or, worse still, to create a negative impression by the way that you present your current situation. If you want to make the most of the openings you create, be sure to follow the advice of Derek Edwards, managing director of Sanders and Sidney: 'Be seen positively'.

"MANY A PERMANENT JOB HAS BEEN FOUND THROUGH CONTRACT WORK."

15 Temporary assignments and part-time work

One of the most fruitful of the hidden approaches, but one which is available only to those who are not currently in employment, is the temporary assignment. As the managing director of one of the leading executive search firms put it, 'Many a permanent job has been found through contract work'.

In the UK, estimates of the number of temporary assignments that turn into full-time appointments tend to vary between one in six and one in ten. In the US, on the other hand, a study by one leading recruitment organisation suggested that the figure there may be as high as one in three – and what happens on that side of the pond more often than not repeats itself, sooner or later, over here.

Before you decide whether or not to pursue this route, however, there are a number of factors which need to be considered. To begin with, there is more than one reason why people may consider temporary work.

 WHY CONSIDER TEMPORARY WORK?

- a way back into full-time employment, when a temporary assignment leads to the offer of a permanent post;
- a short-term stop gap – for financial or other reasons – while looking for a full-time job;
- a longer term filler (e.g. a contract for a year or two) taken on when the market is difficult in the hope that, by the time the contract comes to an end, the economy will be more buoyant and permanent jobs easier to find;
- a career in itself.

While, with the exception of the one/two-year contract, these reasons are not necessarily mutually exclusive, in that you can keep your options open, it is as well to avoid the danger of losing sight of your primary objective. You should also be aware of both the pros and the cons of temporary work.

The advantages are as follows.

- Extended periods of unemployment on your CV tend to generate a negative reaction in the mind of a potential employer. It is easier to get a job when you are in a job, even if that job is a temporary one.

- You may gain valuable additional experience which helps you to market yourself.

- It often enables you to add useful new contacts to your network.

- If your confidence has started to sag, doing a useful job again can boost your morale.

- Psychologically, you will also benefit from the social and intellectual stimulation it provides.

- You can normally take time off for interviews without the embarrassment this may involve for someone in permanent employment.

- It pays the bills.

- For older candidates, who often get screened out on age grounds by headhunters and people who advertise vacancies, it provides the opportunity to get a foot in the door and to prove their worth. Although people who are over 60 may have problems getting even interim work, those in their 50s should not find age a disadvantage, provided that they have a lively appearance and manner, are energetic, and have kept up to date technically – especially with computers.

While the disadvantages are fewer in number, one or two of them have significant implications.

- Temporary work tends to be 'feast or famine' in its nature: you are either going flat out or doing nothing at all. Some people find this difficult to adjust to.

- You may have to tie yourself in to a contract for a period of time which limits your availability to start a new job.

- The prospects of a temporary contract leading to a permanent job can never be predicted in advance. Although you can to some extent make your own luck, there is still a large element of pure chance.

- Most important of all, temporary work is normally full-time work. By its very nature, you may well be expected to do quite long hours. How do you then find time to pursue your hunt for a permanent position?

Given these disadvantages, you may decide to concentrate initially on a full-time job search, turning to temporary work only when the gap on your CV becomes worryingly long, your financial resources become worryingly short, or you simply do not seem to be getting anywhere.

Who's who and what's what

If and when you do decide to take the plunge, you may initially be confused by the number of different terms that are bandied about: executive leasing, contract work, independent consultants, interim executives, interim managers, temporary executives and so on. Apart from the 'adviser' nature of consultancy and the 'doer' emphasis of the other terms – and even that distinction is by no means clear cut – the only differences that go beyond pure semantics relate to the duration and level of the assignments you work on.

At one extreme are the one or two-year contracts whose length effectively takes you completely out of the job hunt for a period of time. At the other end are the one or two-week postings which occur mainly at clerical and secretarial level, filling in for people who are on holiday or off sick. In between are contracts lasting anything from a few weeks to several months and it is into this area that most executive level assignments fall.

The reasons for which such assignments arise tend to fall into two broad categories. The first is the increasing trend towards outsourcing. Having pared their permanent establishments back to the core during the recession, many organisations are extremely chary of increasing their fixed overheads again.

Instead they prefer to bring in independent professionals to cover peak loads, one-off projects, or even – in some cases – ongoing needs.

The second category is the panic measure. For example, an executive may have left an organisation at short notice (voluntarily or otherwise), a manager may have to take a period off work for health reasons or – as more women succeed in shattering the glass ceiling – there could be a need to cover a period of maternity leave.

The first place to look for such work is a company specialising in interim management, which is becoming the most widely accepted term for this business. Such companies may specialise solely in this sector or may be part of an organisation that also handles permanent vacancies. Some may not be too keen on giving assignments to executives who are merely seeking a filler between permanent jobs so, even if this is your true situation, you may be better off keeping quiet about it and suggesting that you are considering interim management as a longer term career.

Unlike temporary agencies, which often specialise in a particular discipline, like HR, IT or marketing, nearly all of the interim management firms cover the whole range of executive functions. Another difference is that, whereas agencies tend to have local branches, most interim management firms operate from a single location, many being based in or around London. Since you will probably not actually have to go to see them, however, until they have an assignment for you, this need not create too much of a problem.

The average length of assignments is around three months, although they can be as short as a few weeks or as long as a year or more. In order to get work from them, interim management companies may insist (for reasons connected with the Inland Revenue and self-employment) on you registering yourself as a limited company.

Do not expect, however, to be coining a regular income as soon as you apply. It may be some time before you get your first assignment. In order to be able to satisfy the wide range of needs which their clients may throw at them, interim management firms need to have a large pool of readily available candidates, by no means all of whom will actually be out at clients at any one time, and downtime tends to be highest among those who are in their first year as interim managers.

It is therefore sensible to register with several firms, and also to take other steps to find contract work. Depending on your seniority, it may be worth contacting temporary agencies. They operate in much the same way as executive leasing firms, but at lower levels. Nevertheless, those that specialise in a particular discipline, such as accountancy, banking, engineering or IT, may handle some assignments which encroach on the lower end of interim management territory.

Bear in mind too that there is a tendency to over-employ when filling temporary positions. Clients need candidates who can hit the ground running. Although this may mean that you are asked to operate at a slightly lower level than you are used to, the temporary nature of the contract means that you are unlikely to be doing this for long enough for it to get boring. In any case, a new environment always provides fresh interest, and there are often stimulating challenges inherent in the assignment itself.

Temporary agencies may well offer you the choice of operating as a limited company or going onto their payroll. (Like interim management firms, they cannot pay you on a self-employed basis.) Operating as a limited company has some tax advantages in that you can reclaim various types of expenses, but this has to be offset against the costs, and time, involved in setting up a company.

In addition to interim management firms and the temporary divisions of agencies, you can also source your own assignments as part of your networking activities by mentioning to contacts that you would like to consider short-term assignments. One thing to remember, however you source the work, is that temporary requirements can be of an extremely urgent nature – you have to be ready, if required, to drop everything else and start at a few days' notice.

A question of commitment

The commitment to being available virtually immediately is not the only one you have to make. It is also vital that you approach the actual assignment with every bit as much commitment as you would put into a permanent job. Think of yourself as part of the company, not as an outsider who is acting as a consultant or doing a fire brigade exercise.

If you adopt this approach, you stand a far better chance of becoming a permanent employee of the organisation in question. Even if the post you are filling on a temporary basis cannot be made into a permanent one, there is always the chance that another position may arise within the company and that you may get a crack at it before it is advertised or put out to headhunters. In fact, if you make a really strong impression, and take advantage of every opportunity to make key decision makers aware of the tangible benefits you could bring to the organisation, a post may even be created for you.

This is the beauty of temporary work. It gives you an opportunity you never get when you apply for a job from the outside. Working within the company, you can demonstrate your ability both to do the work, and to fit in both with your colleagues and with the culture.

A further advantage is the chance it gives you to get the feel of a new business sector, organisation or position from the inside. If you are offered a permanent post, and decide to accept, it is much more likely to be a success than when, as is the normal case with a new job, you start cold on day one. The impression gained at interview is, for a variety of reasons, not always a completely accurate one.

Interims international

Although interim management is established in the US, a British executive is unlikely to get the opportunity to work in America. With the exception of the Netherlands, Western Europe is not particularly fertile soil either, the problem being more to do with attitudes and legislation than with languages – what interim work there is for Brits is likely to be for European subsidiaries of UK groups. The best bet, if you do not mind working there for a few months, is Eastern Europe, where the effects of the sweeping political changes have created a demand, usually through international institutions or global accountancy and consulting firms, for experienced executives.

The best of both worlds?

Because of the disruption full-time assignment work causes to the main priority of finding a permanent job, you may prefer to consider part-time work. This has nearly all of the advantages of temporary assignments in that it:

- plugs a gap in your CV;
- may provide marketable additional experience;
- often adds new contacts to your network;
- can boost flagging confidence;
- provides social and intellectual stimulation;
- helps to pay the bills;
- creates even fewer problems when you want to go for an interview.

Furthermore, part-time work is mercifully free of two of the four disadvantages of temporary contracts in that:

- it tends to come in a steady flow, rather than being feast or famine stuff;
- it leaves you a reasonable amount of time free, on a regular basis, to pursue your hunt for a permanent, full-time position.

Sounds too good to be true? You are right. There is, of course, a catch. In fact, there is more than one.

The first problem is that a lot of part-time work tends to be permanent, rather than temporary. Even if ditching the part-time job as soon as a full-time one comes along does not bother you, it is likely to be a concern to prospective employers, who may prefer to hire a candidate with genuine long-term reasons for seeking part-time employment.

On the other hand, interim management firms do seem to be reporting an increasing trickle, if not yet a flood, of temporary assignments that involve working for anything between one and four days a week. This area is worth exploring.

A second problem is that, with the exception of assignments handled by interim management firms, part-time work may be harder to find. Since the amount handled by agencies is negligible, you will have to rely predominantly on advertisements and on your own efforts – networking and speculative applications.

EMPLOYMENT-SEEKING TECHNIQUES

While the techniques you use will be largely the same as those for seeking permanent employment, do bear in mind the following points.

- Conduct a thorough review of all your skills, experience etc. to assess what is most likely to be saleable in the part-time marketplace. This may not be the same as what is saleable in the permanent, full-time market. For example, you may be able to obtain part-time work lecturing in your technical discipline.

- Do not necessarily expect to find temporary work at the same level of seniority as permanent work. Although your last position may have been largely managerial, be prepared to go back to using your core skills if necessary.

- Think carefully about your targeting. The buyers of part-time services will not necessarily be the same as the people who are likely to have a permanent job for you.

- Use focused letters, rather than your CV, when you communicate in writing. Prepare your letters carefully, ensuring that they highlight the benefits you can offer to the recipients.

While these pointers should increase your chances of obtaining part-time work, there is one further problem to bear in mind. Although it may give you all the advantages listed above, the very nature of part-time work means that the odds against it leading to a permanent job are decidedly longer than those for temporary assignments.

A final thought

If earning a crust has not yet become your number one priority, you could get your foot in the door with a prospective employer by offering the ultimate benefit – something for nothing.

Should you, through networking for example, identify a need but find that the person in question is dubious about committing funds to the project in question without being a little more confident of the benefits, you could offer to do a certain amount of work for no financial reward.

You could explain that the project is something which particularly interests you, or that you simply wish to keep your hand in and this would be an ideal opportunity to do so. The initial work might involve researching a market, or investigating a product and producing a preliminary report on its viability.

You may even stumble across a situation where a company is considering creating a new post, but is hesitant about going ahead until it can be reasonably sure that the investment will be justified. Alternatively, especially if you are an older candidate, they may want to see how you perform before taking you on to the payroll.

Naturally, you have to take care not to be exploited, and to limit the amount you are prepared to do without either being offered a permanent job, or at least a paid assignment. It is a calculated risk, but remember the old saying: nothing ventured, nothing gained.

"THE KILLER CV AND THE PROFESSIONAL ASSASSIN HAVE A LOT IN COMMON."

PART THREE

Your marketing brochure – the killer CV

"What – and who – is a CV for?"

16 Why most brochures don't get read

and how to make sure that your CV does

Have you ever been involved in creating a brochure? If you have, you will be only too aware of how much effort, how much care and how much agonising goes into it.

Now put yourself on the other side of the fence. Think of all the brochures that have landed on your desk over the years. How many of them can you honestly claim to have read word for word? How many did you even skim right the way through, from the front cover to the back? And how many were given little more than a glance before ending up in the bin?

So, what goes wrong? Why does all that effort so often get completely wasted? Here are some of the more common criticisms levelled against marketing brochures:

- too long;

- too much solid text;

- too many different typefaces;

- bad layout;

- poor quality;

- too glossy;

- too much hype;

- boring;

- just like everyone else's – nothing to make it stand out;

- gimmicky;

- all about what they wanted to say, not what I wanted to know;
- it did not explain what the benefits to me of the product or service were.

In case you have not already guessed, most of these criticisms apply just as much to CVs as they do to any other kind of marketing brochure. Some of the faults listed above are to do with the details of how to present a brochure/CV, and Chapter 17 is going to be devoted to explaining the mechanics of producing one which is easy to read and which creates a strong impact on the recipient. Before we get on to that kind of detail, though, we need to take a few moments to consider some very basic, very fundamental points.

A means to an end

To begin with, what – and who – is a CV for?

Get one thing straight, right from the start. Your CV is never going to get you a job. Only you can do that, and in order to do it you have to get in front of the person who has the power to make the appointment. The role which your CV plays in that process varies considerably, depending on which approach you are using and who is going to be reading it.

When you are responding to an advertised vacancy, your CV – together with your covering letter – will be what determines whether you get an initial meeting, usually with a recruiter rather than the ultimate decision maker. The way most recruiters use CVs is as a method of ruling people out rather than in, so you have to pay as much attention to avoiding the snakes as you do to climbing the ladders.

When an appointment is being headhunted, you will normally have spoken either to a researcher or to the executive search consultant who is handling the assignment before you provide a CV – which you may then either send in prior to an interview or take with you to your first meeting. Either way, you will have learned a fair amount about the job on the telephone before you submit your CV. Bear in mind, too, that headhunters rarely pass your CV on to the client. Instead, they prepare their own report on you, which you are unlikely ever to get a look at.

You may, of course, send your CV to headhunters on spec. In that case it will be used either by a search consultant or by someone in the research department as a basis for deciding whether or not to put you on their database.

When you are networking, you may take your CV along to meetings with a view either to asking for advice on it or in order to give copies to your network contacts, which they may in turn pass on to other people who could have a job for you.

When you are making speculative applications, you are initially likely to send a letter, rather than a CV, perhaps taking your CV along to any meetings you obtain. It will then be used in much the same way that slides or handouts are at a presentation – as something to refer to in order to give structure to the session and as a reminder, afterwards, of the key points.

What this all boils down to is that your CV may be used in a variety of different ways and for several different purposes. Which, in turn, begs the question: can a single CV satisfy them all?

Horses for courses

In the dim and distant past, before word processing became widely available, there would have been no point in even asking that question. No one seriously thought of retyping their CV each time they applied for a job. Now, with the opportunity there for you to customise your CV to every single application you make, the point at issue is whether or not the time and effort involved can be justified. If it makes all the difference to you getting the job you want, then it has to be worthwhile. On the other hand, you do have a lot of competing demands on your time. Could you find a better use for that time than endlessly tarting up your CV?

Because everyone's circumstances are different, there is no one answer that is right every time, but there are some simple criteria which can be used to help you make the decision. They just happen to be the same criteria marketing people are recommended to use before they start to write a brochure.

Each time you need to submit a CV, ask yourself the following questions:

- What am I selling?
- To whom am I selling it?
- Why do they need what I have to offer?
- Why should they go for me rather than my competitors?

If you are genuinely convinced that a standard CV is going to do the job, fine – but do be honest with yourself and make sure that you are not just taking the easy option because you cannot be bothered with the editing process. Always remember that, if you are to win the kind of position you really want in today's job jungle, nothing but your very best effort will do.

Vested interests

The standard CV does, of course, have its supporters. However, the worldly wise reader will be only too aware that, in judging how far to be influenced by the views of others, one must always bear in mind where they are coming from and what is in it for them.

Look in the appointments pages of the major national newspapers and you may well see a whole section devoted to 'CV services', with a dozen or so different firms offering to prepare and print your CV for you at apparently very reasonable rates. While these operators may, to be fair, turn out CVs which have a superior appearance to many that pass across the average recruiter's desk, they are inevitably going to be standardised – in more ways than one.

To begin with, when you have a supply of CVs printed off by one of these companies, you inevitably forfeit the ability to customise it, even when there is something you would rather add – or omit – to improve your chances in respect of a particular job vacancy. Secondly, CVs produced in this way often have a mass-produced, and sometimes excessively slick, appearance which can easily give the impression you are conducting a bulk mailing campaign. Finally, recruiters like to get a feel for the individual behind the piece of paper and consequently tend to be turned off by CVs which have obviously been professionally written by a third party.

Exactly the same reaction is created by the CV which comes from an out-placement organisation. Many a recruiter has been heard to groan, 'Oh dear, another three from XYZ & Co.!' It is not that outplacement firms encourage their candidates to produce bad CVs – in general, they are better than average – it is just that every CV from any given firm looks exactly the same.

If you have never sat and waded through several hundred CVs in one day, you have no idea just how boring it can be. While recruiters are not going to be impressed by silly gimmicks like printing your CV on magenta coloured paper or plastering it with graphics that would be better suited to the wall-paper in a toddler's bedroom, they do nevertheless prefer to see some evidence of it having been written by an individual human being.

The personal profile

A lot of outplacement consultants, together with the authors of many articles and books on the subject of job hunting, would have you believe that the way to add this individual impact to your CV is to include a paragraph the inten-tion of which is to summarise, in no more than a few lines, your key selling points. Most commonly referred to as a personal profile, this normally appears either right at the beginning of your CV or immediately after your brief per-sonal details. It is the written equivalent of what one American writer of career books calls the '15-second sales pitch' you are supposed to deliver at the beginning of a networking or speculative telephone call.

Once again, the recipient, the average recruiter, displays considerably less enthusiasm than the outplacement counsellors. The general reaction of selec-tion consultants and HR professionals was summed up by Alan Dickinson, managing director of Michael Page Finance. 'Personal profiles are a waste of space, which could be used more valuably to highlight experience and achievements. Candidates should stick to the facts on their CVs. If your experi-ence cannot sell you, personal views certainly will not. Leave the interviewer to make the subjective judgements.'

Another recruiter, confronted by a profile to which he took particular excep-tion, expressed his objections rather more picturesquely. Casting the offending

CV on to the floor of his office, he exclaimed, 'If I get one more dynamic, results-orientated executive today, I shall throw up!'

PERSONAL PROFILE ERRORS

To be fair, it is not so much the concept which is at fault, but the way it is used. The most common errors which people make in preparing their personal profiles are:

- copying American examples which are too 'over the top' for the British market;
- employing tired, over-used vocabulary, taken from job advertisements or from examples of personal profiles in job search manuals, rather than making the effort to find fresh and individual words of their own;
- being too subjective and insufficiently objective – too many adjectives and not enough facts;
- producing a profile which, far from making them stand out, makes them sound just like any number of other candidates – there is a remarkable tendency for the majority of profiles to highlight exactly the same personal qualities.

In addition to avoiding these errors, you also need to consider whether the same personal profile is appropriate on every occasion. In order to follow the excellent advice of a leading outplacement consultant and 'write your CV as a solution to someone else's problem', you may well need to adapt your profile to each individual target. Although at first sight this may seem unduly onerous, it could pay a double dividend. As well as enhancing the impression your CV makes on the recipient, it will also concentrate your mind on precisely why you are the right person for the job in question.

Naturally, the same added advantage applies to customising your whole CV for each application, rather than just your personal profile – it forces you to focus on those aspects of your experience, skills and achievements which are going to make you the number one candidate for that particular job. You can even go a step further by trying to predict the questions that are likely to be asked about your suitability and then adapting your CV so that it provides the answers to them.

Some job search gurus recommend that, rather than customising the whole thing every time, you use what is often called a performance CV. This includes not only a personal profile, in the form of a paragraph describing your personal qualities and experience, but also a run of bullet points under the subheading 'Achievements', both of which are placed close to the beginning of your CV, before your career history. The idea is that you select different achievements each time, but leave the rest of the CV the same.

While the idea behind this has a certain degree of merit, there are some dangers too. Revamping the opening without changing the main body of the CV may end up sending conflicting messages to the reader. Furthermore, recruiters – who like to be able to home straight in on what you have done and where you have done it – tend to be all too easily irritated if they are delayed from getting into your career history by what they may see as irrelevant clutter. If you lose their interest, you lose the interview.

Which format?

Speaking of which, how does the average recruiter like you to lay out your CV?

The format preferred by the vast majority of selection consultants, personnel managers and line managers/decision makers is as follows.

- Start with *brief* personal details – name, address, telephone number, date of birth.

- If you opt to include a personal profile, keep it succinct and factual – no adjectives, no hype.

- Then give *relevant* qualifications and educational details, i.e. your university degree but not the subjects you passed 20 or 30 years ago at O level.

- Next, and you should by now be only about a third of the way down the first page, go into a reverse chronological career summary.

- Recruiters prefer you to list achievements under the companies they
  relate to. Otherwise, if you summarise them at the start of your CV, the
  recruiter's suspicious mind will probably conclude that you are
  dragging up something you did years ago when you were only just out
  of university and will consequently discount it.

In addition to being the one most recipients prefer, this format has the
advantage of focusing attention at an early stage on your most recent experience which, in the vast majority of cases, will also be the most relevant.

Alternative formats

There are, however, alternative formats, and you should be aware of their pros
and cons so that you can decide whether your particular circumstances make
them worthy of consideration.

A straight chronological CV, starting with your first job and ending with
your current or most recent one, makes it easy for the reader to follow your
career progression, if that is particularly impressive. This advantage, on the
other hand, tends to be outweighed in most cases by the 'most relevant experience first' argument. Furthermore, do bear in mind that the vast majority of
people will initially give your CV only a very cursory glance. Unless you grab
their attention straight away, they are unlikely to read on and may therefore
completely miss your key selling points.

For some candidates a chronological format of either the straight or reverse
kind has inherent disadvantages in that it highlights such matters as gaps
between jobs, frequent changes of employer and switches in career direction.
Furthermore, if your last post is not the most relevant one to the application in
question, the material which is going to sell you really strongly may be buried
somewhere in the middle and could consequently be overlooked.

In an attempt to overcome these disadvantages, candidates sometimes use
what is often called a functional CV. Experience and achievements are classified under functional headings like 'management', 'business development',
'training' and so on, rather than being listed under each job. Career history is

then summarised, towards the end of the CV, giving only company name, position held and dates. People with really patchy careers may even fudge this section, for example by referring to '12 years at senior management level in the retail sector'.

Most recipients dislike this format and there are two reasons for this. The first is because it is unfamiliar and, unable to find the information they are looking for, they get irritated and probably lose interest – which means the end of the line for you. The second reason stems from the fact that recruiters, being cynical types for the most part, will all too quickly suss you out and realise that you are deliberately trying to hide something.

Catch-22?

So, what on earth do you do if you have this kind of problem? Are you going to be a renegade, and risk annoying recruiters and decision makers? Or are you going to give the customers the format they want, in spite of the fact that it may not show you off in the best light?

Furthermore, even if you do not have anything to hide and the customers' preferred option – the reverse chronological CV – presents you with no problems, is using a standard format not going to make you look just like everyone else? How on earth do you make yourself stand out?

The answers are actually remarkably simple. To begin with, avoid focusing on the CV in isolation. It is just one part, albeit an important one, of the whole process of finding a new job. For example, if your CV is going to draw attention to something like a choppy career record, there may be a far better solution than trying to fudge around it by using a CV format which makes people irritated and suspicious.

Start by going back to your targeting. There are some jobs where the fact that you have moved around a lot may actually be seen as an advantage. Take management consultancy firms – they need people who have hands-on exposure to a variety of different situations. Candidates who have spent their entire working life in a single organisation are rarely of interest to them.

Then give some thought to the methods you are using. In the case of advertised vacancies the volume of response often results in CVs being used negatively, as a means of screening people out. If your patchy career history is the reason you are not even getting to the first interview, consider concentrating more on networking and speculative applications, where the CV does not have to be submitted until you have already got yourself a meeting – at which stage it is not being used to rule you in or out but as a basis for discussion.

Talking of which, let us go back to two more of the basic rules about marketing brochures. Firstly, wise marketing professionals always question, right at the start, whether a brochure actually is the best way to achieve their objective. Sometimes it is, while on other occasions it is not. It is exactly the same with CVs. Sometimes you do need to submit one. In other circumstances you may have a greater chance of achieving your purpose by using a letter or a telephone call. For example, while a functional CV is not popular with recruiters, they will be far less likely to react adversely if you summarise your experience in a similar fashion in a letter. Whereas they expect CVs to be in a certain format, against which they can tick off whether or not you conform to what they are looking for, there are no such expectations with letters.

Secondly, marketing people always think carefully about how a brochure is going to get to its target audience. Will it be part of a bulk mailshot, handed over personally at a client visit, sent with a personalised covering letter following a phone call etc.? Again the same applies to CVs.

When responding to an advertisement you use a covering letter. Since this letter will normally be looked at before your CV, it may well be the best place to emphasise your key achievements and to make use of some of the material which might otherwise go into your personal profile. Many recruiters find such material much more acceptable in a letter, although you must still take care to stick to facts and avoid excessive hype.

When you are being headhunted, you either mail the CV, again with a covering letter, after you have had a chat on the phone or else you actually deliver it personally. Speculative applications to headhunters always involve a covering letter as well as a CV and may be preceded by a phone call.

In networking, you hand the CV over personally and if contacts pass copies on they again either do so personally or use a covering letter. Finally, when making speculative applications direct to potential employers, you may initially use a letter which, in effect, summarises selected parts of your CV, the parts you select naturally being the ones which sell you and the ones you leave out being those which might turn the buyer off.

What this all adds up to is that your marketing brochure really consists in many cases not just of a CV, but of a CV which is complemented and enhanced by the letter which accompanies it. There are even instances in which a letter on its own becomes your marketing brochure. That is why we are going to spend the whole of Chapter 18 looking at letters and how to make them work for you in a variety of different situations.

Keeping the customer satisfied

First, however, you will see how you can give the customers the kind of CV they like to receive, yet still create an impact that will put you one step ahead of the competition. Contrary to what some people may suggest, this involves neither the use of overblown hype, nor being devious or concealing information. Instead it is based on employing the inside knowledge which you now have of how CVs are perceived by their recipients, and then on applying yourself to the preparation of your own CV in a professional manner, using the tool kit contained in the next chapter to bring out your individual personality and USPs.

Whichever way you produce your CV, you will always find someone who would like it done differently – it is impossible to please all of the people all of the time. A more realistic aim is to try to please as many people as possible as much of the time as possible and you can do that by observing the following guidelines.

- Always be aware of whom your CV is going to, how it will be delivered to them and how they are going to use it.

- Write your CV as a solution to the other person's problem – not as your personal ego trip.

- Use the format most people want to see: reverse chronological.

- Only insert a personal profile before your career history if it is going to have a stronger impact on the recipient than your most recent experience and achievements. If you do use one, keep it brief, factual and very precisely targeted.

- Prepare a core CV for general use, but study it carefully before each submission and always edit it to whatever extent is necessary in order to present yourself in the best possible light for the specific purpose in question.

- While a covering letter can be used to avoid or limit the extent to which you customise your CV, beware of the risk of inconsistencies between the two documents.

- Never allow a 'second best' CV to go out. It will probably be the end of that particular opportunity as far as you are concerned. Consider the time you spend on getting it dead right not as a chore but as an investment.

**"GOOD PRESENTATION
WILL NEVER MAKE UP
FOR WEAK CONTENT,
BUT IT IS EASY TO RUIN
STRONG CONTENT BY
POOR PRESENTATION."**

17 The killer CV

What it is and how to produce it

The killer CV and the professional assassin have a lot in common. Just as real life contract killers have none of the glitz, glamour and gadgetry of The Jackal, so the killer CV has no truck with being flashy or gimmicky. There are no short cuts, no magic wands. The qualities that make a killer are:

- a clear goal;
- complete single mindedness in pursuing it;
- total efficiency – no waste of either time or energy;
- awareness of risks, and a thorough understanding of how to avoid them;
- outright determination to eliminate the opposition;
- complete mastery of all the tools of the trade;
- total professionalism.

When applying these qualities to the preparation of a CV there are two aspects to consider – content and presentation. Good presentation will never make up for weak content, but it is all too easy to ruin strong content by poor presentation. That is why the first two stages in preparing your CV are all about what you are going to include – and what you are going to leave out.

Getting started

The preparation of your CV involves several stages:

- gathering together the information;
- selecting those facts which will enable you to achieve your purpose;

- choosing a layout which is easy to assimilate and conveys a professional impression of you;
- finding words which get your message across in a vivid and individual manner;
- reviewing your draft;
- editing it;
- checking it.

The reviewing and editing stages must be repeated – over and over if necessary – until you are completely satisfied that your CV is going to do you justice.

The first stage, the assembling of the necessary facts, should involve comparatively little effort. You ought to have all of the information you need in the asset register you compiled right back at the beginning of your job search.

Stage two, on the other hand, is not nearly as straightforward. It is here that so many people start to go astray and, instead of producing a killer CV, end up by shooting themselves in the foot.

The first, and most common, error is to concentrate on the wrong person. Your CV may be about you but it is – or, rather, should be – written for the recipient. Busy recruiters and decision makers do not want to have to wade through your entire life history. Still less do they want to be told irrelevant details about your family and leisure interests. What they do want to know is how you are going to add value to their organisation.

So, before you start to wade through your asset register, put yourself into the shoes of the kind of person to whom you are going to be sending your CV. Take a sheet of paper and write down at the top of it what that person will want to see in order to be persuaded to take the action you are after – calling you in for a meeting, for example. Then, keeping that sheet of paper in front of you all the time, start selecting the relevant facts.

You should find that your problem lies in being spoilt for choice. Be ruthless. Include only those skills, strengths, achievements and so on that really do make you stand out. This will not only ensure that you produce the best possible CV, but will also be valuable preparation for an ultimate meeting, helping you to concentrate your mind on your key assets and the ways in which they will benefit your prospective employer.

If, by any chance, you find that your problem is too little choice, rather than too much, there are two possible explanations. Either you are targeting the wrong kind of opportunity or you did not do your initial self-appraisal thoroughly enough.

CV suicide

If you are to be ruthless in selecting only those assets which are going to ensure that your CV achieves its objective, then you must be even more ruthless in dealing with other matters which probably do not need to be mentioned at all, and in avoiding some of the more common risks and pitfalls. Here are some examples.

- Leisure interests should appear on your CV only if they positively strengthen your application – for example, active involvement in professional and trade associations, or pursuits which demonstrate qualities like fitness and tenacity. Any that are not directly relevant add nothing, except clutter. Oddball interests are a distinct liability – do not risk being labelled a weirdo.

- Political and religious affiliations are even more risky. Keep them to yourself, at least until you find out what your prospective employer's views are.

- Voluntary/community work falls into the same category as leisure interests, i.e. to be omitted unless directly relevant. While some potential employers may admire your public spiritedness, others may fear that you will always be running off to do good works instead of staying late in the office when you are needed.

- It is not necessary to provide references at this stage, except in the case of public sector applications.

- Addresses and telephone numbers of employers are also superfluous.

- Beware of jargon, and of abbreviations which – though universally recognised in your current environment – may be meaningless to the person reading your CV.

- If possible, avoid the risk of either over- or under-pricing yourself by omitting details of your remuneration. Should it be specifically asked for, deal with it in your covering letter, as described earlier, in Chapter 8.

- Reasons for leaving jobs are a potential minefield. Let them wait for the interview.

- Career goals and ambitions are another dicey area. Unless you are sure they match both the specific job and the future prospects in the organisation in question, leave them out.

- Once you have made a statement in your CV, you have invited the reader to ask you to justify it at interview, so do not include anything you cannot prove, if challenged to do so.

- Explain gaps between jobs, otherwise people may jump to an unfavourable conclusion.

- In particular, avoid lies. Be sparing with the truth, if you must, by omitting things completely, but do not risk getting caught in the act of trying to deceive – it will be the end of your chances of the job in question. Professional recruiters check, as a matter of routine, whether candidates actually have the qualifications they claim, while all sorts of other matters – such as dates of employment, and details of salary and benefits – are verified in the course of taking up references.

How to present yourself

You should present your CV the same way you would present yourself for an interview: smart, positive, professional – conveying an image of efficiency but not going over the top by being flashy or too smooth. The following specific points need to be kept in mind.

- **Length**

  A couple of pages should be enough, three at the outside. If you need to list out technical information (this may apply, for example, to IT people, academics or scientists), do so in an appendix attached to the back of your CV. Do not enclose photocopies of reference letters, detailed job descriptions or certificates relating to professional qualifications.

- **Spacing**

  Do not, however, sacrifice legibility on the altar of brevity. Three well-spaced pages, using bullets, indents, clear margins and so on, will produce a more favourable impression on a tired-eyed recruiter than two cramped ones. This is why a one-page CV, for all its apparent advantages, is not generally to be recommended for a mid to senior level executive.

- **Priority**

  Assuming, then, that you are going to have to rely on gaining sufficient interest from your reader to ensure that they do turn the page, remember to put 'first things first'. After providing only the absolutely necessary personal details (name, address, telephone number, professional qualifications, relevant educational details and any foreign languages spoken), go straight into your most relevant experience and achievements.

- **Typography**

  Stick to a single typeface. Mixing them creates a messy effect. Choose a clean, businesslike typeface like Times New Roman and use a size that will not cause eye strain – 12 point is ideal. Achieve variety by the use of capitalisation, emboldening and – discerningly – variations in typeface. Italic is best avoided, so is underlining.

Be verbally lean

Presentation is not just about layout. It is also about the words you use – or, rather, not just the words you do use, but also the ones you do not. The first rule is that every single word you employ in your CV must earn its keep, otherwise it has no business being there.

Start at the beginning. What are you going to put at the top? 'Curriculum vitae'? Does anyone really need telling that? So why put it there? Why not just head the sheet with your name?

Economise on space, as well as words. You want your reader to get to the important stuff as quickly as possible. Your address need take up only one line. Do not forget the post code – its omission is likely to be considered either careless or unbusinesslike. Another single line will be enough for your telephone numbers. Since recipients of CVs may want to contact you during working hours, include not just your home number but also an office number or your mobile. These days contact information should also include your e-mail address.

Avoid, by the way, taking economy with words to the extreme of omitting contact information completely on the grounds that it is on your covering letter. The two documents can, and often do, become separated.

'Age'? No, use 'Date of Birth' instead. There is no more certain way of making a CV look tired than by forgetting to update it when you have a birthday.

Marital status and numbers of children are optional. Include them only if they help. Many employers prefer the impression of stability which is given by someone who is married with two-point-four children. On the other hand, if a job involves a lot of travel away from home, it could be an advantage to state that you are single.

Then, after dealing with qualifications, education and languages, you come to your most recent job – or, if you are really convinced it is going to do you more good than harm, your personal profile. Either way, you need to be aware of a couple more words which should be avoided at all costs: 'I' and 'me'. Once you start using them, you have to go on doing so, and there is no easier way of making yourself sound nauseatingly egocentric. Remember who the CV is for? It is supposed to be a reader-centred document, not a you-centred one.

The way to avoid those two pronouns, by the way, is not to put the whole thing in the third person. Recruiters loathe the kind of CV which has apparently been written by someone other than the subject, e.g. 'Smith spent 10 years with XYZ Co.' The correct method is to eliminate not only 'I' and 'me', but also a lot of other unnecessary little words like 'a', 'an' and 'the' by scrapping full grammatical English and using note form.

CREATING AN IMPACT

Compare the following examples for snappiness and impact:

- I installed a fully computerised accounting system which resulted in a reduction in the amount of time it took to produce the monthly reporting package from thirteen days to seven days.
- **Installed fully computerised accounting system, reducing time taken to produce monthly reporting package from 13 days to 7.**

Writing in note form also ensures that you avoid two more pet hates of people who read a lot of CVs – long sentences and heavy wedges of solid text.

The clearest way to set out your career history is to put dates to the left (months are not necessary, just years are sufficient), and indent the text. State your job title and, unless the company is a household name, indicate its size and what it does. Rather than detailing duties, which are often largely self-evident from the job title, list achievements. Give some thought to why the company was better off for your contribution and get this across in a succinct but striking manner.

Unless an earlier job is particularly relevant to your current application, go into more detail on your current or most recent position and progressively less as you work backwards. If you had several short periods of employment right at the beginning of what is now a lengthy career, you can summarise them rather than listing them individually.

Finding fresh words

If eliminating words that do not earn their keep is one half of the job, then making those words you do use earn not only their keep, but also a handsome bonus, is the other half. The English language is an exceptionally rich one, with many alternative terms for any one noun or verb, adjective or adverb. Do not be lazy. Avoid serving up the same tired old words that everyone else is using. Take the trouble to find the words that precisely describe what you want to convey, words which express the individualism that makes you unique, rather than just another faceless candidate, desperate for a job.

Study the suggestions in the word lists which follow, but do not stop there. Make use of the thesaurus on your word processing package too. Each time you want to describe something, consider all the alternatives. Select the one that sits comfortably on your shoulders, like a well-fitting jacket. Avoid using outlandish terms just to be different – you can achieve a striking impact simply by careful thought and accurate choice.

To take one or two examples of how to make your personal qualities shine through, here are a couple which impressed recruiters who were interviewed in the course of compiling this book.

- A recruitment consultant who was trying to fill a vacancy for an auditor to work for a large European financial institution – not exactly the sort of job that has the majority of people jumping up and down with excitement – was struck by a CV which said, 'Particularly enjoyed audits of international organisations in finance sector'. The applicant had not only drawn attention to relevant experience, but had also personalised that statement.

- Another candidate, working in a business where security was vital, said, 'Regarded by my boss as the safest pair of hands in the whole company'. This applicant had correctly identified the fact that reliability was what the reader of the CV would place at the top of the person specification for the job in question, not executive Rambo qualities like being dynamic and results orientated.

Get the idea? All right, now have a go yourself. Here are the word lists (they are all action words, not adjectives), together with a sample CV layout on pages 201–2.

Achievement	Initiative	Leadership	Problem solving
accelerated	created	controlled	analysed
accomplished	designed	developed	corrected
achieved	devised	directed	cut
attained	established	drove	eliminated
carried out	extended	guided	ended
completed	formulated	headed	evaluated
conducted	generated	inspired	examined
delivered	improvised	led	identified
demonstrated	initiated	managed	investigated
doubled	instituted	organised	refined
effected	introduced	revitalised	reduced
enhanced	launched	undertook	reorganised
enlarged	originated		repositioned
exceeded	pioneered		reshaped
expanded	redesigned		resolved
expedited	set up		restructured
finished	started		revamped
implemented			reviewed
improved			revised
increased			simplified
negotiated			solved
obtained			streamlined
perfected			strengthened
performed			tackled
produced			traced
secured			trimmed
succeeded			turned round
surpassed			uncovered
tripled			unified
won			utilised

At first glance the sample CV overleaf may not look dramatically different from many others you have seen, and this is quite intentional. Gimmicks and unfamiliar formats do more harm than good. What is different from so many CVs that recruiters receive, and reject, is that this CV makes it so easy for its readers to pick out the kinds of things they want to see – Hilary Brown's international exposure, computer systems experience and so on – as well as making the excellent career progression stand out. Careful selection and the elimination of all irrelevancies, combined with clear layout, means that this CV sells itself – or, rather, its writer. Does yours do the same?

Reviews and wraps

In any professional organisation, a draft report always gets reviewed carefully before dispatch, whether it is being presented to a committee or board, or being sent off to clients. This review process usually involves someone other than the writer taking a look at the draft. A fresh pair of eyes often spots things the writer, who has been too closely immersed in it for too long, may no longer have the objectivity to notice.

So, when you have had a first go at reviewing and editing, and have tried to anticipate – and answer – the questions you think the reader might want answered, ask someone else to have a look at your draft. Find someone qualified to pass a reasonably expert judgement. While colleagues or friends may be able to help, you could kill two birds with one stone and actually use your CV to do a bit of networking, especially if you are sounding out a new area you wish to move into.

Get more than one view if possible. Each person will have his or her own quirks, and you will never please everyone 100 per cent, but listen for the consensus. Try asking the question, 'If you were ploughing through two or three hundred CVs, would mine stand out?'

And when, finally, you really do have the best effort you can possibly produce – and have run your word processor's spellcheck over it – take care not to let yourself down with your printing and stationery. The aim here should be for a crisp, professional appearance without going over the top. An excessively

HILARY BROWN, BA, FCA

Address: 23 Laburnum Gardens, Suburbia on Thames, Middlesex MX9 9XM

Telephone: Home: 01999 000999   Office: 01999 989898
                  Mobile: 09090 900990   E-mail: Hilary B @ servprov.co.uk

Date of birth: 17/9/54

Career History

1989 to date   **Global Computer Corporation**
                  (Turnover £4billion worldwide, £600million Europe)

1991 to date   **Financial Controller, Europe**

                  Report to VP, Europe, plus functionally to VP, Finance in Chicago.
                  Control 6 staff in London plus further 12 on continent.

                  Achievements

                  •   Introduced centralised treasury system covering all seven
                      European subsidiaries, reducing interest paid on overdrafts
                      by 24%.

                  •   Reduced average debtor days throughout Europe by 18%.

                  •   Implemented completely new computerised accounting
                      systems, cutting time taken to produce monthly reporting
                      package from 11 days to 7.

1989 – 1991   **Finance Manager, Global France**

                  •   Set up accounting systems in newly established French
                      subsidiary, joining as only the fourth person recruited at
                      greenfield site.

                  •   As member of small management team, helped
                      develop the company to sales of £35million and
                      second highest profitability in Europe.

| 1983 – 1989 | **International Fragrances Corporation** (Cosmetics distributor, Turnover £900million) |

1987 – 1989   **Management Accountant**

Based at worldwide headquarters in London. Responsible for budget preparation and management reporting: setting timetables, ensuring figures received on time from 23 subsidiaries, checking accuracy, consolidating and producing commentary for parent company board.

1985 – 1987   **Systems Accountant**

Co-ordination between group MIS department and users on all new accounting systems, from initial specification through to successful implementation.

1983 – 1985   **Operational Auditor**

Genuine operational auditing, rather than internal checking function. Visited 14 different subsidiaries in Europe, the Far East and Australasia.

1976 – 1983   **Coopers & Andersen**

Articled to this major international firm of Chartered Accountants. Rose to Audit Manager, achieving all promotions at earliest possible opportunities. Audit clients were mainly international groups, both US and UK owned, in the manufacturing and service sectors.

Qualifications: FCA

Education: Bristol University: BA (1st class), History

Languages: Fluent French

Other Interests   Member of Institute's Anglo-French liaison group

Run half marathons

glossy presentation will turn recruiters off just as quickly as a tatty, amateurish one, probably because it smacks of a factory produced bulk mailshot.

You do not, therefore, have to spend a fortune on a laser printer. A decent bubble jet will produce a perfectly acceptable result.

Having taken the trouble to achieve high quality printing, avoid - if at all possible – faxing your CV. The print always lacks crispness, and the paper creates a distinctly tacky impression.

E-mail is a further option for transmitting your CV, but you need to consider carefully the pros and cons, which are explored in detail in the separate section on the internet.

The same need for a balanced approach applies to stationery as it does to print quality. Fancy folders are not appreciated, at least not in the UK, but do print out on a decent quality white paper, even when you are running your CV through a photocopier. White? Yes. Although cream, buff or pale blue are generally acceptable, a main board director of a highly regarded merchant bank was recently seen to cast a CV abruptly aside with the comment, 'Blue paper! No way am I going to employ someone who sends in a CV on blue paper!'

You may not be able to predict all the whims of the people you are targeting, but there is no point in taking avoidable risks. Keep the presentation professional and then let the carefully chosen content do the rest.

International aspects

The first point that needs to be made is that you need to translate your CV into the language in question or, in some cases, languages – plural. In Belgium it is customary to have a CV available in French, Flemish and, if you are dealing with subsidiaries of UK or US corporations, English too.

Custom and practice varies enormously from one country to another. In America you never mention age or date of birth (age discrimination is illegal), and you omit details of marital status, children, religion and nationality. You also print your resumé on an American paper size, not on A4. In Germany you give greater prominence to qualifications. In France it used to be the norm to attach a photograph, but is now becoming less so.

What it all adds up to is the fact that you just have to have local knowledge, gained either through previous personal experience of working in the country in question or through obtaining advice and guidance from people who do have that knowledge.

"**W**HAT YOU NEED TO DO IS WHET THE READER'S APPETITE, NOT CAUSE INDIGESTION."

18 Belles lettres

The other half of your marketing brochure

Letters are far more flexible than CVs. People have fewer preconceived notions about them, and those expectations they do have relate mainly to presentation rather than content. On the other hand, flexibility brings its own dangers. In many ways, it is easier to write a good CV than a good letter. You have a standard format and a set of rules to follow.

This chapter will show you how you can have the best of both worlds, exploiting the flexibility of the letter yet working with some broad templates and guidelines to ensure that your correspondence puts you one step ahead of the average job-hunter. Before looking at what should go into letters which are designed to achieve a whole range of quite different objectives, we will take a look at a set of basic criteria which apply to all letters, regardless of their specific purpose.

- Put yourself in the reader's shoes. Before you even start typing your letter, get clearly in mind what the benefit to the recipient is going to be.

- Be equally clear about what your own purpose is. In the context of job hunting, it is usually, but not always, to get a meeting.

- Remember that your reader is almost certainly a busy person, with no time to waste. Ensure that your first sentence captures the reader's attention. If it does not, then the rest of the letter is likely to be at best skimmed, if read at all.

- Ask your readers questions. This makes them feel that they simply have to read on.

- Do not lapse into excessively formal language. Try to write very largely as you would speak if you were actually sitting in the recipient's office.

- Be short and sweet. Keep the letter to one side of typed A4 if at all possible. Avoid long sentences and paragraphs. Use short, punchy words rather than polysyllabic pomposities.

- Use bullet points and tabulation to make key items stand out, rather than risking them being missed because they are buried in a solid slab of text.

- End your letter with a clear and positive request for action.

- Observe the same presentational rules as for CVs – good quality white A4 paper, businesslike typeface, clear margins and spacing. Go easy, however, on emboldening and variations in type size.

- Finally, do not forget to sign the thing. One recruitment consultant estimated that at least 5 per cent of the jobhunters who write to him forget to add their signature – a sure sign either of carelessness or of bulk mailings.

Now, keeping these points in mind, here are some specifics.

Not just an ad on

Some of the greatest lost opportunities occur when people are responding to advertisements. Perhaps because so many ads end with something like, 'send your CV to . . .' many applicants say little more in their covering letter than that they are interested in the job in question and that they are enclosing, as requested, their curriculum vitae.

Put yourself in the shoes of the recruiter reading a pile of two or three hundred applications, and looking for the handful of key criteria which are going to rule each candidate either in or out. Would you not be pleased if, instead of having to wade through the whole CV each time, you found that the job had been done for you? Example A at the end of this chapter illustrates the principle.

If the advertisement highlights five criteria and you only possess four, just list out those four and ignore the other one. Since most recruiters divide letters into three piles on the first screening – probables, possibles and rejects – you should at least end up in the possibles, if not the probables.

If you match only one or two of the criteria, you obviously cannot use this format – but then, if you are that far off the specification, you should really not be wasting your time applying at all.

Assuming, however, that you are a reasonably close match, here is the way to ensure that you go straight into the 'probables' pile.

- Avoid being too familiar. Although many recruiters put their full name on their ads, they tend to react unfavourably to a letter which starts 'Dear Bill' or 'Dear Sue'.

- Use a clear heading which quotes the title of the advertisement, the publication in which it appeared and any reference number, e.g.:

  Production Director, *Sunday Times*, 21 May 1995, Ref. GP/179.

- Catch the reader's attention in the first sentence by demonstrating that you have a genuine reason for being attracted to this specific position. Do not just say, 'I wish to apply for . . .' Say something like, 'I was particularly interested in your advertisement because I enjoy the challenge involved in extensively restructuring manufacturing facilities while continuing to operate to tight deadlines'.

- Then go straight into the main body of the letter, in which you show how you match the requirements of the post. Do be sure to use a tabulated format rather than solid text. It is so much easier for the reader to take in.

- End with a brief but positive sentence like 'I look forward to hearing from you and to having the opportunity to discuss this position with you'. While this can be preceded by a statement that your CV is, as requested, enclosed, this is somewhat superfluous. Recruiters have seen enough CVs in their time to be in little doubt as to what the document attached to your letter actually is.

A letter without a CV

Sometimes an advertisement simply says, 'Write to . . .' In these circumstances your best bet might still be to use the kind of letter discussed above and to send it off together with your CV. On the other hand, in the following situations a letter on its own is likely to have a greater chance of success.

- The advertisement may have said little, or have been vague about, the required criteria and it may therefore be difficult to produce a 'You require – I have' response.

- Your most recent experience may not, in this particular case, be the most relevant, and you may prefer to avoid your CV sending the wrong message.

- If your career history is a bit patchy or has gaps, you may not wish to draw attention to this, which both a chronological and a functional CV do in their different ways.

- Just occasionally there may be a case where you fall somewhat short of the advertised requirements, but it is clear from what is said in the ad that you do have other qualities which mean that you could make an exceptional contribution. If – and only if – this really is the case, then it will take a well thought out letter to demonstrate your suitability.

While this kind of letter is to some extent a letter and CV combined, the last thing you should try to do is to get the whole of your CV into the letter. Quite apart from the fact that that would make it far too long, the whole essence of the exercise is to be selective.

In order to ensure that you select the right things, keep firmly in mind the purpose of the letter. Assuming that this is to get yourself a meeting, then what you need to do is whet the reader's appetite, not cause indigestion.

LETTER FORMAT

The format of your letter should be as follows:

- Clear heading.
- Attention-grabbing opening sentence explaining why you are interested in the advertised position.
- Succinct summary of your strongest USPs. Highlight your most relevant achievements and give a brief rundown of those aspects of your career which are going to get you an interview. For example, if you have 25 years' work experience of which 10 are in the advertiser's industry (publishing), all you need say is, 'My last 10 years have been spent in the publishing industry'.
- Better still, use at least some bullet points and tabulation – especially for the key, factual items.
- End with a positive statement saying what you want, i.e. a meeting.

This kind of letter not only emphasises the points which sell you most strongly, it also enables you to avoid drawing attention to any points which may be considered to be negative, such as the fact that you may be above or below the advertised age parameters. A CV, on the other hand, inevitably draws attention to such matters.

Writing on spec

A speculative letter to a potential employer may have a number of similarities to the kinds of letters we have just been looking at, but it needs even more thought before you launch into it. When you respond to an advertisement, you know that there is a position to be filled and you usually have a reasonably clear set of criteria (the person specification part of the ad) to use as a structure for your letter.

In the case of a speculative application you may be writing because you have noticed a news item which suggests that the company is likely to have recruitment needs, or you could simply be applying to a company to which you believe you could make a contribution, in the hope that they just might either have a current vacancy or be sufficiently interested in your background and achievements to create one for you. Furthermore, you will certainly not have a person specification to which to relate your selling points. You will have to identify, by intelligent research, the potential problem to which you could be the answer, and then decide which of your assets to highlight in your letter.

Your research will also have to include identifying the person to whom the letter should be addressed. This should be the most relevant decision maker – usually the chief executive in a smaller company, or a functional head, such as the finance, production or sales director, in a large one.

As we explained in Chapter 13, if you are to achieve your objective of obtaining a meeting it is better not to ask, in so many words, for a job, but rather to use phrases like 'seeking a new challenge', which imply that you would welcome a job offer but also leave the way open for a more general discussion.

This leads to the question of whether you are more likely to achieve your defined purpose by sending a letter on its own or whether to accompany it with your CV. There is no hard and fast rule – you have to make a separate judgement on each occasion. Where only limited aspects of your career are relevant, use a letter on its own. Where there are a number of areas which could appeal to a prospective employer, include the CV as well.

Whichever choice you make, the format of the letter will be broadly the same.

Headhunters and agencies

The main difference when you are writing on spec to headhunters and agencies is what you say in the opening paragraph. Whether you like it or not, recruitment consultants always want to categorise you. Partly because of the way their minds work, and partly because of the way their computerised databases are constructed, they like to be able to define you in terms of:

- your core discipline, e.g. finance, HR, IT, production, sales;
- the business sector(s) in which your experience lies;
- the kind of job you are looking for;
- your salary expectations;
- the locations you will consider.

Define these at the outset and you will get off on the right foot. Fail to do so, and you risk irritating your reader, who will inevitably be a busy person with only a very limited amount of time to spend on each application.

Another thing which at best irritates recruitment consultants and at worst completely scuppers your credibility as an applicant is being too vague about what you want to do. It is instant death to say, 'I am open to anything' even if, in your heart of hearts, you are. Headhunters expect you to be focused and even agencies, who want to be able to market you widely, expect you to be clear about those options you will consider and those you will not. This goes back to what we said at the beginning of the book: it is all a question of targeting.

Examples and excesses

The rest of this chapter is taken up with examples of the different kinds of letters that have been discussed. However, before you start rubbing your hands in glee and assuming that you can get out of all the hard work, a word or two of warning.

First, never copy anyone else's letters parrot fashion. If your letters are going to work for you, then it is essential that your personality shines through them. Make sure that they reflect your individual attitudes and feelings. Use your own words and phrases.

Secondly, it is worth repeating that you should never copy American examples. They tend to be so over the top as to make the average British recipient cringe. Avoid anything that sounds insincere or over familiar. It ought to be possible to achieve an effect which is both positive and professional.

Finally, here are a few words about the examples.

- **EXAMPLE A**

  Advertised vacancy, covering letter to accompany CV – comes from a candidate who meets all main requirements specified in the advertisement and who therefore has only to be sure not to be missed in the screening process. This is achieved by clearly tabulating how the key criteria are met.

- **EXAMPLE B**

  Advertised vacancy, application letter without CV – comes from a candidate who in fact lacked one of the key advertised requirements, a professional qualification, but did possess some exceptionally relevant experience. Whereas a CV would have highlighted the lack of qualification, the narrative format of the letter emphasises the candidate's pluses without drawing attention to this shortcoming.

- **EXAMPLE C**

  Letter to headhunter, with CV – is a straightforward letter to an executive search firm, highlighting an impressive career record and relying on this, plus careful targeting of a headhunter operating in the areas in which the candidate has been working, to attract interest.

- **EXAMPLE D**

  Letter to headhunter, alternative approach – was suggested by a leading outplacement consultant and plays on two factors: the natural curiosity of headhunters; and their eagerness not to miss out on any opportunity to pounce on new business.

- **EXAMPLE E**

  Speculative letter to potential employer, referring to a news item – comes from a candidate who has spotted the fact that a company is entering a phase of regional expansion and who, having excellent experience in the business in question, is getting one step ahead before jobs are advertised or put out to headhunters.

- **EXAMPLE F**

  Speculative letter to potential employer, vacancy likely to exist – is aimed at a firm of management consultants. Such firms tend to recruit on a frequent basis and are therefore a good bet for a speculative approach.

- **EXAMPLE G**

  Speculative letter to potential employer, creating a vacancy – is from a jobhunter who has identified a benefit which other firms of a similar nature to the one being targeted have already seen and exploited. Bringing this to the attention of the firm may well result in the creation of a new position for which the writer of the letter could be the one and only candidate.

EXAMPLE A

Advertised vacancy, covering letter to accompany CV

1 The Pines
etc
etc

31 May 2000

Mr L Challis
Managing Director
Templar Hotel Group
etc
etc

Dear Mr Challis

IT Manager, Sunday Times: 28 May 2000, Your Ref. CD/749

Your advertisement caught my attention because it offers a new challenge in an environment which I find extremely stimulating and enjoyable. What is more, as you will see from the following summary, my background is particularly relevant to your requirements:

Hotel Experience	Last 8 years in this sector, with major UK and US groups
IBM AS400	Implemented AS400 in both current and penultimate jobs
International Exposure	Have worked in 7 different European countries plus USA
Languages	Fluent business French, working knowledge of German

I would welcome the opportunity to discuss this appointment with you and look forward to hearing from you.

Yours sincerely

Advertised vacancy, application letter without CV

2 Chestnut Lane
etc
etc

31 May 2000

Mr J Bunyan
Managing Director
Progress Construction Co. Ltd.
etc

Dear Mr Bunyan

Financial Controller, Daily Telegraph: 25 May 2000, Ref: DT/431

Your advertisement was of particular interest to me, since I have a proven success record in implementing improved management information systems in the construction industry.

During my five years with O'Reilly and Mulholland, we made several acquisitions of companies which had systems ranging from the outmoded to the virtually non-existent. In each case I upgraded management reporting in such a way as to achieve compatibility with group accounting policies whilst retaining the flexibility to provide executives in each company with information in a format which reflected the individual characteristics of their particular businesses.

Having spent this period with a mechanical and electrical sub-contractor, I have gained an excellent understanding of the relationship with main contractors and feel that, by becoming a poacher turned gamekeeper, I could make a strong contribution to your own organisation.

My earlier career included articles with a firm of accountants which had a number of construction company audits. Then, prior to joining O'Reilly and Mulholland, I gained valuable computer implementation experience in an American engineering group where I was exposed to exceptionally tight reporting deadlines. Now age 35, I am looking for a Financial Controllership in a group offering opportunities for long-term career development.

I would be pleased to discuss this position with you.

Yours sincerely

EXAMPLE C

Letter to headhunter, with CV

2 Cedar Grove
etc
etc

31 May 2000

Mr H Hunter
Eurosearch International
etc
etc

Dear Mr Hunter

As Business Development Director of Cormorant Holdings I have, over the last four years, been instrumental in increasing sales sixfold, and in broadening the base of the group's activities to protect it against cyclical influences in any one market. However, with the group now entering a consolidation phase, I cannot see the same level of challenge being available to me in the immediate future, and I am therefore considering alternative career options.

As you will see from the enclosed CV, my experience has been primarily in the distribution and service sectors, and I see myself as being most marketable in those areas. Being aware that you have a number of major service industry clients, I wondered whether you might be handling any suitable opportunities for me.

I am willing to relocate anywhere in the UK or continental Europe and am currently earning £85,000 plus the usual executive benefits.

I would be pleased to meet you at any time to discuss this matter further.

Yours sincerely

EXAMPLE D

Letter to headhunter, alternative approach

3 Willow Walk
etc
etc

31 July 2000

Mr H Hunter
Eurosearch International
etc
etc

Dear Mr Hunter

You may well already be aware, through your usual grapevines, of the recent events at the Hawkswell Group which culminated in my decision to tender my resignation after eight very successful years, the last three of which I spent as Sales and Marketing Director.

However, in the event that the full ramifications of the boardroom reshuffle, and its effects on the various divisions, have not yet reached your ears I wondered whether you would be interested in meeting so that we can catch up on things.

Naturally, I would also appreciate your advice on the direction in which my own career should now be heading.

I will call your secretary within the next few days to see if we can find a mutually convenient date and time to get together.

Yours sincerely

EXAMPLE E

Speculative letter to potential employer, referring to a news item

4 The Oaks
etc
etc

31 May 2000

Mr B King
Chief Executive
Fast Food Inc
etc
etc

Dear Mr King

My interest was aroused by the recent article in the Financial Times indicating that, now you have outlets throughout Greater London, you are planning to extend your network into the regions.

As you will see from my enclosed CV, I have fourteen years' experience in the fast food business in the UK, having worked my way up to Area Manager with one of the most successful burger chains.

Whilst I could go further with my present employers, their growth has levelled out. In any case, what I enjoy most is building up new operations from scratch – hence the attraction of your expansion plans.

Whilst I can easily travel to most parts of England from my current base in the Midlands, I would be happy to relocate, if required, for the right career opening.

I would welcome the opportunity to meet you to discuss this matter further and will call you early next week to see if we can arrange an appointment.

Yours sincerely

Speculative letter to potential employer, vacancy likely to exist

6 Beech Close
etc
etc

31 May 2000

Mr O Richards
Chairman
Interconsult
etc
etc

Dear Mr Richards

In the course of my fifteen years as a Human Resources professional, I have worked in both manufacturing and service industries and have gained wide exposure to all aspects of the HR function. Since I particularly enjoy new challenges and the problem solving aspects of my work, I am seriously considering developing my career in the field of management consultancy.

As one of the leading firms of consultants in the UK, I wonder whether you might have a requirement, either immediately or in the foreseeable future, for someone with my background.

I enclose my CV and would welcome the opportunity to talk to you, or to the appropriate manager within your firm, both about my interest in management consultancy generally and about any possible openings within Interconsult.

I will call you next week with a view to arranging an appointment.

Yours sincerely

EXAMPLE G

Speculative letter to employer, creating a vacancy

7 The Limes
etc
etc

31 May 2000

Mr F Cholmondeley
Senior Partner
Beauchamp & Farquharson
etc
etc

Dear Mr Cholmondeley

I have noticed that many leading law firms are recruiting professional managers to run their 'back office' functions, thus leaving partners free to generate increased fee income. Although, as far as I am aware, your own firm has not yet taken this step, I wonder if you may be considering doing so.

Should this be the case I would, as the enclosed CV demonstrates, be well equipped to take over responsibility for your finance function. Four years ago I was appointed to what was then a newly created appointment as Financial Controller of a firm of chartered accountants with thirty-five partners. Having now upgraded their computerised work in progress and billing systems, streamlined management reporting, and introduced cash flow forecasting, I feel ready for a new challenge.

I would welcome the opportunity to discuss this matter with you and will call within the next few days to see if you would be interested in arranging a meeting.

Yours sincerely

"Do not skip this section if you already have a near perfect CV."

19 Building a smarter CV

The CV example on pages 201 and 202 speaks for itself. University degree, professional qualifications and languages spoken all stand out. It takes only a glance at the work history to identify impressive achievements, relevant experience of working overseas and of implementing computer systems, and consistent career progression. The content was there to begin with. The presentation has ensured that its impact is not lost.

It is not everyone, though, who has such an impressive career. What do you do if your pedigree is somewhat less pure?

If the content is not there, presentation can help only to a very limited extent. Rather more can be achieved by:

- concentrating on your most marketable qualities;
- targeting your search carefully;
- using the telephone and letters rather than a CV where this highlights, even if only by the omission of what people normally expect to see, your shortcomings.

An even more positive contribution, however, can be made by consciously building a better CV. You may not be able to change the past, but there is an enormous amount that you can do to influence the future. Furthermore, while some of the actions you may need to take will involve too long a timescale to help in the immediate job search, there are others which can have an impact in the relatively short term.

Do not, by the way, skip this section if you already have a near perfect CV. Right now you may well be all set up to make your next career move, but what about the one after that? Career progression is largely about looking ahead and choosing the right stepping stones. What looks like the obvious step at this point in time may not be the best one in terms of finding the most effective route to your longer term goal.

Past, present and future

The first thing you need to do in order to build a more marketable CV is to make sure you are looking in the right direction. There is nothing to be gained by worrying either about mistakes you have made in your career to date or about things you should have done but have failed to get around to. Even professional recruiters do not expect you to be perfect. They will overlook the odd minus, so long as it is outweighed by enough pluses.

Take a piece of paper, then, and – bearing in mind the kind of job you are looking for – write down everything you could do to give yourself a better chance of getting it. You will probably find it useful to divide the paper into two columns or halves, one for the short term (things you can do within the next few months) and the other for the longer term (things which will take years rather than months and will therefore help you to get the next job but one, rather than assisting with the immediate job search).

Take professional qualifications, for example. If you have continually been putting off taking the last set of exams, a determined effort to get them out of the way could be a relatively short term aim. For those who have never even made a start on their studies, on the other hand, the objective of becoming professionally qualified has to go into the longer term category.

A similar situation exists with languages. If you were once fluent but have become rusty through lack of practice, a quick refresher may well be sufficient. Learning from scratch, unless you can afford the time and cost of a highly concentrated language lab course, will inevitably take some time.

Many skill updates, on the other hand, fit comfortably into the short-term category. It need not take very long to become familiar with a new spreadsheet package or to get yourself up to date on any recent legislation which is particularly relevant to the area in which you operate.

If you are in work, you may be able to get your employer to send you on appropriate courses, or at least to help with the cost. If you are unemployed, you may have to think twice about investing significant sums of money but there are usually ways round this, like subsidised adult education classes or home study packages. When you are out of work, learning something new has the added advantages of providing intellectual stimulation which may otherwise be lacking, of making you feel that you are achieving something and, where it involves going to classes or courses, of giving you the chance to meet some new people.

The experience factor

Perhaps the most important single factor, though, is your actual work experience. Think about all the years you have been at work. How much of the time were you actually doing things which added to the marketability of your CV?

Some people are lucky. They can point to a long history of new challenges. Many, on the other hand, will, when they sit and think about it, realise that there were periods, often long ones, when they were just doing the same thing over and over again. Think about your own last five years. Were they five years of added CV value, or just one year's tasks repeated five times over?

Now come even closer to the present day. Consider your last 12 months of work experience. If you had written your CV once at the beginning of that period, then again at the end of it, how much more marketable would you have become? Would that second CV, in fact, have looked noticeably different at all?

If concentrating your mind on these questions has made you realise that you have been getting into a rut, now is the time to do something about it. Do not waste time crying over spilt milk, just start adding to your marketability right away. You can do this regardless of whether you are currently in work or unemployed.

Taking the initiative

The proactive approach starts with a 'gap analysis' – a look at where you want to get to, the experience you need in order to get there, what experience you have already and, by comparing one with the other, where you fall short. If the gap is relatively small, you may be able to fill it by undertaking some short-term, project type work. Where it is larger, you may need to consider tailoring your immediate job search to finding a position which will provide a stepping stone to achieving your ultimate goal in a few years' time.

If you are in employment you can often volunteer to undertake a particular project, or join a committee or working party, which will give you the experience you seek. It may also be possible to organise a secondment for a few months, or even a year or two, either within your organisation or outside it. Management consultancy firms, for example, sometimes make secondments of senior staff, or even partners, to major clients such as banks or government departments. The consultancy practice benefits from the contacts and inside knowledge gained, while the individual in question obtains valuable experience, expands their network, and earns a good few brownie points into the bargain.

Ideally, of course, there should always be a mutual benefit, a win-win situation. In practice this is not difficult to achieve. If you are expanding your capabilities by breaking new ground, you are not only likely to be providing an immediate benefit to your employers, but will also be of greater value to them in the future. The people who are at greatest risk of being made redundant when times get tough are those who have ceased to add value to themselves, the organisation or its customers.

If you are out of work, you can use interim or temporary work, whether full-time or part-time, as a means of increasing your marketability. While in these situations clients inevitably want to hire people who, by dint of their existing knowledge and experience, can hit the ground running, it is rare for an assignment not to add something to your value to a future employer.

Some further angles

Looking into the longer term, those who really want to broaden their experience should give serious consideration to a spell in management consultancy. A major practice once ran a recruitment advertisement which said, 'If you want to pack ten years' experience into the next five, have you thought about a spell in management consultancy?'

The broadest experience is normally to be had in the generalist practices which have not yet grown so large that consultants have become pigeon holed into narrow specialist divisions. When attending interviews for consultancy jobs be sure to check not only on the range of work which you will be expected to undertake but also on the duration of assignments. If you get stuck on a single assignment for two or three years, your learning curve will start to look more like a horizontal line.

Those whose work, whether permanent or temporary, does not provide the opportunities they seek to plug the gaps they have identified in their experience should consider looking outside the field of paid jobs. Professional societies, trade associations, voluntary organisations, sports clubs and other leisure groups can all offer openings for the proactive individual to acquire new skills and experience.

Finally, while your first thought should be to plug identified gaps, do keep an eye open for any chance that arises to gain additional experience which, though not on your immediate target list, could be useful.

Take the case of Tim, who worked for a large accountancy practice. As part of his ongoing development, he was asked to help out from time to time with the firm's training programme, working alongside professional tutors who were brought in from outside. The immediate benefit to Tim was an improvement in his presentation skills and in his general confidence with groups of people. However, when Tim's division lost its biggest client and he was one of a number of people made redundant, he used one of the trainers he had worked with as a network contact. The outcome exceeded his wildest expectations. The training firm asked him if he would like to consider switching careers and coming to work for them. That was four years ago. Tim is now one of their most successful tutors.

The moral of Tim's story is that it never does any harm to acquire new skills and experience – or new contacts.

New frontiers

In the mind of many an ambitious executive, the most attractive of all new horizons may well be an international career and, to judge by the writings of some business journalists, you would think that opportunities for such careers grew on trees. In reality, unfortunately, this concept currently has about as much substance as that other great love of the business media, the paperless office.

In spite of the remorseless expansion of multinational corporations and the somewhat more hesitant progress of the EU (European Union) towards European integration, most organisations still prefer to fill senior positions with a national of the country in which the job in question is based. The reasons for this include the following.

- Cultural differences, which make it difficult for – say – a German to be a successful manager in an Italian company, or vice versa.

- Knowledge of local markets.

- Fear that the appointee, or their family, will not settle. Due to factors ranging from climate and culture to children's education and spouse's career, failure rates – especially for those lacking previous overseas experience – are high.

- Even if short-term problems do not arise, there tend to be concerns over length of tenure in the medium term, since overseas nationals are seen as being likely to want either to return home in due course, or to move on somewhere else.

- Costs of relocation.

- Language – to fill a managerial role, complete business fluency is required, and that is almost impossible to achieve without actually working in a country.

- Difficulties in obtaining work permits – although EU nationals can move freely within member states, moves elsewhere present far greater difficulties. The US, for example, has very tough legislation, while it is about as easy to get into Switzerland to work as it is to discover the identity of the holder of a numbered bank account.

Being realistic

In order to overcome such a long list of handicaps, there have to be some very positive benefits to justify employing an overseas national. The situations in which the advantages do outweigh the disadvantages fall mainly into the following categories:

- people with rare technical skills;
- high performing chief executives;
- developing countries importing expertise which they cannot find at home;
- multinational corporations making internal transfers of existing staff.

Assuming that you are neither one of the world's leading biotechnologists nor one of the world's most sought after chief executives, we can concentrate on the last two options.

Back in the 1960s and 1970s, even into the early 1980s, plenty of opportunities existed for UK citizens, and other nationals of the more developed countries, to take a two- or three-year contract in places like Africa and the Middle East, and come back with a greatly improved bank balance. Localisation, together with the prolonged worldwide recession, has largely seen an end to that. The relatively few opportunities which do exist these days are in different locations, places like South America, China and Eastern Europe which – unlike Britain's former colonies – are not English speaking. What is more, they are not paying the inflated salaries which used to be on offer in the oil-rich Gulf states.

In any case, emerging nations are interested in expatriates from developed nations only in the short to medium term, until they have their infrastructure in place and have used the expats to train up their own nationals to take over. This kind of experience will not necessarily do wonders for your future marketability back home.

Your best bet is therefore to obtain a job in the UK with a British, US or European group and then work yourself a transfer overseas. Some multinationals have a positive policy of developing teams of mixed nationalities, usually based at their worldwide or, in the case of US companies, European headquarters. This is particularly likely to happen in marketing. International companies may have a central marketing team made up of representatives of each of the major countries in which they operate so that products and strategies take account of consumer preferences in the various local markets.

While English may well be widely spoken at the continental HQ of, say, a US corporation, your chances of getting a posting will nevertheless be significantly enhanced by some existing linguistic accomplishments. You can then use a spell in Europe to acquire true business fluency. An MBA will also help you on your way, especially if it comes from an internationally renowned business school like INSEAD in Fontainebleau, France.

Once you have had one spell in a foreign location, and have proved that you can adapt both at work and in domestic terms to a different culture, you will then find it easier to make subsequent international moves. It is breaking the ice for the first time that is the greatest problem.

"Can you do the job, will you fit into the organisation and do you want to do the job?"

PART FOUR

Closing the sale

"EACH TIME YOU ATTEND AN INTERVIEW, YOU ARE IN A MAKE OR BREAK SITUATION."

20 Interviews

The myths and the reality

You are not going to get that new job without having an interview. Even when an opportunity arises directly out of networking or a speculative application, rather than through an advertisement, headhunter or agency, there will be an interview. It may be less formal, but do not be fooled by that. No one is going to invest tens of thousands of pounds a year in you without checking you out. Nor, if you are sensible, will you accept a new position before you have found out as much as you possibly can about the company, the job, your boss, the way your performance will be measured and so on.

Before a senior position is offered and accepted there will, in practice, normally be not one, but two or three interviews, sometimes even more. The length of an interview can vary from 30 minutes or less to several hours, although 1 to $1\frac{1}{2}$ hours is about average. There is just as great a variation, too, in the interviewers you will face, both in their approach and in their quality. What is more, while some organisations rely on interviews alone, others use tests, assessment centres, presentations, report writing and a variety of other aids to the selection process.

The bottom line, however, is that each time you attend an interview, you are in a make or break situation. The future of your career, to an extent your whole life, depends on the outcome of the brief amount of time you spend in that inevitably artificial situation. Perhaps it is this that has given rise to the many myths which surround the interview – myths which need to be exploded if you want to get ahead of the competition and increase your interview success rate.

The big fight

The first, and most dangerous, myth is that the interview is a contest between you and the interviewer, the object being to score points off your opponent. While an interview may be challenging – indeed it is in your interests, if your strengths are to be brought out, that it should be – there is a world of difference between a stimulating discussion and a punch-up.

The outcome of a properly conducted interview should be the same as that of a successful negotiation: win-win. The negotiations which get locked into a situation in which one party is perceived as beating the other are the ones that have failed. All too often, in fact, their ultimate outcome is not even win-lose but lose-lose, with neither party really gaining anything. A professional interviewer will aim not for confrontation but rapport, and you should be prepared to reciprocate. The two of you can then use the limited amount of time at your disposal productively, rather than wasting it by playing silly games.

The Gestapo

Another myth, favoured by the less combative, rather more defensive, kind of candidate, is that the term 'interview' is really just a euphemism for 'interrogation'. They ask the questions, you answer them.

Anyone who suffers from this misconception should substitute 'meeting', not 'interrogation' for the word 'interview'. To treat the interview as a one-way process is a fundamental error. If the process is to work effectively, then it must operate on a two-way basis.

In a sense, of course, it is easy to see how this myth arises. You are summoned to their offices. The interviewer seems to be in control of everything from the layout of the chairs to the length and structure of the session. You seem to be at a disadvantage right from the start.

If this is how you feel about interviews, try adopting a different approach. Imagine that you have been invited to someone else's home as a guest. Since it is their home, you naturally observe the basic courtesies. You arrive when you said you would, let them show you in, wait to be asked to take a seat and so on.

They show you the same courtesies, offering tea or coffee, making sure you are comfortable and outlining the programme they have arranged for you. Then you both get on with enjoying each other's company.

Enjoying? What – an interview? Yes. Why not? If, when you say goodbye, both you and the interviewer can genuinely say, 'I enjoyed meeting you', then you probably succeeded in establishing the kind of rapport which is the bedrock of a good interview.

The stress interview

So, is there really no such thing as a stress interview? Given that senior executives need to be able to cope with stress, do interviewers not try to simulate it in an attempt to see how well you cope?

The short answer is that the stress interview is talked about far more than it is actually used. Professional recruiters know that the way people deal with simulated stress in an interview is a poor predictor of the way they will actually respond to stressful situations in real life. The pros also know that they have far more to gain by making you feel relaxed and opening you up, than by putting you on edge and making you defensive. If they do challenge and probe in the course of a discussion, this will normally be done in a firm but fair way.

You are more likely to experience stress when you meet an untrained interviewer. Although the majority will be affable, probably displaying more warmth than the brisk and efficient professional recruiter, it has to be said that a proportion of people who get to the top do behave in a manner which is overtly aggressive, even boorish and downright belligerent. Regardless of whether this is simply put on in order to test your mettle, or whether it is how they always treat people, the golden rule in responding to such behaviour is to remain calm, courteous and businesslike. Never allow yourself to be dragged down to their level.

You should also keep your cool if you encounter a problem like finding, on taking the seat which is offered to you, that the sun is shining right in your eyes. Rather than getting paranoid and assuming that it is a deliberate stress ploy (it probably is not), simply move the chair, explaining politely why you are doing so, or ask the interviewer to pull the blind across the window.

Turning the tables

Having examined the myths about interviewers, let us turn for a moment to the equally prevalent misapprehensions which exist about the behaviour of interviewees.

It is often said that the person who gets any given job is not necessarily the most suitable candidate, but the one who performs best at interview. To be fair, there is an element of truth in this. However well qualified you are for a job, you can ruin your chances if you blow the meeting with the potential employer or the recruitment consultant.

This does not mean, on the other hand, that you can wheedle your way into a job for which you are totally unsuitable just by becoming a slick, practised performer on the interview stage. It is very much the same as the situation which exists with CVs: poor presentation can ruin good content, but a polished presentation will never make up for a lack of underlying substance. What is more, just as recruiters are put off by over-glossy CVs, so they are suspicious of interviewees who come across as too smooth or glib.

But don't be passive

This does not, however, mean that you can just sit back and wait for the interviewer to draw out all your strengths. Even professional recruiters, working to a carefully prepared plan, may miss key areas. The risks with line managers, who may well have had no training at all in interviewing skills, are very much greater.

All too often the decision makers, the people who have the final say in which candidate to hire, are notoriously bad interviewers. They frequently fail to prepare for the meeting, in many cases not even reading your CV thoroughly, let alone thinking about how they are going to structure the interview in order to elicit the required information. They do too much of the talking themselves and ask closed or leading questions when they should be using open ones.

If you are to overcome the problems posed by the clumsy amateur, you need to be extremely well prepared, having a clear idea of exactly what you need to get across and making sure that none of your key selling points are missed. Never fall for the myth that the interviewer can be relied on to do the job for you.

The truth, the whole truth

Another myth, perpetuated by writers of articles about the recruitment business, is that candidates can, and often do, lie their way to interview success. There are, no doubt, some who try it. Very few succeed.

Professional interviewers spend every day of their lives sorting fact from fantasy, true substance from hype. To get one over on them, you have to be an extremely good liar. Very few people indeed are that good.

One of the problems is that once you start lying it is difficult to stop. The first lie leads to a second, the second to a third and so on – until, sooner or later, you trip yourself up. That leads to the next problem. Get caught out once, even on something relatively insignificant, and nothing else you say will be believed. It is just not worth the risk.

Being economical with the truth, on the other hand, is a different matter – at least, to an extent. If there are topics you would prefer not to have to discuss, then clearly you do not raise them.

If a difficult subject does come up, the situation is more complex. In general, it is best to say no more than you have to and to change the subject as soon as you can. On the other hand, you have to avoid making any discomfort you feel obvious to the interviewer. Like dogs, interviewers smell fear and, once they get their teeth into something, they will not let go.

Being smart

Another school of thought says that there is a far smarter approach than telling lies. All you have to do is to anticipate the awkward questions you are likely to be asked, prepare clever answers to them and then trot these out at interview in response to the appropriate cues. This theory has become part of recruitment folklore, which is where it belongs, because its relevance to reality is, at best, decidedly limited.

In spite of this, the concept does get perpetuated by journalists. There has even been a whole book published on the subject, entitled *Great Answers to Tough Interview Questions* (Martin John Yate, Kogan Page), which lists over 100 questions ranging from the fairly sensible to 'What would you say if I told you your presentation this afternoon was lousy?'

PAT ANSWERS

There are several reasons why mugging up pat answers to what one writer describes as 'the tough, sneaky, mean and low-down questions the interviewers love to throw at you' does not work in practice.

- Pat answers sound just that, and this will do you absolutely no good at all.
- Most interviewers do not ask catch questions.
- If a question seems tough, it is most likely to be because your interview preparation has paid insufficient attention to the company, the job and your own relevant background.
- Thorough interview preparation would be a far better use of your time than trying to memorise over 100 questions, let alone the smart answers to them.
- You will, in any case, never predict everything you might be asked. If you rely on having all the answers, rather than on a sound knowledge of your own CV, you are likely to get thrown by the first question you have not anticipated.

While you will never be able to foresee every question you may be asked, you should put yourself in the interviewer's shoes and try to predict the key areas they are likely to concentrate on. Some of these will be determined by the requirements of the job in question, others by your own CV. Any reasonably competent interviewer is obviously going to want to discuss your career progression, your reasons for leaving jobs, your aspirations for the future and the extent to which you fit the specification for the post you are being interviewed for. The ability to discuss matters like these confidently is what you need to concentrate on, rather than clever replies to smart questions.

A confidence trick?

Mention of the word 'confidently' raises a further issue. The last thing many people feel when they attend an interview is confident. So what do you do? Put on an act? Pretend to be something, or someone, that you are not?

The idea that you should do that is just one more myth. The candidate who walks in with a cocky, 'I'm God's gift' kind of manner is going to get off on completely the wrong foot. Interviewers expect candidates to be a little nervous initially, and consequently allow for this by taking deliberate steps to break the ice and relax them. In fact, if you do not feel slightly keyed-up before an interview, you probably will not give of your best. As a famous stage personality once said, after years and years of appearing before the public, 'The night I don't have butterflies in my stomach before I go out there is the night I ought to give the business up'.

Too keen?

A related issue to that of confidence is the matter of how much enthusiasm you display. There is an argument which says that it is wrong to appear over-eager at an interview because this weakens your negotiating power if you are eventually offered the job.

The only grain of truth in this is that you should not actually appear desperate. People who have been out of work for some time, especially those who have heavy financial commitments or who believe themselves to be victims of ageism, can fall into this trap. Even if you actually are beginning to feel desperate, you will certainly do yourself nothing but harm by letting it show.

This does not mean, however, that it is smart to go to the other extreme and project an attitude which suggests that you really do not care a toss, and that, if they want you to join their organisation, they had better make all the running. This is another example of playing silly games, which will not help you one bit.

In any case, do remember the three basic items on any interviewer's agenda: can you do the job, will you fit into the organisation and do you want to do the job? It is not uncommon for interviewers to ask, towards the end of the meeting, why you are interested in the position in question. Unless you have been displaying a reasonable amount of enthusiasm, you may find it difficult to give a convincing response.

Winning ways

If you want to succeed at interviews, there are three basic principles to follow.

- First of all, forget all the tricks and games.
- Secondly, be yourself. By all means show your best side, rather than going out of your way to draw attention to your warts, but do not try to be something you are not.
- Finally, remember that the only way to be certain that you will present a positive and confident image when it comes to the crunch is to invest the time and effort beforehand in making sure that you are really thoroughly prepared.

On video

As technology makes an increasing impact on the recruitment process, there has been talk of using 'video interviewing', which would have the advantages of:

- saving travelling time and costs for both candidates and members of an interview panel

- allowing employers to edit interviews for subsequent play-back
- enabling employers to get through more interviews in a shorter space of time.

However, there are also distinct disadvantages, including:

- loss of the ice-breaking and rapport building which occurs in face-to-face interviews
- limited ability to pick up body language
- loss of eye contact
- an increase in the risk of hiring decisions being made on the basis of physical appearance rather than ability to do the job
- candidates do not get the opportunity to get a feel for the place where they would, if successful, be working
- it is more difficult for employers to sell the job and their organisation.

Consequently, the use of such techniques is at present very limited and is currently unlikely to be encountered by the executive job hunter.

"THE MOST VITAL STAGE OF PREPARATION IS RESEARCH."

21 The chapter you can't afford to skip

Preparing for the interview

Before you start beavering away at researching the company or matching your CV to what you know about the job, sit back and ask yourself the following questions.

- ❏ What is your objective – what do you want out of the interview?
- ❏ Whom are you going to be interviewed by?
- ❏ What do they want out of the interview?

The answer to the first one may seem obvious: you want to be offered a job. However, you also need to find out enough about the company, the person who will be your boss, the responsibilities involved in the job and the performance measures by which you will be judged to be able to decide whether you will accept the offer if you get it.

Some career advisers say this does not matter. Concentrate on getting the offer. You can always turn it down – or arrange a further meeting to obtain the additional information you need to make your decision. In practice there is more to it than that. If you do not show enough interest at interview, you are unlikely to get the offer to begin with. Many interviewers 'mark' candidates, even if only subconsciously, on the number and relevance of the questions they ask. They also respond, again often without necessarily being conscious of it, to the amount of enthusiasm the candidate displays.

What interviewers are actually looking for are the answers to three questions.

- ❏ Are you capable of doing the job? In other words, do you have the technical ability, the experience and so on?

❑ Will you fit, both in terms of organisational culture, and in terms of getting on with your boss, peers and staff?

❑ Will you be motivated by the job? Does it make sense in terms of career progression and does it match with what you say you enjoy doing?

Unless you score highly on all three counts, you are unlikely to get the offer.

But who are they?

We have, however, skipped one of the original questions. Who is the interviewer? It could be:

- your potential boss, who may be the owner of a business, its chief executive, a director heading up a function or a senior line manager;

- the person to whom your potential boss reports, who is vetting the appointment;

- another line manager, who is giving a second opinion;

- the organisation's banker, auditor or lawyer, or a non-executive director, being used either for a second opinion or for their 'approval' of an appointment on which things like provision of finance may depend;

- a personnel or HR manager;

- a headhunter;

- an executive selection consultant, who is handling an advertised recruitment campaign on the company's behalf;

- an agency recruiter.

Depending on whom you are seeing you will find, and therefore need to be prepared for, significant differences in style, expertise and the emphasis which is put on different areas of the interview agenda.

Line managers often lack training in interview techniques and tend to be less skilled at eliciting information from candidates. Often egocentric, especially if they own or run the business, they frequently do more of the talking than they should and may be more aggressive in their questioning. They will, however, usually be the best people from whom to obtain the information you need about the company and the job. They may well ask questions with a greater technical bias and will certainly be particularly concerned with personal chemistry.

Professional advisers – bankers, auditors and lawyers – tend, both by their training and their relationship with the company, to be cautious, concerned primarily with avoiding a mistake being made rather than with the more personal or positive aspects of the selection process.

HR managers are normally skilled and structured interviewers, who often give little away about their own feelings. They are the people who will provide you with the best run-down on company policies and benefits, areas about which line managers are often vague and out of date.

Headhunters tend to be more affable than other outside recruiters. Used to having to seduce people away from existing secure jobs into the arms of the search firm's client, they often start an interview with a relaxed chat about your present situation and your aspirations, then, having established what you are looking for, embark on a soft sell of their client and the job they are trying to fill.

Selection consultants have the task of reducing the vast response to an advertisement down to a short-list of probably about four to submit to their client. Although they need to ensure that you are sufficiently interested in the job to attend an interview with the company, if short-listed, they will be concerned mainly with whether you match the specification, and whether you are likely to fit in with the personalities and culture. If in doubt, they tend to err on the side of caution rather than taking chances.

Agencies, being paid only if they succeed in making a placement, may in some cases be more willing to bend a specification. You may also find that, if they have not met you before, they may kill two birds with one stone, combining an interview for a specific job with a more general chat about the kinds of opportunity you would consider.

Where it's at

The assumption thus far has been that there is already a well-defined job, with a specification against which you can be measured. That, however, is not always the case.

If you have been networking or making speculative applications, you may have identified an organisation which is interested in what you have to offer but which does not have a vacancy as such. The object of the interview may be to discuss and enlarge on the needs and benefits you identified in your approach to the company. You may then find yourself, either at that meeting or a subsequent one, participating in the preparation of your own job specification.

A variation on this theme is when you identify one of those windows of opportunity, a vacancy which has been approved but not yet advertised or put out to consultants. Depending on the stage things have reached, there may be a well-defined specification or they may still be knocking ideas around, in which case the initial interview may still have an element of writing the spec about it.

Even when there is an apparently clear specification, things are not always set in stone. A company may already have tried one recruitment campaign and failed to find the right person, in which case they may be considering amendments to either the job responsibilities or the candidate requirements. Or they may be trying to fill a vacancy where, by its very nature, it is unlikely that they will find someone who can do all aspects of the job equally well. They may know that they will have to compromise somewhere, but be adopting a suck it and see approach, waiting until they meet some suitable candidates before deciding exactly where that compromise will be.

Doing your homework

Only by being aware of what stage things are at (preliminary screening interview, short-list etc.), whom you are meeting, and what both you and they want out of the interview, can you focus your preparation to maximum effect.

The first and most vital stage of that preparation is research. Never skimp this stage. Comprehensive research gives you at least four major advantages:

- it enables you to ask pertinent questions;
- it puts you one step ahead of the competition by demonstrating to the interviewer that you have done your homework;
- it gives you much greater confidence;
- it helps you to be more certain that you are making the right choice of your next job and employer.

So, what do you already know about the company and job? What do you need to know? What ought you to check out prior to interview and what should be left for that moment in the interview when you are given the opportunity to ask questions? And how can you find out what you need to know in advance?

Begin by gathering the information you have already: the advertisement, what the headhunter told you over the telephone, the information your network contact gave you, the research you did before making a speculative approach. Compare it with what you need to know.

Here is a checklist of things to find out about the organisation.

❏ How long has it been in existence?

❏ How has it changed and developed from its inception to the present day?

❏ What is its current situation?

❏ What are its future plans?

❏ Who owns it?

❏ If owner managed, what about succession or likelihood of a sell-off?

❏ What is its legal status – quoted PLC, private company, partnership etc.?

❏ If unquoted, any plans for a flotation?

❏ How many locations, and where?

❏ Range of products/services.

❏ Markets – split by level (e.g. quality or cut-price) and geography (percentage exported, and where).

❏ Market share and details of main competitors.

❏ Financial details: sales turnover, profitability, return on capital employed, order book.

❏ Number of staff employed.

❏ Funding: analysis of borrowings (from whom, on what terms) and gearing.

❏ Where will future funding come from, especially for any expansion plans?

❏ Assets, e.g. are buildings owned, leased or rented?

❏ Liquidity and solvency.

❏ Organisation structure.

❏ If part of a larger group, similar details to above for rest of group, plus information on how autonomous or otherwise the part you are being interviewed for is in terms of decision making, funds etc.

❏ Details of operations, e.g. depending on the type of job you are going for, you may need information on production processes, distribution networks and methods, customers, suppliers, sales/marketing policies, credit terms.

❏ Major risk factors, e.g. vulnerability to foreign exchange rate fluctuations, changes in government policies, the weather, fashion swings.

❏ Key people in the organisation.

❏ Any recent news items about either the organisation itself or the business sector in which it operates.

As far as the job is concerned, you need to know the following.

- Job title.
- Reason for vacancy.
- Urgency of filling it.
- How many incumbents over, say, last five years and reasons for leaving.
- Whom it reports to – position, name and personality.
- Where it fits into the structure.
- Where it is based geographically, and how much travel.
- Main purpose of job.
- How performance will be measured.
- Detailed responsibilities.
- Budgets controlled.
- Limits of authority.
- Reporting methods and frequency.
- Staff supervised: how many, their quality, staff turnover etc.
- Systems and equipment in use.
- Opportunities for future career development.

Filling the gaps

The length of these lists may look daunting, but in reality the task need not be too onerous. Put it into perspective.

- Some of the information you have already, from research you have already carried out, or from what you have learned from an advertisement or a headhunter.
- Quite a lot may be provided automatically by the company or the recruitment consultants they are using. It is becoming increasingly

common for job applicants to be supplied with an information pack, including details on both the organisation and the job.

- Where this is not the case, or where you need more, you can get a lot just by asking. Company reports and accounts are freely available. So too are sales brochures and catalogues. There is also a lot of information on the internet and the company's own website is an absolute must. In some ways it is better when organisations do not send this kind of information out to everyone, because those who display the initiative to ask for it or access it get ahead of the competition.

- You can get a further step ahead by ringing up the person you will be meeting, or their secretary, and asking a few pertinent questions – which will provide you with the ammunition to get yourself better prepared for the interview itself.

- Some of the questions you have, like those about the company's plans for future development, or questions about your boss, peers and staff, are actually better left to be asked at the actual interview. When you are given the opportunity to put your own questions, you want to make sure that you have some good ones, so that you score maximum brownie points. For instance, always ask at least one question that shows that you have read the company's annual report and accounts.

- At executive level, another key area for scoring, or losing, points is business awareness. If the interviewer makes a reference to recent press coverage of the company or the industry in which it operates and you do not have a clue what this was about, your credibility will immediately plummet. Keeping abreast of business news should in any case be part of your regular routine on networking and speculative applications.

- You can also double up on your time utilisation by combining research with networking. Although some of your research will be of the 'desk' variety, either at home or in the library, calls to people who might know the company in question are a vital part of the process. The facts come from reference books like *KBE, Kompass, Who Owns Whom?* and *Who's*

Who? The gossip and opinions come from people who know the industry, from the company's customers and suppliers, from its competitors, from headhunters and recruitment consultants.

- You may even know, or be able to network a contact with, someone who works for the organisation itself. Do, however, be discreet, and do not be tempted by the more outrageous suggestions made by some job hunting articles, like hanging around the pubs near the company's premises in the hope of striking up conversations with its employees!

The glass slipper

Once you have gathered as much information as possible, you can set about ensuring that your foot is the one that will fit snugly into the glass slipper. Keep constantly in mind the three things that the interviewer will be looking for.

- ❑ Can you do the job?
- ❑ Will you fit into the organisation?
- ❑ Will you want to do the job?

Remember, too, the 'added value' test. What problems and needs does the company have? What benefits can you bring to the party?

Go back to your asset register. Select from each section – qualifications and training, interests, experience, skills, strengths, achievements – those assets which are going to make you someone the organisation cannot afford not to hire. Tattoo these points onto your mind so that, when you are at the actual interview, you can mentally tick them off as the opportunities arise to get them across. If there are any which you do not get the chance to mention in response to the interviewer's questions, make sure you take the initiative. You normally get an invitation to raise any further points or questions towards the end of an interview. On the rare occasions when you do not, create one rather than risking underselling yourself.

It is also useful to encapsulate your USPs in a carefully prepared, succinct presentation since it is not uncommon for an interviewer to ask something like, 'What do you think you could contribute to our organisation?' or 'Tell me why we should hire you for this job'.

Watching your back

Scoring goals, though, is only half the battle. You also have to avoid conceding them. Put yourself into the interviewer's shoes. Take a careful look at your own CV. What would you home in on? Get someone else, a friend or network contact, to provide a second opinion. Give some thought to any Achilles' heels. How are you going to defend against them?

Areas which interviewers commonly pick upon include the following.

- **Speed of career progression**.
  Why did you stay so long in that job? Valid reasons could include the interesting projects which provided the icing on the gingerbread of the same core duties, loyalty (staying with the company to see it through a tough patch even though the recession meant a lack of personal progress), or the fact that, although the job title remained unchanged, the job content was in fact developing all the time.

- **Logic of career progression.**
  People expect to see a rational development. Be ready to demonstrate the reasons for any apparently sideways moves. For example, they may have plugged a gap in your experience which would enhance your long-term prospects.

- **Reasons for leaving jobs.**
  Be sure to have explanations which are both credible and positive. Do not bend the truth – this is an area which will be checked out when references are taken up, so be aware of what your former employers will say. If you did have a bust-up with your boss, discuss it objectively, e.g. 'We simply had diametrically opposed views on the way the company should develop'. Be particularly on your guard if you feel

yourself getting angry or displaying any other negative emotions when you discuss such matters. Skilled interviewers are adept at picking these up. Above all, never knock either a person or company you have worked for.

- **Gaps between jobs.**
  Be prepared both to explain why they arose and to show that you made positive use of them.

- **Gaps between what they want and what you have.**
  Provided that you meet the bulk of the requirements, do not worry about the odd shortfall, so long as it is not in a vital area. After all, if you could do the whole job standing on your head, where would the challenge be in it? Whatever you do, avoid getting defensive and making claims you cannot justify. That will damage your credibility not just on the item in question, but in every other respect as well. Instead, be prepared to show how you could readily acquire the necessary skills, experience etc. to plug the gap.

- **Your strengths and weaknesses.**
  Although this question may be asked in exactly these general terms, you should obviously gear your reply to the specific situation under discussion. The strengths aspect gives you the opportunity to summarise that list of reasons, which you have committed to memory, why you are the ideal candidate for the position. Being asked about your weaknesses is a bit more tricky. Try to come up with one or two which are really the reverse side of strengths, like 'I sometimes get impatient with people who aren't pulling their weight', and do be sure to avoid any that might prejudice your suitability for the post in question.

Some people find it useful to practise an interview by getting a suitably qualified friend to role play the recruiter or potential employer, while others feel that this is too artificial to be of real value. Whether you actually act it out or not, there certainly can be mileage, if you have the opportunity, in getting someone else to give a second opinion on your preparation, and particularly on the areas of potential difficulty, like those listed above, which you need to be prepared to deal with. Another person will always spot one or two things you have missed, and that could make all the difference between success and failure.

Looking to the future

Although interviews inevitably concentrate largely on the past – your education, career history and so on – a powerful method of setting yourself apart from the other candidates is by being prepared to talk about the future. The more astute interviewer will in any case raise questions like these.

- How would you go about this job?
- What do you see as the major challenges (or opportunities) in this role?
- What is the first thing you would do if you were appointed?

If questions such as these do get raised, you may well be the only candidate who has thought about them in advance and prepared answers to them. If the interviewer fails to ask them, you can lead into these topics yourself. A particularly appropriate point to do this is when you are being quizzed on one of the potentially difficult areas listed above, like your career progression. Switching the discussion away from what you should have done, but failed to do, in the past, and moving on to what you intend to do in the future, has a double benefit.

Do also, by the way, be ready for a question about your own future, as well as any about how you would do the job. 'Where do you see yourself in five years' time?' is a popular one. If the interviewer is your potential boss, be wary of responding with the pat answer, 'I'd like to be sitting where you are now'. The individual who is occupying that seat may still be ten years off retirement with no obvious promotion prospects.

And other gaffes

That gaffe is by no means the only one you have to watch out for. Having taken all the time and trouble to prepare yourself so carefully, take care not to wreck it all by slipping up on what may appear to be minor details. Here are some examples.

- If you do not get a letter confirming the interview details, send one yourself. A small but steady percentage of candidates insist on turning up either on the wrong day or at the wrong time.

- Likewise, make sure you have the right address, especially when an organisation has more than one office building.

- Unless you know an area well, check your route out carefully.

- Make sure you have plenty of change for parking and, if you are on a pre-payment meter, buy plenty of time. You do not want to be sitting in an interview worrying about whether you have been wheel-clamped.

- Allow for Murphy's Law. Road works, wide loads and accidents always occur when you have a vital appointment. And do not feel smug if you are using public transport: when did the trains ever run on time when it really mattered?

- Give yourself plenty of time at the other end of the interview, too. You are not going to be thanked for cutting a meeting short because you have another appointment. If in doubt, call the company and ask approximately how long the interview is likely to last.

- Avoid going into an interview on either an empty stomach or an over-full one (you do not want to feel sleepy) and avoid alcohol. For obvious comfort reasons, it is best not to have too much tea or coffee either, even if you have arrived early and need to find somewhere to kill a bit of time.

- Arrive about five minutes before the appointed time and, even if you do not need a comfort break, make use of the cloakroom – to check your appearance. First impressions are crucial.

"INTERVIEWERS ARE HUMAN. THEY CANNOT HELP PICKING UP SIGNALS ANY MORE THAN ANYONE ELSE."

22 A professional image

You never get a second chance to make a first impression. Recruiters, it is often claimed, make up their minds about candidates within the first four or five minutes of an interview. Is that really so? And if it is, what can you do about it?

In some ways, the position is even worse. A lot of judgements are made within a matter of seconds. Think about it. What do you do when you meet someone for the first time? The moment you clap eyes on them you start pigeon holing them without even thinking about what you are doing. Pin-stripe suit? City gent. Twin set and pearls? Middle-class shire county lady. Long-haired bloke with beard? We could go on for ever.

But it is not just clothes. We also make assumptions based on build, posture, vigour and a host of other factors. And that is before people even open their mouths. When they do speak, more judgements are made, based on accents, vocabulary, fluency, confidence, voice pitch and so on.

Like you, interviewers are human. They cannot help picking up all these signals any more than anyone else can. The only difference is that professional recruiters are trained to be aware of the processes which, in most people, take place purely subconsciously. Particularly when a candidate makes a very strong first impression, they try to be objective, even playing devil's advocate for the rest of the interview in an attempt to validate, or repudiate, that initial judgement.

At least, that is what they should do. It does not always happen in practice, especially if they are tired, or pushed for time, or having a bad day – or because they already have a good short-list and are, without necessarily being aware of it, looking for reasons to rule people out rather than in.

Once a first impression has been formed, it is all too easy to filter all subsequent information, rationalising each item to fit the judgement which has already been made. When the initial impact is favourable, this is called the halo effect; when unfavourable, the reverse halo effect.

If highly experienced, professionally trained recruiters find this behaviour pattern difficult to counteract, imagine how much more likely it is to occur when the interviewer is an amateur, like the typical line manager who will claim with great conviction, 'I know how to judge people. That's how I got where I am today.'

Mirror, mirror

What kind of an impression do you make? Dressed as you would be for an interview, stand in front of a full-length mirror. Take a good look at yourself. Try to be objective. If you find that difficult, get a second opinion. In fact, get a second opinion anyway – no one is that honest about themselves. And do not ask your partner or your children or your parents. Find someone who is both independent and who can angle their opinion from a business viewpoint. It could be a networking contact or one of the people you meet at a job club. The main thing is that it must be someone who understands what is expected in business circles and who will not be embarrassed about being completely honest with you.

If you have the opportunity to be put on video, do not be afraid to take it. Disconcerting though it may be to watch yourself on the box, you can learn an awful lot from it. This is what happened to Brian when he attended a session on interview techniques. Although he was impeccably dressed and highly articulate, Brian habitually talked into his boots rather than projecting towards his audience. As soon as he saw this on video, he realised what he was doing and, by correcting it, was able to achieve what was little less than a complete transformation in the impact he created.

Bearing up

There is, of course, a lot more to posture than the angle of your neck. What is more, the importance of good posture lies not only in the effect it creates on the interviewer, but also in its influence on the way you feel and, in particular, on your confidence.

We cannot all have the kind of height and build which creates that automatic physical presence that enables some individuals to dominate a whole room full of people. Fortunately, this is not at all necessary. It can even be a disadvantage, in that some people actually find it threatening and that is not the effect you want to have on interviewers.

A POSITIVE FIRST IMPRESSION

When you greet the interviewer you must, however, achieve that positive first impression, which means the following.

- An upright, but not stiff, stance.
- Looking the interviewer in the eye – which will also ensure that you do, in fact, keep your chin up.
- Smiling warmly, with your eyes as well as your mouth.
- Shaking hands firmly. The wet fish handshake creates such a negative impression that many interviewers will reject a candidate on that factor alone. Do not go right to the other extreme, though. If you see the blood rushing to the other person's eyes, let go.
- Making sure that your first few words are clear and positive. A lot of candidates are too eager and either gabble or fall over themselves. If you are prone to this all too common tendency, try steadying yourself by taking a breath before you speak.

Being too keen can also be a danger if the interviewer comes to collect you from a reception area. Be sure to get out of your seat in a businesslike, but not rushed, manner. One recruiter commented on the number of candidates who, in their eagerness, dropped the magazine they were reading or slopped the cup of coffee they had been given, while another interviewer had clearly not been impressed by the candidate who leaped out of the chair like a guard dog going for an intruder's throat.

What to wear

If anything, your clothes are even more important than your posture. Certainly clothing, and other aspects of appearance like hairstyles and accessories, cause far greater problems. While there is general agreement on what constitutes a businesslike bearing, what clothes to wear on any given occasion can be far more complicated.

One problem is that there are so many different prejudices. Asked what would turn them off a candidate before a single word was spoken, a diverse group of line managers came up with long lists which included (for men) beards, white socks, grey shoes and strong after-shave and (for women) no make-up, too much make-up, bare legs and trousers. The safest bet is therefore to err on the side of neutrality and conservatism, avoiding the inherent risk of making yourself instantly forgettable simply by being that bit more crisp and professional than the competition.

You should, of course, give some thought not just to your own image but also that of the organisation you are being interviewed by. Different expectations do exist in a City bank, a factory, a housing association, an advertising agency and so on. Normally, if you have been working in a given environment, you will be aware of its standards.

If, on the other hand, you need advice on the kind of appearance that would be appropriate, there are always people you can turn to. Network contacts are a useful source, especially where you are transferring your skills from one business sector to another. Alternatively, when you have had a first interview with a headhunter, selection consultant or agency, you can always ask them for tips about how to present yourself when you meet their client. It will be as much in their interest as your own to ensure that you create the right impression.

Finally, there are the professional image consultants, who – for a fee – will do for you what they have done for politicians and other public figures. Whether ordinary mortals like job-hunters need this kind of service is a somewhat moot point. Power dressing, like the excessively glossy CV, may be seen by interviewers as over the top.

Furthermore, although a session with an image consultant will cover all aspects of your appearance, a significant chunk of the time is usually devoted to the colours that are right for you and the impression that you make as a result. Since executive males are effectively limited to dark grey or navy suits and a restricted range of shirt colours, and many women have a natural sense of the colours that suit them best, the value of this is questionable.

Unless you can get a free image session – some companies run courses for their employees, either just on image or as part of training in things like presentation skills – it is probably worthwhile only if you have reason to believe that your appearance is having a seriously detrimental effect on your job prospects. For those whose appearance is broadly acceptable but who could just do with a bit of extra polish, the following extracts from what the image consultants would probably charge a three-figure fee for telling you ought to suffice.

Unisex tips

The following ground rules are valid for both men and women. Like the gender-specific tips that follow, they are based on the views of image consultants, who tend to be somewhat conservative in their views. However, in spite of dressing down days and a general tendency towards more casual clothing, an interview is a formal occasion on which it is safest to err on the conservative side.

- Quality rather than quantity applies once again. It is better to buy two good suits than four cheap ones. Quite apart from their better appearance and fit, good clothes actually provide better value in terms of cost per wearing because they last so much longer.

- Having invested in good clothes, look after them. Brush suits after wearing, keep them on the proper type of hangers and have them cleaned regularly. Get shoes re-soled and heeled before it is overdue and use shoe trees so that they keep their shape.

- In the vast majority of business environments, you should avoid being trendy. Classic styles are not only more acceptable, but also mean that you do not have to keep throwing clothes out and replacing them with the latest look.

- Do not ruin a good suit with tacky accessories such as nylon shirts and cheap acrylic blouses. In particular avoid juvenilia, like pink elephant ties, teddy bear brooches and watches that say Mickey Mouse past Donald Duck rather than ten past two.

- If your body shape is less than ideal (join the club), choose clothes that compensate for its failings, rather than accentuating them. For example, short people can achieve an illusion of greater height by wearing vertical stripes.

- Even if the interviewer does not see you arrive, someone else will. Anoraks and plastic macs are the pits. Invest in a decent coat.

- Carry only a briefcase (a handbag is an alternative for women, but do not carry both). Go to the bottom of the class if you arrive with one or more plastic carrier bags. Do your shopping after the interview.

- Never neglect personal hygiene. Dirty nails are a killer. So is lank and greasy hair.

- Even worse are odours. Use a (fragrance free) deodorant and, particularly if you smoke, a mouthwash. Women should apply perfume only very discreetly, if at all, and men are definitely advised to leave the after-shave for the weekend.

International aspects

Do not be fooled by the fact that in some continental European countries dress is apparently more casual than it is in the UK. Although men may wear jackets or blazers rather than suits, these are carefully co-ordinated. The overall effect is often smarter than the average British businessman's appearance. Style is particularly important in Italy.

In any case, at an interview you will rarely go wrong by erring on the side of formality.

Women only

While women have rather more freedom, or quandary, of choice than men, the following broad guidelines will apply in most cases.

- Whilst a suit is not obligatory, a jacket is – at least in all bar the most casual of environments. Women should take advantage of the fact that, unlike men, they can choose a variety of jacket lengths. Short women should normally wear a short jacket to keep them visually in proportion, but any women who have large thighs or hips should avoid jackets which accentuate these features by ending at the widest point.

- Do not try to wear the trousers at the interview, at least not literally.

- Skirts, like jackets, need to be selected carefully, bearing in mind your figure shape and the features which you consequently wish either to emphasise or conceal. You must also ensure that the skirt co-ordinates with the jacket.

- While a shorter skirt will give a woman who lacks inches a leggier look, it is generally better to err on the conservative side with regard to length.

- With all garments, but particularly skirts and jackets, a good fit is vital – neither baggy nor too tight. The latter is the greater sin. Never let anyone apply to you P. G. Wodehouse's tart comment: 'She looked as if she had been poured into her clothes and had forgotten to say "when"'.

- Belts give authority but must be the right width for your waist.

- Blouses sit right next to your face, so choose them with care, and make sure that pattern, colour and collar all go with your jacket.

- Knitwear is casual and reduces the amount of authority you convey.

- Classic shoes, enclosed and with leather uppers, are the most professional bet. Heels, which should never be scuffed, should strike a balance between the frumpy flattie and the 6-inch stiletto.

- Unless you are being interviewed in a heat wave, and your legs are smooth and tanned, always wear tights. They should be plain, not patterned, and do carry a spare pair – remember Murphy's Law?

- It should not be necessary to mention underwear, except that panty lines can show and dark lingerie may be visible through light clothes. Make sure that you are not the one to let yourself down.

- Make-up is considered to be an essential for the executive image, but not too much – and do take care to ensure that it never gets onto your collar.

- With jewellery, the rule, once again, is quality rather than quantity. Always wear earrings, but not dangly ones. A smart brooch can liven up a sober suit.

- Make sure that your hairstyle suits both your face shape and your professional image. You also need one that will still look good when you arrive at the interview, not just for five minutes after you have set it.

- If you wear glasses, select them with care – interviewers are going to be looking at your eyes for more of the time than all of the rest of you put together. They should complement the shape of your face, and you should avoid both old-fashioned and gimmicky designs.

- Scarves, gloves, watches, pens and so on should all be tasteful and of good quality. Do not spoil the ship for a ha'p'orth of tar.

Men only

The impression a man's clothes make can vary just as much as a woman's, even though his choices are fewer. Watch the following points.

- Suits are *de rigueur* for interviews at executive level in the UK.

- Darker shades give increased authority but black makes you look like an undertaker. Browns and greens give a rustic impression, as do tweeds.

- If you buy suits off the peg, do make sure that the jacket fits properly across the shoulders and that the sleeve length is correct – when your arms are by your sides the sleeves should end at the thumb knuckle, where hand meets arm.

- Trousers with turn-ups make legs look shorter.

- If your trousers have belt loops, wear a belt. Braces may be more flattering if your waist is not exactly trim, but avoid trying to emulate those worn by Sir John Harvey-Jones unless you can also match his personality.

- Waistcoats do not go with double-breasted suits. If you do wear a waistcoat, the done thing is to leave the bottom button unfastened.

- Buy good quality shirts in colours that complement your complexion. Shirt sleeves should be long enough to show about $\frac{1}{2}$ to $\frac{3}{4}$ inch of cuff below the jacket. A correct collar size will enable you to insert one finger between the collar and your neck.

- Ties offer the greatest opportunity for the male to make a personal statement and are consequently also the greatest potential hazard. Try to strike a balance between being deadly dull on the one hand and ruining an otherwise professional impact on the other by being patently crass. Pre-matched shirts and ties are out unless you actually want to be labelled a chain store clone. Prefer silk to polyester, and take the trouble to tie a neat knot which stays in place.

- Socks are the next most hazardous area. Wear plain ones rather than the pair the kids bought you for Father's Day, and remember that an expanse of hairy leg is unlikely to enhance the interviewer's opinion of you.

- Black is the safest colour for shoes. Suede is distinctly naff.

- Identity bracelets come into the same category as suede shoes. The only permissible items of jewellery, unless you count your watch (not plastic, please), are a signet ring or wedding band and cufflinks – tasteful, good quality ones.

- Hair must be cut regularly and in a businesslike style. Sorry, but you cannot be an executive and look like a rock star.

- If you are thinning on top, do not make yourself look silly by combing a few lonely strands across a shining bald pate. Be equally wary of hairpieces, unless you can afford to spend a fortune on one that really does look natural.

- A significant proportion of interviewers are prejudiced against facial fuzz, especially beards.

- Glasses are a key area. The interviewer will be looking into your eyes for at least half the time. Pick a style which not only complements your face shape but also avoids being either fuddy-duddy or trendy.

- Do not let yourself down with cheap accessories. Bic pens and scuffed briefcases do not fit with the senior executive image.

Looking your age

First impressions become even more important, if that is possible, as time goes on. One recruiter used to get his receptionist to guess the ages of candidates when they arrived for interview. On one occasion, she put two candidates as, respectively, 40 and 60. In reality they were both within a few months of 50. The older you get, the more attention you need to pay to your appearance.

 TELL-TALE SIGNS OF AGE

Here are a few of the most telling factors.

- **Glasses.** Bear in mind the amount of time the interviewer will be looking you in the eye. Half-moon glasses add a good ten years to your appearance, while specs on strings consign you to the Darby and Joan club.

- **Hair.** If you do colour grey hair, make sure it is not blatantly obvious. Keep your hairstyle reasonably modern, but do not try to emulate a 20-year-old, as you will only succeed in looking ridiculous. Men should bear in mind the comments under 'Men only', above, about bald patches and hairpieces.

continued overleaf

TELL-TALE SIGNS OF AGE – continued

- **Weight.** It is natural to put on a few pounds as you get older. Some put on a few stones. Take care to choose clothes which minimise the effects on your contours.
- **Posture.** If your chin or shoulders begin to sag, people will assume that you are wilting. Keep your chin up and your back straight.
- **Vigour.** Show that, even if you can no longer match the energy levels of your youth, you are far from having run out of steam. Move briskly and positively.
- **Speech.** It is important not only to maintain a lively voice, but also to watch the words you use. Derogatory references to young people and new-fangled ideas are a dead giveaway.
- **Attitude.** You really are only as old as you feel. Think young and you will feel young and give the impression of actually being younger. Think old at your peril.

Health and fitness

All of this will, of course, be a lot easier if you keep yourself in good shape. Rightly or wrongly, interviewers do discriminate against candidates who are overweight, seem to have trouble with their breathing, are subject to coughing or just look unhealthy.

Getting in shape does not have to mean gruelling sessions in the gym or running a marathon. Particularly if you have been neglecting exercise for longer than you wish to admit, overdoing it may well be positively dangerous. Gentler pursuits like golf, swimming or walking can, if practised regularly, do wonders for your skin and body tone, and for the way you feel about yourself.

Keep your mind in trim, too. Always be learning something new. Seek out the company of stimulating people and avoid associating only with your own age group.

Nutrition is another important consideration. There is a lot of truth in the saying, 'You are what you eat'. Forget the freaky diets. Rapid weight loss is all too often followed by an equally rapid weight gain. Cut down on sugar and fat if you need to, but maintain a balanced regime including adequate supplies of protein, as well as plenty of fruit and vegetables.

Finally, do not assume that this section is just for those who are in, or approaching, their middle years. Health and fitness affect the first impressions made by candidates of all ages.

"IF YOU WANT THE JOB, YOU WILL BE SOAKING UP EVERY FIRST IMPRESSION YOU CAN OF THE INTERVIEWER."

23 Why the best candidate doesn't always get the job

Establishing rapport and controlling the interview

Try answering this question: while the interviewer is absorbing all those (hopefully positive) first impressions of you, what are you doing? If you want the job, what you will be doing is soaking up every available first impression you can of the interviewer.

Are you too nervous to notice anything about the interviewer? Well, here is your chance to kill two birds with one stone. The most effective way of avoiding being preoccupied with yourself and the impression you are making, which is what is at the root of nervousness, is to concentrate completely on the other person, leaving no room for self-consciousness.

The reason for paying all your attention to the signals being given off by the interviewer is to help you to establish as much rapport as you can in the shortest possible period of time.

Professional recruiters will be trying to do exactly the same thing themselves, so you should have an easier time with them than with line managers, who probably conduct interviews less frequently than you attend them and consequently may well be more nervous than you.

In order to achieve rapport you do not have to be sycophantic. The last thing you want to do is give the impression that you are a Grade A creep. In any case, it does not matter if you and the interviewer are very different in terms of background, attitudes or personality – opposites can, and often do, attract. You do, however, have to establish an effective working relationship, and this embraces such factors as courtesy, consideration, respect and trust. If you are attending a screening interview, with a recruitment consultant or personnel manager, the amount of rapport need only be sufficient for the purposes of that brief meeting. If you are meeting your potential boss, on the other hand, it clearly needs to go a lot deeper. Personal chemistry will be a major factor in the ultimate hiring decision.

In making your initial assessment of the person you are meeting, it helps if you can learn to recognise the different types of individual you may be dealing with and respond to them appropriately.

For example, the affable type of interviewer may want to spend several minutes chatting about what sort of journey you had, whether you are familiar with the area and so on before even beginning to get down to business. A busy, hard-nosed line manager, on the other hand, may keep the preliminaries to the bare minimum, diving almost straight into the matter in hand. If you have any sense, you will clearly play along in both cases.

Spotting the clues

In the above examples, the behavioural differences would have been self-evident from the first few words spoken. In practice, you can often pick up the signals before interviewers even open their mouths, especially if they are seeing you in their own office rather than an impersonal meeting room. For instance, the affable type would probably have had photographs of spouse and children on the desk, plants on the window sill and a plaque commemorating some sporting or business achievement on the wall.

Clothes, pens, briefcases, the tidiness or otherwise of the office – these, and a host of other factors, are all part of the non-verbal communication on which, consciously or otherwise, we base so many of our decisions.

You can continue to make use of the non-verbals as the meeting progresses. By watching the interviewer's body language, you should be able to tell how things are going. An alert posture with the body leaning slightly forwards, the occasional encouraging nod of the head, good eye contact and so on will indicate that the other person is attentive and interested. If the interviewer slumps back in the chair and fails to make much eye contact, this may well be a warning that you are waffling. Sudden movements such as a jerking of the head or a pronounced blinking of the eyes often indicate surprise or disbelief.

Experienced interviewers will, of course, be picking up the same signals from you, checking whether your subsequent behaviour validates their initial judgement. Although a bad first impression may be difficult to wipe out, a good first impression is not necessarily so readily sustained. You must therefore stay on your guard and continue to give off the right signals, displaying an alert, positive manner and trying to avoid sending any negative signals. While it is difficult to control your own body language for any length of time, here are a few things to try to steer clear of.

- Sitting with arms crossed, which looks defensive.

- Covering your mouth with your hand when you are speaking.

- Lounging in your chair instead of maintaining an upright, but not stiff, posture.

- Fidgeting, which makes you look either uncomfortable or nervous.

- Insufficient eye contact. It is acceptable to avert your eyes while considering the answer to a question, but look at the interviewer when delivering it – and do pay attention when you are being spoken to.

- Too much eye contact. While you should be looking at the interviewer for about two-thirds of the time, do glance away intermittently. When your eyes are meeting the interviewer's, avoid staring – instead send a positive message such as interest or enthusiasm.

What's in a question?

Although first impressions are based heavily on non-verbal signals, and body language certainly continues to play an important role throughout an interview, as the meeting progresses an increasing amount of the interviewer's judgement will be based on what you say. If you got off on the wrong foot, it may be difficult to talk your way back in, but it is very much easier to do the opposite and, having started well, then proceed to talk yourself out of the job.

The biggest danger is doing just that – talking too much. It is a far more common problem than saying too little. In case this sounds as though you will be damned if you do, and damned if you don't, a few words of explanation are probably required.

It is, quite obviously, vital that you find the opportunities to get all of your key selling points across. What is more, good interviewers will ensure that you do more of the talking than they do. On the other hand, you must, at all costs, avoid waffling. Be particularly wary of open questions. If the interviewer says, 'Give me a brief summary of your career' and, 10 minutes later, you are still talking about things that happened 20 years ago, you have blown it. Efficient executives communicate clearly and succinctly. That question you were asked may have had more to do with testing your communication skills than finding out about what was, in any case, largely self-evident from your CV.

Although open questions have their dangers, they do at least give you the chance, provided that you stick to the point, to say what you want to. Professional recruiters use open questions a lot, both as ends in themselves and as the first stage in what is known as an interview funnel.

The open question with which the funnel begins gets you talking freely. The interviewer waits for something interesting to come up, such as a major success you claim to have achieved, then latches on to it, probing more deeply by saying something like, 'That's interesting – could you just tell me in a bit more detail exactly what you did?' Further probes close you in further and further – hence the funnel analogy – until the interviewer finally pins you down and you either substantiate your claim or it is shown to be unjustified. This technique works to your advantage if you can back up your claims, but to your detriment if you cannot.

Open questions can be particularly tricky when you are on sticky ground, such as explaining why you apparently resigned from your last job without having another position to go to. Rather than asking openly if you were fired, the interviewer may simply say, 'Why did you leave XYZ?' It is all too easy to say far more than you intend, especially if the interviewer employs reflective questions (encouraging you to go on by repeating words or phrases you have just used) or, worse still, saying nothing in reply when you stop speaking. Most people feel uncomfortable when faced with a silence, and consequently proceed to fill the empty space – frequently blabbing themselves into ever deeper water – rather than sitting it out and forcing the interviewer to pick up the baton.

While you should avoid saying too much, it is equally dangerous, on the other hand, to leave obvious doubts or suspicions to fester in the interviewer's mind. As in any sales presentation, objections do need to be identified and dealt with. If you have prepared thoroughly, you should have spotted potentially difficult areas and have decided in advance the best methods of dealing with them. This in itself should enable you to respond clearly and concisely when they come up, rather than talking yourself into trouble.

The other side of the coin

Professional recruiters use questions skilfully. If you are right for the job and have prepared thoroughly for the interview, this can only be to your benefit. Untrained interviewers, on the other hand, can make it more difficult for you to demonstrate your worth because they are prone to making greater use of what are all too often the wrong kinds of questions. These include the following types.

- Leading questions, e.g. 'Wouldn't you agree that . . .' Although the desired answer has been flagged up for you, simply sitting there and agreeing will hardly advance your campaign to show what you can offer the company, unless they are simply looking for a 'yes person' – in which case it is probably not the job you want anyway. Occasionally, canny interviewers may use leading questions to see whether you have sufficient character and conviction to disagree. Body language, especially the expression in their eyes, may be the best way of sussing this out.

- Multiple questions, i.e. asking two or more questions at the same time. This can be confusing. Unless you want to cop out of the difficult part of a multiple question by answering the easy bit, the best way of dealing with this is to say that you will take each point in turn and then proceed to do precisely that.

- Closed questions. Sometimes a question which can be answered only by 'yes' or 'no' is appropriate. More often it is not. At the very least it limits your opportunity to sell yourself. At worst a closed answer could be positively misleading. Do what politicians do when the media try to trap them in this way. Insist on opening the question out by saying something like, 'That is actually quite a complex issue' and then exploring it fully.

In addition to using inappropriate questions, untrained interviewers also have a tendency to do far too much of the talking themselves. This can be a real problem, facing you with the dilemma of either failing to get your USPs across because you cannot get a word in edgeways or of appearing rude by butting in. Since it would give offence to interrupt and blatantly switch the discussion from what the interviewer was rattling on about to what you want to say, the best approach is to display interest while biding your time then, when you see an opportunity to link what the interviewer has said to something you wish to say, seize the initiative without appearing to break the flow of the conversation. The professional recruiter's trick of reflecting the other person's words back to them can be invaluable in this kind of situation.

The mob scene

So far we have been talking in the context of the one-to-one interview – the most common kind. Sometimes, however, and especially when the job is in local government, with some official body, or with a professional partnership, you may have to face the dreaded group, or panel, interview. This is inevitably more stressful, but you can minimise the stress if you follow a few basic ground rules.

- When you are being asked a question, maintain eye contact with the person who is speaking.
- When you reply, concentrate mainly on that person, but include all the others by glancing round and establishing intermittent eye contact with them too.

- Take care not to ignore members of the panel who are seated to one side or the other of you. It is all too easy to pay most attention to those within an easy line of vision.

- Although the implication of a group interview is that the decision will be made by consensus, there may be a first among equals and it is sensible to pay this individual proportionately greater attention. If you cannot identify the *primus inter pares* from titles (e.g. chairperson, senior partner), watch body language. The rest of the group will probably tend to turn their bodies and eyes towards the key person in subconscious deference.

- If, before you have finished answering one question, someone else chips in with another, say politely that you will answer the second one in a moment, as soon as you have responded fully to the first. As a result of poor preparation or chairing, this is unfortunately an all too common hazard.

- If you feel yourself getting flustered, cool it by taking a breath, or a sip of water, before responding to a question or continuing with what you were saying.

- When you are given the opportunity to ask questions, try to draw in as many of the members of the panel as possible.

- As you continually move your eye contact round throughout the interview, try to get a feel, by their body language, of which members of the panel are on your side and which have still to be won over. Try to get their doubts out into the open, so that you can deal with them.

Don't relax

After a formal interview, whether it is with one person, two or three, or a whole gang, you may be given the opportunity to have a guided tour of the organisation's premises. Although this may genuinely be primarily for your benefit, do not treat it solely as a one-way situation. You will be expected not only to display genuine interest, but also to ask relevant questions and make sensible comments. While you should avoid offering instant, and probably ill-informed, solutions to any problems that are raised, going to the other extreme and just wandering round looking relieved that the interview is over could equally well blow your chances of the job.

Another situation in which it is all too easy to drop your guard is the social meeting. You may be invited to lunch or dinner, or asked to meet some of your future colleagues over a drink. Since it is important to be sure that you will fit into the culture of the organisation, these occasions can be mutually beneficial, but they do also have their dangers.

Although it is important to relax a little and be less formal than you would be in an interview, you still need to be cautious. This applies particularly to alcohol. The best rule is to say that you have to drive your car later on (even if you do not) and either stay off alcohol altogether or limit yourself to a single drink, taking care to sip it extremely slowly. If you are having a meal, avoid any dishes which are messy to eat, even if they are your favourites. Pay your host the compliment of enjoying the meal but do not make a pig of yourself.

Finally, do prepare for this kind of meeting just as thoroughly as you would for a normal interview. While there will be a certain amount of purely social chat, you should also be ready to advance your candidature by discussing relevant business issues.

International aspects

When you are being interviewed in an overseas country, or for that matter even in the UK but by someone who is not British, you need to be aware of the cultural differences and their implications. For instance, while it is common nowadays to use first names in an interview in the UK (once the interviewer has taken the initiative), people are much less familiar in Germany, addressing each other by formal – and often complex – titles. The French will probably get onto first names eventually, but not as quickly as the British, and the 'tu' form would certainly never be substituted for 'vous' at an interview.

Another difference relates to the fact that although a touch of humour might be considered desirable in an interview in the UK, as a means of relaxing the atmosphere, it would be thought frivolous in Germany where meetings of all kinds tend to be more formal and serious. A further example to watch out for is when a Japanese executive gives you a business card. Do not just pop it into your pocket. You are expected to sit and gaze at it in reverence for a few moments. Ideally, you should have one of your own to give in return, so that this gesture of respect can be reciprocated.

Body language has some major differences too. In terms of interpersonal space, people from the Middle East tend to stand much closer to each other than we do. While they may make a European feel uncomfortable, the distance a European maintains seems positively aloof to them. Crossing the legs is considered rude in the Middle East, while showing someone the soles of your feet is positively insulting.

Gestures may also have different meanings. There are even countries where nodding the head means 'no' and shaking it means 'yes'. What it all adds up to is that you need to mug up on such matters – there are books and even courses available – if you are to avoid misinterpreting behaviour or, worse still, giving offence.

Thanks for the memory

Since last impressions are, in many ways, just as important as first impressions, do be sure to end on a positive note. Without being insincere or nauseatingly gushy, thank the interviewer for their time, and say that you enjoyed the meeting and look forward to hearing about the next stage. If you have not already been told what that is, there is no harm in asking.

There are, however, two things you should not ask about. One is whether you have got the job, or a place on the short-list if it was just a screening interview. The other mistake is to ask for expenses. If the company is going to reimburse them, they will make the offer. If it has cost you a lot of money to attend the interview and you feel strongly about it, at least wait until you have heard the outcome before raising the matter.

Finally, when the moment comes to say goodbye to the interviewer, do so with a firm handshake and a warm smile. That is the very last impression you will leave, so it needs to be a good one.

After the interview, ignore the advice sometimes given to send a letter thanking the interviewer and confirming your interest in the position. The vast majority of people in this country regard such behaviour with distaste. A telephone call is even worse.

However, where you have been to an interview arranged by a headhunter, selection consultant or agency with one of their clients, it is a good idea to ring the consultant and report back on how it went. The consultant will appreciate being kept informed both about your ongoing interest and about your reaction to the client. If you leave it a day or two before you call, you may in return be able to obtain some feedback on your performance at the interview.

After that, it is unfortunately just a matter of being patient. Although news often seems to take far longer than it ideally should, chasing the interviewer is likely to do you more harm than good. The majority of prospective employers will tell you why you have finally been ruled out, so to an extent no news is good news – even if it only means that the delay is due to the job having been offered to someone else but you being held in reserve in case the first choice declines.

Should you be rejected, there is equally little to be gained by ringing the interviewer and asking why, even if you do phrase it as a request for advice as to what you might do better in future. Such requests are embarrassing to the interviewer, who will probably not tell you the truth in any case.

Dos and don'ts

The chances of being successful, rather than rejected, can be increased significantly by keeping in mind the key dos and don'ts. Here are some of the things that most commonly turn interviewers off.

- Arriving late, especially without the courtesy of a phone call.
- Unprofessional appearance.

- Weak or clammy handshake.
- Over-familiarity, e.g. using first names without being asked to.
- Lack of eye contact.
- Fidgeting.
- Lounging.
- V.D. (verbal diarrhoea).
- Jargon.
- Name dropping.
- Knocking previous employers.
- Being evasive.
- Failing to keep to the point.
- Playing games.
- Raising the question of remuneration at an early stage.
- Being more interested in what you can take than what you can give.
- Concern with trivialities like hours of work.
- Indecisiveness.
- Apathy.

And now for the dos.

- Prepare thoroughly.
- Keep your objective firmly in mind.
- Put yourself in the other person's shoes.
- Consciously seek to establish rapport.
- Watch – and respond to – not only what interviewers say, but also their tone of voice and body language.
- Treat the meeting as a two-way conversation between equals who respect each other's professionalism, not as a question and answer session controlled by the interviewer.

- Ensure that you cover the whole of your agenda and do not fail to communicate any of the ways in which you can add value to the organisation.

"A MINEFIELD FOR
THE UNWARY."

24 Interview add ons

Tests, assessment centres and
other selection tools

If you have ever wondered, after attending a badly conducted interview, just how good an indicator of future performance the interview actually is, you are not alone. Various surveys have shown that the predictive success rate of the average interview is in fact not much better than pure chance.

Untrained interviewers score particularly badly, but even professional recruiters do not exactly produce ratings which inspire very much confidence. Since the tendency to make instant judgements in the first few minutes – or even seconds – of an interview probably has a lot to do with this, it emphasises just how important it is to ensure that you make a good first impression.

While many employers continue to rely solely on the interview, in spite of its obvious shortcomings, an increasing number are supplementing it both with tests and with a variety of other selection aids, ranging from assessment centres to graphology. If you are not to be thrown out of your stride by these techniques, you need to know what to expect and how to handle them.

A testing time

Tests are the most commonly used form of interview add on. Their (at least pseudo-) scientific nature appeals strongly to employers who have been rattled by scare stories about interview unreliability. The idea of being able to allocate people marks, and offer the job to the one with the highest score, has the attraction of taking the onus off the decision maker – although, in practice, by no means all tests permit this kind of simple comparison and very few recruiters would, in any case, recommend such a simplistic approach.

Reliable information about the validity of tests as predictors of job performance is difficult to come by, since most of the statistics are produced by the people who develop and sell the tests – not exactly an independent source. The picture is hardly made any clearer either by the obsession the testing fraternity has with using a volume and complexity of jargon that makes computerspeak seem like plain English, or by the acrimonious rows between the supporters of different kinds of test.

What is perhaps an even greater problem than whether tests actually do what they claim to do, however, is whether employers select the correct test for a given purpose. The failure to do this is often compounded by a tendency among employers to interpret the output of tests negatively, paying less attention to indications of a candidate's plus points and potential, than to the odd word in a report which sows a seed of doubt and suggests that a hiring may involve a risk which could subsequently rebound on the decision maker. No wonder that the Institute of Personnel and Development (IPD, formerly the IPM) has described psychometric testing as 'a minefield for the unwary'.

What is a test?

The term 'test' gets applied very loosely to a whole range of instruments. The main types you are likely to encounter in the selection process are pencil and paper (or computer keyboard) exercises, in which you answer a number of questions; and activity tests, in which you simulate tasks you would carry out in the course of a job. The latter, which include, for example, in-tray exercises and group discussions, will be examined when we look at assessment centres.

The former can be further subdivided into performance-based tests, under which you are scored on the basis either of the time you take to complete tasks or of the number of correct answers you achieve; and self-description questionnaires, the output from which is a profile, describing your temperament in terms of a range of parameters such as introversion and extroversion. Performance-based tests are used to measure abilities, aptitudes, attainments and skills, while self-description questionnaires are used to assess rather more subjective areas like interests, motivation and personal qualities.

Most such tests are of either the multiple choice variety, in which you have to choose your answer to each question from several alternatives, or the forced choice variety, in which you have to choose between just two options. The problem with the forced choice type is that you often find either that neither of the two options really applies, or that both do with almost equal relevance. You may occasionally come across free response tests, in which you can give answers in your own words, but these are difficult to mark and consequently not greatly favoured.

Ideally a battery of tests should be used, rather than just one, preferably with a qualified psychologist on hand to interpret them and discuss the results with you. In practice, however, a day, or even half a day, spent with a psychologist is expensive in terms both of candidate time and company money. Many organisations just throw in the odd test, selection being based in the better cases on proper trials and experience to verify its predictive value, and in the less laudable instances on its specious appeal or on the persuasiveness of a salesperson.

Presumably also for cost reasons, some companies test just the final one or two candidates, and only do this at the end of the selection process, as a kind of insurance policy against having missed some fatal flaw. It would be much more useful to apply tests at an early stage, and use the output as a basis for discussion at interview.

Test types and tactics

So much for categories and formats, but what kinds of test are you likely to encounter and how should you deal with them? The types you may come across in the selection process at managerial levels include the following.

- **Ability**
  The most commonly tested ability being intelligence, often incorrectly referred to as 'IQ'. These tests usually involve solving a number of problems which are often divided into sections such as numerical, verbal, logical and spatial. Your performance on such tests, like your ability to solve crossword puzzles, can be improved sufficiently with familiarity and practice to make the difference between being above or

below the pass mark. If you cannot get hold of actual test blanks, you can buy books containing tests of this type. Apart from preparing you for any tests you may encounter, they are useful for sharpening up your mind generally.

- **Interests**
  These are more likely to be encountered at a career guidance session than as part of a selection process.

- **Management style**
  Questionnaires may be used to assess whether your style is autocratic, consultative or somewhere in between. There is not necessarily any one right style. Even within a given organisation and culture, different managers may be equally successful, even though their styles vary greatly.

- **Motivation**
  Not too often found in practice, due both to the complex cocktail of factors which comprise motivation, and because it is so dependent on the relationship between an individual and an organisation. The same person might be highly motivated in one environment and completely demotivated in another.

- **Personality**
  A number of personality tests may be encountered in the selection process, including some which were not designed for use in recruitment at all. Unfortunately the ones which appear to candidates to be most plausible tend to be the least reliable, and vice versa, so do not be surprised if you cannot see the relevance of some of the questions you have to answer. These tests, or – more correctly – questionnaires or inventories, are usually of the self-description variety. Although their designers claim to build in 'lie-detectors', candidates may be tempted to answer with what they perceive to be the desired, rather than true, answers. For example, if a job seems to call for an extrovert and there are questions like 'Do you prefer to spend an evening (a) reading a book, or (b) going to a party', you do not have to be Machiavelli to plump for the latter.

- **Team building**

  The most widely used questionnaire, Meredith Belbin's Self-Perception Inventory, classifies people into various different team roles, each of which has its value. Even if you were to familiarise yourself with these roles, and to guess which one would make you the ideal candidate for the job, the nature of the questionnaire would make it difficult to fake. It is probably, therefore, best to answer honestly.

At managerial level you are unlikely to encounter either aptitude tests (used to assess people's potential for such roles as computer programming or operating machinery) or attainment tests (again used mainly at lower levels, e.g. word processing tests given to interviewees for secretarial jobs). Executives' aptitudes and attainments are more likely to be evaluated by technical questions or by the kinds of participative exercises used in assessment centres.

Activity tests

The fundamental principle behind assessment centres is job simulation. Given that it is impracticable to put a bunch of applicants through a trial period in a job in order to decide who is going to produce the best performance, it is argued that the next best thing is to create situations which, though inevitably artificial, do replicate as closely as possible the job in question, or at least key elements of it. Therefore, while a full assessment centre programme may well include interviews, and pen and paper tests, the emphasis will be on what are often referred to as activity tests – the sorts of things you may have done on management training courses. There will also probably be group discussions.

These attempts to simulate the work situation are both a strength and a weakness of assessment centres. The idea makes a lot of sense, but it is difficult to put into practice because it involves getting a bunch of job applicants, the four or five people on a short-list for example, together for at least one whole day, quite possibly two. This may be practicable when a large company is making an internal promotion, but it presents major problems when the candidates are all currently employed in demanding jobs of their own – and, of course, bringing together such applicants also raises the thorny problem of confidentiality.

This difficulty, combined with the inevitably high costs of running assessment centres, results in them not being as widely used for external selection purposes as you might expect. However, because the principle behind them is sound, individual elements of them – the activity tests and group discussions – may well be encountered as part of an executive selection process.

Group exercises

When short-list interviews for a position are being set up, candidates may be asked to leave the whole day free so that, in addition to being interviewed by one or more people, they can participate in a group exercise or discussion. The dynamics of this are, to say the least, interesting. Although the task or problem with which the group is presented may involve the need to work together as a team, the candidates for the position in question will be aware that they are being observed and will consequently feel the urge to compete with each other to make the best impression.

Such exercises vary a great deal in structure, depending on such factors as:

- whether objectives are tightly defined or are expressed only in general terms, leaving the group to define them more precisely;
- whether a leader is nominated in advance or simply left to emerge;
- how much preparation time is allowed – if any;
- the extent to which competition and co-operation are deliberately built into the briefing;
- whether or not specific roles are assigned to the various participants.

Since the variation is so great, no perfect formula can be provided for dealing with such situations – you need to be ready to think on your feet. Nevertheless, here are a few basic rules which will stand you in good stead.

- Keep your cool. Careful study of the briefing you are given will often reveal information which is deliberately designed to be missed by those who dive in feet first.
- While you need to make a contribution which will be noticed, do not

try to monopolise the show. Yes, you have guessed, it is quality rather than quantity that you should aim for once again.

- In choosing how to contribute, try to relate the exercise to what you know, from interviews, from the job spec and so on, about the type of person they are looking for. Aim to demonstrate these qualities in what you say and do.

- Do not openly knock the other members of the group. You are likely to score more brownie points by acknowledging the value of someone else's contribution – then going on to make your own.

In-tray exercises

One of the most popular individual, as opposed to group, selection aids is the in-tray, or basket, exercise. You are asked to assume that you come into the office one morning to face either a series of crises in your normal job or the need, due to some emergency, to take over someone else's job. There will, needless to say, be a number of conflicting priorities – far more than you can possibly deal with single-handed in the time available. You will be assessed on both the decisions you take and the reasons you give for making them.

Once again, the first requirement is not to go into a flat spin. Beyond that, it helps to know what the exercise is trying to assess, so that you can aim to demonstrate the required qualities. These include:

- your ability to work under pressure;
- your skill in prioritising a number of conflicting requirements;
- the ability to sift the wheat from the chaff – the in-tray will usually contain a certain amount of information which can be binned straight away;
- how good you are at delegation;
- whether you can distinguish between fact and opinion;
- how sensitive you are;
- your capacity for logical reasoning, and analytical and critical thinking;
- how flexible and imaginative you are.

Reports and presentations

If the job you are applying for is one in which report writing is a key element, you may be asked to bring with you to the interview a relevant piece of written work you have produced. Alternatively, since the prospective employer has no way of checking that such a sample is entirely your own work, you may be asked to write a brief report or essay, based on information, or a subject, which will be given to you. Essay subjects can range from topics of general interest to current issues relevant to the industry in question, and they may even be as specific as 'How would you tackle your first three months in this job?'.

As yet, it is rare for candidates to be asked to submit a video but, when oral presentations are important in the position in question, you may be asked to make a presentation, either just to the interviewer or to a small group of people. Sometimes you are given the opportunity to prepare visual aids such as flip charts or slides for overhead projection. On other occasions you may be given very little time to prepare anything at all.

These occasions are inevitably nerve-racking but remember that everybody is in the same boat. Keep your head and do, in particular, take care to ensure that you have understood the briefing properly. If you are faced with a demand to make a presentation at zero notice, you can always gain a breathing space by asking to use the cloakroom before you proceed.

Eyes and ears

Other forms of activity test which are sometimes encountered include fact-finding and listening exercises. The former, which test things like analytical and reasoning ability, involve you being given a certain amount of information to start with, then having to obtain more, usually with a view to making a decision or recommendation – which may be used as an opportunity to make you give a presentation. Listening exercises use either film, tape or a live presentation to provide you with information, then test your perceptiveness of it by using questionnaires.

You may also, occasionally, be presented with case studies. For example, candidates for a finance director's position may be asked to compare the profit and loss accounts and balance sheets of two companies, and to comment on such matters as the comparative performance and strategies of the two businesses. An exercise like this – which will probably have one or two 'tricks' built into the information provided – tests the ability to:

- keep calm and analyse the information thoroughly;

- consider not only technical, but also commercial, aspects;

- make a brief oral presentation with minimal preparation.

Then there is the dreaded role play. You may be asked to participate in such scenarios as a client meeting, a negotiation or a staff appraisal, with a representative of your potential employer playing the other role. While many people seem to be thrown by role plays, they do normally represent situations which you should have encountered many times before in your everyday work experience, so they should not present undue problems if you simply ignore the pressures of the selection process and behave as you normally would in real life.

How to respond

Tests – using that term in the very broadest sense – seem to throw candidates far more than the interview does, however nerve-racking that may be for some people. The reason for this may well be primarily the fear of the unknown. Interviews are at least something most of us are familiar with. Tests tend to be shrouded in an element of mystery.

Occasionally candidates do refuse to take tests. In some cases they may actually be justified in doing so. The potential employer could well be using a test that is totally unsuitable for the purpose in question, or may be failing to observe accepted administration procedures. Unfortunately, though, the assumption is likely to be that, if you refuse, you must have something to hide. It is rather like ducking a question in an interview. Generally speaking, therefore, you would be advised to be prepared by acquiring in advance a knowledge of the kinds of tests you are likely to be faced with, then, when you do get presented with one, to keep a cool head and give it your best shot.

One exception to this rule is where you believe you may be disadvantaged, perhaps because English is not your first language or because you have a disability. Such factors should be brought to the attention of the potential employer, who should make arrangements to compensate for them. There is also evidence that some tests contain built-in cultural biases which may discriminate against women or ethnic minorities, but you would have to be an expert on test construction to be able to identify and prove this so it is probably best left to those who do possess such expertise – test publishers, HR professionals and equal opportunities bodies are aware of the potential problem.

The ethics of the testing business dictate that anyone who is given a test is entitled to feedback on the results and a chance to discuss apparently erroneous assessments. Primarily for cost reasons – it is very time consuming – this is rarely volunteered. If you do decide to insist on your rights and ask for feedback, you may prefer to play safe and wait until you have heard whether you have got the job or not, in case you are seen as a nuisance, or even as a troublemaker.

Graphology

Widely used in France, and also in Switzerland and French-speaking Belgium, graphology is still not generally accepted in the UK as a selection tool. Its theoretical basis actually seems eminently sound. At any given school, it is argued, all the children will be taught to write in exactly the same script yet, by the time they reach adulthood, they will all be writing in a uniquely different way, as identifiable as a fingerprint. Graphology argues that the development of each person's individual script must be driven by subconscious factors relating to their different temperaments and that, by analysing the various elements of a person's handwriting, it is therefore possible to deduce relevant information about their personality, and physical and mental health.

While many people would probably agree with the first part of this argument – something, after all, must cause the change from a standard to a uniquely individual script – the second part is more contentious. Some practitioners in graphology do produce remarkably accurate analyses, identifying factors ranging from basic personality traits to disorders like heart problems, alcoholism and sexual perversions. On the other hand, there is a strong subjective element. Two or more practitioners cannot always be guaranteed to agree on an analysis of the same handwriting sample. Graphology seems to be as much of an art as a science and, as such, may have as much in common with the interview as with the psychometric test.

"THE WHOLE THING CAN GET A BIT LIKE A GAME OF POKER."

25 The bird in the hand

Job offers: decisions and negotiations

Congratulations! You triumphed at the interview, you survived the tests, you have got the offer. What you have to ask yourself now is, 'Should I accept?'.

To those readers who have been unemployed for some considerable time, that may seem like a rather silly question. Yet they are the very ones who run the greatest risk of either making a disastrously wrong decision or, by jumping at the offer, of failing to negotiate the best deal. When you have spent months out of work, devoting yourself full-time to the job search, it is very tempting to accept the first offer you get, especially if it arrives just as you are starting to become desperate.

Those who currently have jobs are likely to be more careful. Even if their progress is blocked where they are, or their company is in a parlous state, they know how easy it might be to jump out of the frying pan into the fire.

So, when the elation has died down, you need to take the time to consider carefully every aspect of the situation before you commit yourself. If the offer is made face to face, or over the telephone – either by the potential employer or by a recruitment consultant – acknowledge that you are pleased to have received it but say that you would like to think it over before giving your decision. Ask for it to be confirmed in writing – that will buy you a bit more time. When, on the other hand, the first you hear of the offer is a letter arriving on your doormat, you are spared the need for an instant response and automatically get time to think it over.

How much time you have to consider it varies widely, but several days would normally be reasonable and, at a push, you can get away with up to a couple of weeks. Some companies actually put a limit on it, saying that the offer is only open for a given amount of time. While you need a sufficient breathing space to talk things over with your partner and do any checking around which is required, do not take more time than you need. Put yourself in the position of any other candidates who are being held as reserves in case you decline and be considerate to them. Do, on the other hand, be wary of any company that demands an immediate decision on a 'take it or leave it' basis.

What to check

By the time you get to an offer, which will probably be after two or three rounds of interviews, you might think you would already have all the information you need to make a decision. In reality, however, there are a number of reasons why it may only be at this late stage that vital information becomes available. Private companies may be unwilling to release their detailed accounts until they have narrowed the field down to the last candidate and know that they are genuinely interested. Professional partnerships are still more secretive. Even public companies may be wary of early disclosure of key facts, especially if – for example – these relate to plans regarding an expansion programme or the introduction of a new product.

Make sure, therefore, that you have all the information you need about the following.

- The company's financial situation – its profitability, liquidity and sources of funds (especially for financing any planned growth).

- The industry in which it operates, including both the general prospects for that business sector and the company's position in relation to its competitors.

- The company's power structure – how are decisions made and who really calls the shots?

- The key people – have you met all of the individuals who really count as far as the position you have been offered is concerned? If the company is part of a group, have you met relevant people from the parent company?

- If the ownership is in the hands of an individual or a family, what are the plans for succession? Is the company likely to be sold off?

- The culture – joining a new organisation inevitably involves an element of culture shock. Have you really got a feel for the likely extent of that? Especially where you are making a major change, for example from a large corporation to a private company, or from a British organisation to an American one, are you sure that you are going to be able to adapt?

- The reason for making the appointment – have you been told the truth? Has the position been imposed on the company, for example by the parent organisation or at the insistence of the company's bankers? If so, what kind of resentment are you going to face?

- Are there any other problems? Have you asked what difficulties face the company as a whole, and the person accepting this job in particular? Have you been given a 'warts and all' view or just the sunny side of the picture?

- Job title – if, for example, you are a 'director (designate)', how long will it be before the 'designate' is removed?

- The job – has it been defined fully and precisely enough for you to be sure it is the right move? Be particularly wary with newly created positions. Is there any overlap with posts held by other people and, if so, what are the implications?

- Performance measures – do you have a clear and detailed understanding of how your performance will be judged?

- Reporting lines – are there any ambiguities which need sorting out in order to avoid problems later?

- Authority – has the amount of authority you have, and any limits on it, been clearly defined? Is the authority you have been given in line with the responsibilities which you will be accepting?

- The resources you will need in order to do the job successfully – what guarantees do you have that they will be adequate?

- The remuneration package.

How to check

The first source of information is the company itself. If you do not have all the information you need, then do ask. There is nothing wrong with requesting either additional facts, or a further meeting to discuss pertinent matters. It is in both parties' interests to avoid making what could be an expensive mistake.

If you have concerns, or need reassurance, about the company's financial situation, you could ask for the opportunity to meet its professional advisers – the partner in its audit firm, or its bankers or lawyers.

For independent advice, do use your network. By now you should be familiar enough with networking to get any additional information you may need on the company itself, the industry it is in and its competitors. Try to get views on key people, too – especially the person you are going to be working for and, if it is not the same individual, whoever runs the company. When you meet people at interview they will, like you, probably be deliberately displaying their best side and many successful individuals can be highly charismatic, at least until you get to know them better.

If the selection process was handled by recruitment consultants, they may also be useful, but do not expect their advice to be totally unbiased, especially if part, or all, of their fee is dependent on filling the job. You are more likely to get impartial advice from any headhunters or consultants whom you know well but who were not involved in this particular assignment.

Finally, do talk the offer over fully with your partner, especially any implications on your domestic life like a longer journey to work, absences from home due to business travel, or the need to relocate. It is better to confront any problems before you take the job, rather than when it is too late.

Negotiating the package

Often, a company takes the initiative on the package and makes you an offer, leaving you with the options of either accepting, turning it down or negotiating. Sometimes, however, they will tell you they want to make you an offer, but ask you to attend a further meeting to discuss terms. At such a meeting, they may make the first move, or they may ask you what you expect to be paid, perhaps in the hope that you will bid low.

The whole thing can get a bit like a game of poker, which may suit you if you enjoy bluffing and gambling, and terrify you if you do not. In a game of poker success depends partly on the cards you have in your hand, and partly on how you play them.

By the time you come to negotiate on the remuneration package, you probably have the stronger hand. The company has identified you as the favoured candidate. Should you decline the offer, they will have to consider either turning to someone who is only their second choice or, if there are no other suitable candidates, starting all over again. This advantage is, nevertheless, balanced by the fact that the company probably has more experience in conducting negotiations than you do – unless, of course, you have done a lot of hard negotiating in the jobs you have previously held.

Where selection has been carried out by recruitment consultants, it is possible that they may act as intermediaries in the salary negotiations. This could have two advantages. Not only are they likely to be more experienced in such matters than you are, but they also have a vested interest in achieving a satisfactory outcome. In order to achieve this, they may try to persuade the company to up the ante. Indeed, where they are paid on a percentage of the salary which is finally agreed, rather than on a fixed fee, it will be in their own interest to do this.

Evaluating the offer

Regardless of who actually does any negotiating, however, you need to know whether you are being offered a fair figure for the job in question. How do you find out?

Salary surveys are not a great deal of use for this purpose. At best they will give only broad markers. They are usually out of date by the time they appear, they quote very wide ranges, and you have to take into account so many different factors – like size of companies, the number of levels of management, regional pay variations and so on – that you will be lucky to arrive at any conclusions which are sufficiently precise.

To be fair, by the time you get to a senior level of management, there is no precise rate for any given job. The same job title may mean very different things in different companies – and that is before you start taking into account the variations in performance between one individual and another. There are, however, two groups of people who will be able to give you a pretty good view on the matter.

The first group are professional recruiters. A headhunter or recruitment consultant who is handling the job in question may not be entirely impartial, but it is worth asking any others that you know well enough, although you should obviously be discreet, maintaining confidentiality about the name of the company from whom you have had an offer, and just describing its size and the nature of its business.

The other source is your good old network contacts. Speak to people who are in the same business sector. You can do this at the same time as you ask them for any other information or advice about the position in question.

You will, naturally, also be comparing the offer you have received with what you are currently, or were last, earning. If you are currently employed, you may well feel – unless you are making a sideways move to enhance your long-term career progression – that you require an increase to justify the risk of moving and the increased responsibilities of the new job.

You will want to take account, too, of any disadvantage you may suffer by leaving before you reach the end of a bonus or profit sharing period, or as a result of missing out on either a salary review or the chance to exercise share options. Those who are unemployed, on the other hand, may be willing to move sideways, or even to take a drop, in order to re-establish their careers.

The main consideration will, of course, be the total value of the package, but you and your potential employer may be able to negotiate to mutual advantage over the various elements of it. Smaller companies are often more flexible over the way the total cost to them of employing you is divided up. Large companies tend to be more bureaucratic, although some do offer cafeteria benefits, i.e. the opportunity to pick and choose assorted benefits up to an agreed value.

Elements of the package

In looking at the various elements of the package, there are a number of points you need to be aware of.

- **Salary**

  As well as the basic offer, check the frequency and date of reviews. If a review is due a few months after you start work, will you miss that and have to wait over a year for your first one, or can you negotiate an interim review? An agreement to a review being undertaken after, say, six months can also be used as the means of achieving a compromise if you cannot get the company to match your expectations on the salary at which you will start.

- **Bonus or profit share**

  A scheme based on a formula is generally to be preferred to one which is purely discretionary, although the latter may pay well if you have a generous boss. Check whether the amounts earned depend solely on your own performance, or that of a team, or even the whole company or group, and ask for figures on what has actually been paid out in the past rather than relying on pie in the sky expectations.

- **Share options**

  Get full details of the scheme and check the current tax situation. In evaluating this benefit, bear in mind both the plus of the fact that it can make you a lot of money, and the minuses of the uncertainty of this and of the long timescale involved.

- **Equity participation generally**

  Whether you acquire shares via options or in some other way (e.g. bonuses), take an objective view of their marketability. Shares in unquoted companies may be saleable only to the individual who owns the bulk of the business, in which case you need to examine the relevant provisions extremely carefully. Beware too of the promise of shares in a business which is owned fifty/fifty by two people. When it comes to the crunch, you often find that neither is willing to put a small but potentially controlling interest into someone else's hands.

- **Cars**
  Check which running costs are paid by the company and which you have to meet. Although most people still find it tax efficient to have a company car, you may wish to consider a cash alternative, if one is offered.

- **Pension**
  What do you contribute, and how much does the company put in? If you opt for a private pension, will they contribute to that? If you are currently in a company scheme, what will you lose by moving, especially if capping rules come into play? Will other elements of the package compensate for this?

- **Insurances**
  Does medical insurance cover just you or your whole family? How much life cover is provided? What about permanent health (long-term disability) cover?

- **Relocation**
  If this applies, what will the company pay for? Just legal and estate agents' fees plus the actual removal costs? Or will they contribute to the equally large sums you could end up paying out, as a result of having to move home, on new carpets and curtains? You also need to consider a host of other factors, like whether the salary differential reflects comparative house prices, and whether educational standards in the new area will necessitate incurring the cost of private school fees.

- **International relocation**
  The number and complexity of factors, including different tax regimes as well as considerations like housing, education, the cost of groceries and other everyday items, and your partner's earning potential, make it imperative that you obtain expert advice.

Final details

Before you finally accept an offer, it is vital to get it all in writing, including any amendments you may have negotiated. However much you may trust the person you are dealing with, never accept promises made orally. What would happen if the individual in question had a heart attack or went under the proverbial bus?

Do also bear in mind that offers may well be made subject to a medical check and satisfactory references. Surprisingly, only a minority of employers seem to insist on medical examinations, although rather more use medical questionnaires and the majority do appear to check references. This raises some interesting questions about how honest you should be.

Unless you have to fill in an application form, the question of your health is likely to arise only if an interviewer asks specific questions, if you display obvious signs of having a problem, or if you raise the matter yourself. Since prospective employers tend to run a mile at the slightest whiff of a health problem, you may, so long as you are quite sure that the matter in question will not affect your ability to do the job, prefer to be economical with the truth. You need to be aware, though, that if you are asked to take a medical examinations or complete a questionnaire, there could be problems, so you should be very wary of being blatantly untruthful. If direct questions are asked it is generally better to explain the situation fully and thus put it into its proper perspective.

The situation regarding references is rather more clear cut. It is likely that your current or most recent employers, and probably one or two earlier ones, will be asked to act as referees, and very few refuse, even if they limit what they say to objective, factual matters and avoid committing themselves to subjective opinions. If, therefore, you have fudged dates of employment to conceal a gap in your career history, or have erred on the generous side in quoting your remuneration, hoping that this will enable you to negotiate a better deal in your next job, you are almost certain to be caught out. Such dishonesty would represent grounds for your prospective employer to withdraw the offer.

While some companies are very guarded about giving references, many are not. There is consequently a fair chance that the company which has made you an offer will phone up your current or most recent boss, and have quite a lengthy chat about everything from the factual items like dates, job titles and salary to your achievements, your personal relationships with superiors, colleagues and staff, your integrity and sobriety, and even the stability of your personal life.

Naturally you will avoid, if at all possible, giving as a referee anyone from whom you expect to get a bad reference. If, however, the company which has offered you the job insists on speaking to a former employer whom you left under a cloud, alert them to this and explain the situation, e.g. that there was a disagreement over some fundamental matter or simply a clash of personalities.

In any case, you should never allow referees to be contacted until you have given them the courtesy of a call to explain who will be contacting them, and you should use this opportunity to brief your referees about the company and job in question. With the exception of the public sector, where openness about job applications means that references are supplied on application and taken up before interview, it is rare for referees to be contacted until an offer has been made and it is advisable, therefore, to decline to supply them any earlier in the process unless it is to your advantage to do so – for example, if you are out of work and wish to reassure a potential employer as to your performance in your last job or your reasons for leaving it.

Buy-backs

If you are in employment it is possible that, when you hand in your notice, your employers will try to dissuade you from leaving them. In some cases they will actually try to buy you back with inducements of one kind or another. You may be offered more money or you could be told that the company had been on the point of offering you a promotion. How should you respond?

Some people feel that, once they have accepted an offer of a new job, they should honour their decision. Others are happy to encourage an auction between their current and prospective future employers.

If you find yourself in this situation, you may wish to seek advice from disinterested third parties. Remember, though, that any recruiter who is directly involved does not fall into that category, being paid by your future employer and probably being dependent for at least part of that payment on you accepting the job.

The decision you make will inevitably reflect circumstances which are different in every case. If you are tempted to succumb to a buy-back, you should, however, bear in mind that, if it took the threat of losing you to make your present employers recognise your true worth on this occasion, you may find yourself back in the same undervalued position once again in the not too distant future.

"THE MORE EFFORT YOU PUT INTO PREPARATION, THE MORE POSITIVE AND CONFIDENT YOU WILL FEEL ON DAY ONE."

26 Keeping one step ahead

Your new job, and the one after that

When it is finally all over – offer accepted, medical and references cleared, start date fixed – your first reaction may well be relief. The job hunt is over. You can ditch all the files and other bits you have accumulated, or at least shove them into the back of a drawer or cupboard.

Yes, you can indeed do that – if you want to be complacent, if you are willing to risk being in the same position again even sooner than you need to be. If, on the other hand, you would rather be wise, stop and think about:

- what you have learned about yourself and the job market, and how you can use this knowledge;
- what you can do between now and the time you join your new company to help you to settle in quickly and successfully;
- how you are going to tackle the job when you do actually start and during the vital early stages;
- the plans you need to make for your longer term career development, whether that proves to be within the company you are about to join, or elsewhere.

Self-awareness

The self-appraisal you undertook at the beginning of this book, together with all the advice you have received in the course of your job search, ought to have brought about a significant increase in the level of your self-knowledge. If you are to make the optimum use of this, you need to check the following.

- Whether you now have a strategy for your career development, and if this is in turn a coherent part of a strategy for your whole life.

- If you can learn anything from your last job, especially if you lost that job without another one to go to. Even if you did not actually make serious errors, were you guilty of sins of omission, of complacency, of not consciously working to make yourself an asset the company could not afford to be without?

- Whether you have weaknesses which you need to do something about, now that you have the time, in order to make yourself more marketable in the future.

- Whether you understand clearly both what your strengths are and how you are going to use them.

Before you join

While you are waiting to start your new job, prepare yourself as thoroughly as you possibly can. This should include:

- reviewing all the information you already have from the research you carried out, from what you learned at your interviews and from what the company has provided subsequently;

- asking your new employer for any further information which may be useful, such as systems manuals, details about products and services, company newsletters and so on;

- getting up to date on any technical matters relevant to your new job;

- undertaking any general background reading that may be useful, e.g. about the areas in which the company operates.

The more effort you put into preparation, the more positive and confident you will feel on day one and the less steep your learning curve will be thereafter.

Settling in

Things to learn about as quickly as possible include:

- key people, and how to handle them;
- communications, both formal and informal, and in all directions – upwards, downwards and sideways;
- how decisions are really made;
- the unwritten rules of the organisation as a whole, and of its various parts;
- how to cut through red tape and get things done.

Some dangers to avoid are:

- trying to set the world to rights before you have taken the trouble to find out how it operates;
- repeatedly telling your new colleagues how this, that and the other was done so much better at your last company;
- knocking your previous company, boss, colleagues or staff;
- getting dragged into company politics – you could well end up on the wrong side.

Your boss

The most crucial relationship in your new job will inevitably be the one you form with your boss.

Bosses expect you to be:

- capable
- co-operative
- efficient
- hard working, in terms both of effort and, when necessary, hours
- honest

- loyal
- keen
- reliable.

They do not like:
- indifference
- insobriety
- intrigue
- irresponsibility
- surprises.

Getting feedback from your boss is vital. You do not have to ask openly, but do not wait for the first annual appraisal either. Listen actively, being receptive not only to what your boss says to you but also to all the non-verbal signals.

Other people

While your boss is inevitably the most important person in the organisation as far as you are concerned, you also need to get on with your colleagues and your staff.

Colleagues expect you to be:
- co-operative
- friendly
- loyal
- trustworthy.

They do not like:
- deceit
- one-upmanship
- selfishness
- unreliability.

Staff expect:

- consideration
- leadership
- recognition
- support.

They do not like:

- autocracy
- being patronised
- distrust
- favouritism
- having their boss take all the credit for their ideas and hard work
- indecision
- insecurity.

Building for the future

As well as looking outwards, at other people, you also need to look inwards, at yourself. If you are to keep yourself marketable in a rapidly changing world, it is vital that you write into your diary a regular review session – say, once every six months – at which you look at what you have achieved in the period just ended and plan ahead – in broad terms for the next few years, and in detail for the next few months. Using your long-term strategic plan as the backdrop, set yourself targets in terms of the following.

- **Experience** – aim to make every day a CV building day.
- **Keeping up to date** – have a regular programme of reading both general and technical matter pertinent to your job, and attend relevant courses and conferences.

- **Learning something new** – identify areas which will advance your career (e.g. learning a new computer application or a foreign language) and set yourself targets to achieve these objectives.

- **Interpersonal skills** – aim, too, to develop your skills in management, and in dealing with people through reading, workshops and practice.

- **Raising your profile** – start by publicising your new appointment, then go on to join trade and professional bodies, get yourself into print, be seen in public etc. (see Chapter 14).

- **Developing your network** – thank all the people who have helped you and let them know about your new appointment. Use the fresh contacts you will make in your new company to expand your network. Keep in touch with people through calls to exchange information, invitations to business functions, Christmas cards etc. Take advantage of your new position to be seen as a potential client by headhunters and other recruitment consultants – and do not forget to send them a copy of your updated CV.

Talking of your network and your CV, use them at your regular review sessions as a measure of what you have achieved in the preceding few months. If your network has not grown, and if you do not have additional achievements, experience and skills to add to your CV, then you have not been maintaining your marketability. Keep working at it. Remember that, in the long run, you make your own luck.

A final thought

A lot of people have probably helped you in your search for a new job, whether it be with advice, encouragement, information or specific leads. You may never be able to repay all of those individuals directly, but there is one thing that you most definitely can do. Next time someone who needs a job asks you for assistance, however busy you may be, please find the time to do what you can to help them.

INDEX

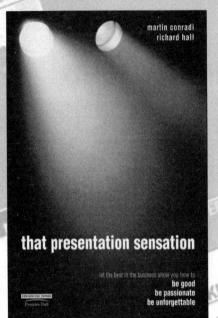